THE
EARTH'S BEST
STORY

A Bittersweet Tale of Twin Brothers
Who Sparked an Organic Revolution

— *by* —

RON & ARNIE KOSS

CHELSEA GREEN PUBLISHING

WHITE RIVER JUNCTION, VERMONT

Project Manager: Emily Foote
Developmental Editor: Cannon Labrie
Proofreader: Helen Walden
Designer: Peter Holm, Sterling Hill Productions

Printed in the United States of America
First printing January, 2010
10 9 8 7 6 5 4 3 2 1   10 11 12 13

Our Commitment to Green Publishing

Chelsea Green sees publishing as a tool for cultural change and ecological stewardship. We strive to align our book manufacturing practices with our editorial mission and to reduce the impact of our business enterprise in the environment. We print our books and catalogs on chlorine-free recycled paper, using vegetable-based inks whenever possible. This book may cost slightly more because we use recycled paper, and we hope you'll agree that it's worth it. Chelsea Green is a member of the Green Press Initiative (www.greenpressinitiative.org), a nonprofit coalition of publishers, manufacturers, and authors working to protect the world's endangered forests and conserve natural resources. *The Earth's Best Story* was printed on Natures Book Natural, a 30-percent postconsumer recycled paper supplied by Thomson-Shore.

Library of Congress Cataloging-in-Publication Data
Koss, Ron, 1951–
 The Earth's Best story : a bittersweet tale of twin brothers who sparked an organic revolution / by Ron and Arnie Koss.
    p. cm.
  ISBN 978-1-60358-239-1
  1. Koss, Ron, 1951- 2. Koss, Arnie, 1951- 3. Earth's Best Baby Foods. 4. Baby foods industry--United States--History. 5. Natural foods industry--United States--History. I. Koss, Arnie, 1951- II. Title.

HD9332.U64E275 2009
338.7'66462092273--dc22
[B]

                              2009043272

Chelsea Green Publishing Company
Post Office Box 428
White River Junction, VT 05001
(802) 295-6300
www.chelseagreen.com

To the memory of
MILTON KOSS AND JUDITH WEISS KOSS
our devoted and loving parents

Contents

Prologue

Organic baby food is ubiquitous today. It can be found in glass jars, portable squeeze tubes, and frozen cubes. Once upon a time there was no organic baby food. There was only Gerber, introduced in 1927, and then Beech-Nut and Heinz, both introduced in 1931. Almost sixty years later, in 1987, Earth's Best was introduced. Most product categories do not stay as untouched for generations as baby food did. We, Ron and Arnie Koss, did not set out to find why this was the case, but we did nonetheless.

The word "grok" is freely scattered throughout this story. Robert Heinlein coined the expression in his 1961 classic *Stranger in a Strange Land*. To grok is to know deeply and in a greater way than that which can be sensed by an outside observer. To grok is to understand something so well that it is fully absorbed into oneself. Those who are grokking are momentarily vibrating on the same frequency and wavelength.

It was the power of this shared immersion and cohesiveness between us, this grokking, that brought Earth's Best into being. And it raises the question, what else that seems so improbable today on Planet Earth is possible with a little more of it?

The brand name "Earth's Best" was one of several concepts presented to us sometime in 1985 by a graphic-arts designer from the Burlington, Vermont, area. Visually and emotionally, the name was an instant powerhouse, but the awkwardness of pronouncing the possessive form of "earth" (as in "earth's") caused us angst and indecision for some time.

Out of necessity, we started to use the name Earth's Best in various communications. It was a work-in-progress name that never stopped working for us.

To help protect the privacy of others (where we thought it was advised) we have used fictitious names throughout the story and altered in places identifying information.

The many events and chronologies that follow reflect our best efforts to recall and reconstruct meetings, conversations, and circumstances that have spanned many years. As such, there may be some inadvertent errors and misstatements made for which we apologize in advance.

And last, our entire story precedes the involvement and purchase of Earth's Best Baby Food by The Hain Celestial Group in 1999.

RON KOSS AND ARNIE KOSS

Introduction

Earth's Best began as a speck of alluring light on a distant shore. It was a complete fantasy, and, like any good fantasy, achieving the impossible (as in reaching that light) was central to the plot. For some reason, Ron saw this light in 1976, well before it became visible to the collective naked eye. Maybe it was a destiny thing. Maybe it twinkled just for him and he happened to be looking.

Or was it me who saw that light way back then? Ron and I have endlessly debated this question. This is a twin thing. Sometimes our lives inexplicably merge, and it's hard to tell whose experience was whose. Regarding that alluring light in 1976, Ron is more certain than I am about the moment, so for the record it's his light.

For fantasy to take form, it insists on dreamers with a hell-bent passion to take center stage. Success may bring accolades such as "visionary" and "genius." "Failure" and "fool" are also possible associations if the dream is a bust. The entrepreneurial personality tends to envision only success. If failure is more the preoccupation, it's a red flag indicating some kind of mismatch between the venture and the prospective adventurer.

How does an idea successfully journey across the wasteland separating fantasy and reality, a vast expanse littered with the wrecks of fantastic ideas, brilliant people, and sure things, a place where colossal failure and entrepreneurial heartbreak is recorded? It would be fantasy in its own right to be tricked by the mirage that the best ideas, the best educated people, and those with the most money and experience are the most likely to navigate through this wasteland. Strangely, but perfectly, that is not the case.

The Earth's Best Story is the tale of our journey from fantasy, through the wasteland, and into reality. It is as much a "how-not-to" story as a "how-to" story. More so, it is a "how-we-did-it" story. It will be an eye-opener for those who feel both righteous about the greatness of their ideas and entitled to a free Advance Directly to Go card, as we sometimes did, or for those who straight up seek the gold and power of entrepreneurial success.

On the face of it, our story is the tale of a journey to launch the first organic baby-food company in the United States. While of course true, our inspiration soared beyond baby food to a grander, multidimensional imagining, an imagining where the face of agriculture was transformed and the chemically dependent agribusiness paradigm was reduced in its prominence.

We envisioned a world where organic foods would become dominant, with an organic avenue right through the mainstream food thoroughfare. And in our dreams organic baby food would be a catalyst for that paradigm shift: a shift that would support and protect our fragile ecosystems, safeguard farm workers and their families, and walk the talk about doing right by those who are most vulnerable and precious to us—our children.

More personally, this book reflects the voyage of the Koss Brothers, Ron and Arnie. It is a story about our battle to overcome generations of encoded Koss family defeat and bitterness in business. It is also a story about our twin-ness and the unbreakable bond that began during the nine months we shared our mom's womb.

Unbeknownst to us, as we traversed childhood and adolescence, a foundation of trust was laid that would one day become the bedrock to support the incalculable weight of an emerging Earth's Best. And unexpectedly, we would discover the immense potential of the synergies resulting from this trust and leverage them in all ways possible. No energy would be wasted or sleep lost wondering about the other's intentions, commitment, or integrity. We were free from such distractions and free to immerse ourselves in what really mattered— bringing Earth's Best Baby Foods to life.

Interestingly, Ron and I could not retell our story in one voice, because despite the sameness (i.e., identical genes) it really is two unique stories, merging dynamically together. The writing process has been cathartic for both of us. You will soon clearly understand why.

Our shared hope is that *The Earth's Best Story*, while in many respects a sobering tale, will inspire others to smartly venture off and do something amazing and positive to make a difference in a world that needs difference makers.

We invite you to take the Earth's Best journey with us.

Buckle up!

Arnie Koss

— PART ONE —

The Boys Behind the Men

Segue: Middlebury, Vermont, Summer 1990

ARNIE:

The celebration of local Vermont organic-food producers was bitter-sweet. We had lost control of the company. Ron and I sat under the white billowy tent, gazing out at the farmers, local dignitaries, employees, and investors and admiring the amazing baby-food processing plant that we had built. In the back stood the president of Earth's Best, the man who had replaced me.

How did this happen, the feeling of accomplishment and failure, all in the same moment?

"Fear and greed drive us. The bottom line is money," exalted one of the keynote speakers, representing a large supermarket chain. I couldn't stand it. What nonsense! Ron and I shot each other quick and quizzical looks. What to do? We could not let this dead-end paradigm be the last word and impression of the day.

I watched Ron move to the edge of his seat, as the speaker concluded. I didn't exactly know what was coming, but I knew Ron was not going to be silent. He stood and turned to the audience.

"There's another line, below the bottom line," Ron responded. "And that line is love. Love is what Earth's Best is about, love for children and love for this planet. We have to join together and be this love."

Ron sat down to a rousing round of applause.

Who was this contrary twin brother of mine, who took such an unscripted stand for love in such a public forum? It was just, as you will see, Ron being Ron.

"Grow Up and Get Real"

RON:

When I was growing up, my parents made a solid effort to instill morality in me. I don't think their effort was out of the ordinary. The Golden Rule stands out as a memory, and the Ten Commandments were well learned in Hebrew school. But basically the message was to be a good boy; do the right thing; don't curse; don't be selfish; don't be greedy; be compassionate; be thoughtful; be sensitive; be loving. Love definitely held a place of prominence in my life as a kid. It was good and right, and I know how fortunate I was.

I took all this grown-up advice to heart. I believed every bit of it completely and quite happily. I liked being good. My parents were good. It all seemed simple and straightforward and sensible.

I rolled along the track toward adulthood with very few outwardly apparent glitches until I reached my junior year in college (1972). I remember it well. As usual, I went to the library to study, this time for my marketing midterm exam. I was a pathologically driven student. I opened my notebook and started flipping through the pages, just to size up the task at hand. I felt nauseous. The material was so dry and lifeless to me. I ignored the feeling, which wasn't a new one. I tried to focus and memorize something. I gagged and dry heaved.

I stood up and walked away from the notebook. I had to study, but my body was saying no. Every time I returned to study, I gagged. For the first time in my life I faced a fundamental truth about myself. I was sick and tired of trying to be good (actually perfect is more like it). My actions in life to this point were completely controlled by the fear of failing, making mistakes, and letting my parents down. Suddenly I could no longer act on their behalf or obey the demands of those deeply seated fears. The track was disappearing.

In those profound moments of nausea, I took, in a very real sense, my first baby steps into my own life. Some very fundamental questions reached my conscious mind for the first time. What am I doing with my life? Where am I going? And who's driving this cavernous womb of a bus I'm mindlessly riding?

I answered myself much as you might expect: I'm going to college just like my friends and just like my family and teachers expected me to. I'm doing the right thing. And if I stay on track and get my degree, I will automatically have a successful and financially secure life and live happily ever after. Not bad.

And then I saw that the bus was being driven by the inertia of past lemming migrations. I wasn't so sure that I wanted to catch the next wave over the cliff and into an ordinary life. Suddenly the strife and cultural upheaval I was surrounded by made an impression on me. I picked my head out of my marketing notebook and saw the Vietnam War, the civil rights movement, environmental decay, and the aftershocks of Woodstock.

Those rock-solid "answers" crumbled. They seemed disconnected and irrelevant. And it all happened instantly while I stared in vain at those four p's (products, place, price, and promotion) in my marketing notebook. That class woke me from a deep sleep, a great example of an unintended consequence. I wasn't groggy or disoriented. I felt exhilarated and ecstatic, and I did something I had never done before, the unthinkable. I knocked myself off the track to my future. I dropped my marketing class. This was a sea change for a guy like me.

So I started to look at the world for myself and by myself for the first time. I did this just by sitting in that same library with an empty notebook and a pen and no other agenda but to discover myself and my destiny. Everything that I was supposed to do stopped, and everything that I wanted to do started. And all I wanted to do was to sit still and wait to see, hear, and feel what happened.

I never knew until those moments of disrupted parental and cultural inertia that I was bursting with wonder, joy, and love for this Universe, this Earth, and all of its creation.

I experienced myself reborn, a newborn at the age of twenty-one. I was not reborn into any particular dogma or spiritual belief. Rather, I became newly born in the sense that I discovered a door to myself, and for the first time began to listen, think, and feel for myself in a more complete way. I sat in that library oohing and aahing and wowing with a happiness I had never experienced.

Epiphanies aside, all of this was simply translated by my parents as "Ronald went off the deep end." I was genuinely sympathetic. Their "sure-bet" son derailed just short of success.

Those days in the library led me to the discovery of food. It was as if after twenty-one years of eating I had never appreciated, savored, or realized that food had anything consequential to do with my life, short of starving, if I stopped eating. My first trip into a natural-foods store was something like a moon walk: strange, fascinating, and otherworldly. "Let's see, I know I'm walking by food, but what do you do with it?" Good-bye Uncle Ben's, hello brown rice, tofu, and hiziki. I reported my discoveries to my parents with endless enthusiasm, and while somewhat appalled, I think they got by okay by rationalizing that I was just going through a "rabbit phase."

I became an environmentalist in that library. I discovered what is now referred to as "Gaia." I not only intellectually understood pollution, but felt the pain of the earth, felt my own pain and distress. I loved the earth and I knew that love would never fade into a phase, because I had discovered a piece of my own self-love.

It all seemed so simple and so important to me. Yet rather than taking a giant leap toward adulthood, toward becoming a peer with my parents and teachers and friends, I became more distant and removed. I was the one who was regressing, going backward, not growing up. I was the dreamer, the idealist, the naïve one. I was failing in life.

My father lectured me about not worrying about pollution or the world's problems. I should think about myself and my own life. And of course I was. What I failed to communicate was that my connection to the earth was as deep as my dad's love and concern for me.

When I was a kid, it was okay to be a kid. And kids hear from their parents, family, and culture the laudable things that kids are supposed to hear. But when you get to be or are perceived to be a grown-up, the rules and the messages change drastically and dramatically. The Golden Rule mutates to "He who has the gold rules," and the Ten Commandments are condensed to simply "Might makes right." And so I understood that the warm, mushy, sensitive stuff is for kids, and the hardball, bare-knuckles, cover-your-ass ethic is for grown-ups. Grown-ups can curse, sweep their dirt under the rug, be deceitful, insensitive, selfish, corrupt, greedy, self-destructive, and ignorant and (until recently) still become president of the United States. Kids who fit such a description are emotionally disturbed juvenile delinquents and burdens to society.

I discovered for myself, heart and soul, that the enlightened values of my parents, imparted to me as a kid, were not the real, day-to-day, nine-to-five, adult values. Rather, they were the values that go nicely with church and synagogue; the values that would be nice to live by if the world was fair and just. With that in mind, the message from family and friends back then was "grow up and get real."

I left college in 1973 with 111 credits, 9 shy of graduating, and spent the better part of two years traveling throughout the United States hitchhiking, camping, sleeping in cheap motels, and finding a nice assortment of floors to crash on. I checked out communes in Taos and community-living groups in San Francisco, looking for an expression, a manifestation, of life that survived the transition into adulthood, heart and soul intact. It wasn't to be found, and I didn't understand it. I was the innocent fool questing for the Grail Castle. To my parents I was a just a plain fool, but a nice one. We were all in pain together. They could not ease mine, and I could not ease theirs.

I was homeless during these wandering years. My childhood home in Ellenville, New York, had been sold in 1970. My parents, Milton and Judith, moved to south Florida. And the close circle of friends and community in Ellenville, which nurtured me far more than I ever realized, disappeared virtually overnight. It was not just the physical place or home that was missing. I was lost in the darkness of being overwhelmed by seeing no new tracks to get my life onto. The counterculture seemed to be infested with drugs and escapist indifference. The old career tracks, which were the only path in life I had known or imagined, continued to have that scent of a doomed lemming migration. The pain of seeing the earth raped and trampled was too great and the idea of a career too small. I felt alone and abandoned and paralyzed. For some reason, karmic or otherwise, I shared this paralysis with Arnie.

There were two green plush swivel chairs in my parent's south

Florida condominium. They sure could spin. Around and around Arnie and I went, talking in circles and going nowhere. So much energy to live and yet everything was pent up inside. The world seemed inaccessible, unapproachable, hostile, dishonest, and superficial. Around and around, searching intently for a place to stop and start our lives, to jump in, get wet, and escape from the stifling angst of being unexpressed, unfulfilled, and dependent upon my parents and their condo reality. My dad hated the idea of us wearing out those swivels. So did we.

For the sake of movement, I enrolled at Empire State College's independent study program (in 1975) to complete my bachelor's degree. I remained lost throughout the process, pretending as best as I could to be in my life and hopefully finding my way. It beat the swivel chair!

Interestingly, I started my first business during this time—a natural-foods lunch cart that I set up near the capitol building in downtown Albany. This was the summer of 1975. I liked being independent, and I liked being next to those hot-dog guys. Total investment was probably under $100. There were no stockholders and no debt. I was brilliant back then. My first taste of entrepreneurship was mostly satisfying. I didn't need a lot of money, and, most importantly, I saw a way to express my values and politics in the world. This was empowering.

I also worked part time in a natural-foods store called "The Store." It was during the winter of 1976 that the idea of organic baby food was conceived. I remember standing in front of The Store talking to Arnie about this great idea. I just couldn't imagine how to pull it off on a wood cookstove. The complexity overwhelmed the fantasy in five minutes, probably less, but we both knew the idea was right and necessary.

Arnie has imagined a different story about how Earth's Best was conceived, although at long last, he has yielded to me in the introduction to this book. Twins sometimes seem to confuse each other's reality. Arnie does this more often than me.

During the summer of 1976, I became a houseparent at Highland, a group home in the Adirondacks. One of the kids there was a fiery sixteen-year-old named Donna. I was scared of her, but I tried to out-nice myself to win her approval. The harder I tried, the sweeter I was, the more antagonism and verbal abuse came my way.

I was raised to believe that "Nice guys finish first." Donna was telling me that "Nice guys finished last." My worldview was not holding up, and I wanted to leave this job for safer territory. On a warm summer day, I found myself face-to-face with Donna in a confrontational situation. She threatened me by saying, "Ziggy (my nickname at the time), cross this line and you are a dead mother-you-know-what-er." I was scared, but also tired, and tired of being abused, and I do have my pride. So I took a step across this imaginary line drawn on the living room floor. Donna broke into a big smile and spontaneously told me how she couldn't trust me and didn't feel safe around me, because I was scared of her and wasn't honest. She didn't trust my "Mr. Nice Guy" persona and was angry with me for bullshitting her. She was right.

I didn't know a thing about genuine relationship until that moment. I learned that niceness for the sake of being safe and toughness for the sake of being in control (and again safe) will not solidify or deepen human relationship. It was not the act of being nice or tough per se that was problematic, but the fear (of rejection) that controlled my nice behavior. I did not want to be vulnerable, and as long as the nice-guy charade worked in my life, I could hide. Donna nailed me, and I am very grateful.

As a historical aside, I met Ben Cohen (of Ben & Jerry's) at this group home in a rather amusing away. It was my first night at Highland, and I was temporarily staying in a very nice log home on the property. I had just completed a three-day meditation retreat in Albany with Amrit Desai, and I was full of chanting energy and 5:00 a.m. wake-ups. I thought I was alone in this house; at least I was when I fell asleep. I woke up at 5:00 a.m. and began to loudly chant these beautiful melodies that I had just learned. I was full swing into my thing when I heard a few bearish groans from the loft area. There stood a very groggy Ben wrapped in a blanket, wondering who this chanting idiot was. I was embarrassed and apologized. I don't remember chanting for the rest of the summer.

Ben, who was the resident potter, and I were so different. We had to take note of each other. He was always eating junk food and I was always eating brown rice, tofu, and hiziki. I think we grossed each other out in a friendly way. Our paths did cross again as Arnie and I journeyed into the Earth's Best story. But that story will have to wait until we get there from here.

I felt pretty good about myself when I left the group home that fall of 1976, but still very much on the fringe of identifying a career path, a future plan, and a life direction. I wanted to live Helen and Scott Nearing's *The Good Life.* I wanted to retreat into simpler times and a simpler life. And I came to Vermont with Arnie in January 1977.

Sprouting in Vermont

Arnie and I rented a big house in Plainfield. I think noting the size of the house is important because a characteristic of our relationship has been thinking big, dreaming big, and in the case of Earth's Best, doing big. And big certainly has its glamour and allure, but as I have learned, it does not come cheap.

Once we got the big Vermont house under our belt, we attempted to heat it with two small wood stoves. We didn't know what we were doing. First we bought log-length green wood, and then we tried to cut it all with a crosscut saw. The logs were all frozen together and covered with snow, and we could barely get enough wood into the house to keep the fires going. The water in our toilet bowls kept freezing and so did our pipes. But I loved using that crosscut saw. It was real and invigorating, and I felt alive. It seemed that almost every moment was in the present.

Looking for a job was out of the question for both Arnie and me. We dreamed up our first business enterprise together, called the "Vermont Sprouting Family"—alfalfa sprouts, mung-bean sprouts, and lentil sprouts (my favorite). We designed our sprout room in one of the second-floor bedrooms and tried to keep it warm. We came up with a sweet little package, thanks to a Goddard College student, and we set our sights on the P&C supermarket chain.

These were exciting times. I loved the adventure of doing my own thing.

Our sprouting room was my first experience with production. Stuffing each bag with a quarter pound of sprouts with tongs was an art in itself. It was tedious. Sifting through twenty-five pounds of lentil seeds searching for little stones was a chore. Arnie was a great partner.

We set up an appointment with the buyer at P&C, and we dressed up ourselves and our little sprout bags as best as we could. There were several other salespeople also waiting to present at P&C's headquarters in White River Junction. They looked pretty snazzy with their three-piece suits and leather cases. Arnie and I held our future in a medium-size paper bag. The bag itself wasn't much to look at. We knew that, but I think we were also feeling a little smug about the dynamite package and product we had hiding inside. We also desperately needed this business to generate some money.

Finally it was our turn to present the Vermont Sprouting Family product line. I think the buyer was amused by our appearance. Long, bushy brown hair, full beards, no ties or jackets, and a wrinkled, brown paper bag holding our product line.

I can't remember too much more about our P&C meeting. Arnie pitched the product. The buyer seemed skeptical and reserved. He took a wad of our alfalfa sprouts, put them to his mouth like he was about to kiss a spitting cobra, grimaced, and politely refilled the bag. "It's an acquired taste," Arnie reassured him. I thought to helpfully add that we carried anti-sprout venom with us, but wisely held my tongue. When there was no more to be said by us, I heard him state matter-of-factly, "Give me 48 of each." That was exciting. As we stood up to leave, Arnie restated what he heard the order to be: "You want 48 alfalfa; 48 mung; and 48 sprout mix with lentils." The buyer said, "Yes, 48 dozen each."

Unbelievable euphoria. I thought he wanted 4 dozen of each. With a 144-dozen order, we had established our business as a going concern. I was passing Go and about to collect $200. Despite this great (relatively speaking) entrepreneurial accomplishment, our parents were still devastated, believing that both their precious boys were still refusing to grow up, lost in a phase that others had already left for medical school, and still eating like rabbits.

It was a scramble to deliver the sprouts. The house was cold and the sprouts grew slowly. The packing kept us up late into the night, but we did it with the help of some friends. And on the appointed day, we proudly drove to White River Junction with our Chevette packed to the gills.

There were problems. The sprouts got stranded in warehouses and were old and ugly by the time they got to the stores. Sometimes they weren't refrigerated properly. Arnie and I raced around, talking to the produce-management people and fluffing up and beautifying our little bags as best as possible. P&C reordered, and we kept stuffing our wood stoves with green wood and watching expectantly to see if our little sprouts were growing.

They did grow, and we did deliver, but the cash did not flow in on time. We didn't ask about payment terms in our interview presentation. It's hard to ask for what you need when you feel vulnerable and dependent. Arnie and I assumed that the money would come in time, but we never imagined waiting months and more for a check.

One of the greatest challenges for an entrepreneur is to be willing to see, to bring into focus those things that tarnish, spoil, and threaten the vision, the ideal, the dream. Avoidance is deadly and yet very understandable and perhaps even necessary at times. An entrepreneur needs to learn to recognize that the red flags, voices, twitches, and butterflies that surface momentarily are gifts from your entrepreneurial angel and present opportunities to "morph" now so as to succeed later. Unfortunately, I hadn't met my wife yet. She can see a red flag before the red paint dries. Actually, even if I had met her I probably wouldn't have listened. I had to learn humility the old-fashioned way—through experience.

Our cash-flow dilemma was demoralizing. There was nowhere to go for help, and the sucking sound that most every entrepreneur has heard at one time or another, as he or she descends into the swirling vortex that leads to the business graveyard, was in earshot. This sound is not a rhapsody.

But businesses have a life of their own and seemingly, in my experience, a will to live apart (and even in spite of) any intention of the businessperson. This was certainly true in the case of Earth's Best, and I think it was true of our fledgling Vermont Sprouting Family.

Two friends purchased our business for $1,000 and moved it to New York State, where it thrived for many years and even made a star appearance in *Mother Earth News* magazine.

There was no entrepreneurial encore to follow the sprouts. Arnie reluctantly fell back into estate and caretaker work and left Vermont to care for an elderly gentleman in Connecticut. I fell back into working with adolescents and applied for a group-home job at the top of Maple Hill in Plainfield, Vermont.

I liked group-home life, because I liked feeling a part of a community. I liked the camaraderie with the other staff. It did have its hellish moments, and the pay was inconsequential, but Maple Hill served as a haven for me, a place to hang out and avoid the regular nine-to-five world and routine that my dad belonged to and that alienated me.

The Land

November 3, 1978, was the brightest day in my life since that Florida-bound U-Haul truck sat darkly in our Ellenville driveway stuffed with whatever wasn't thrown away from a wonderful childhood. Arnie and I plus a friend plunked down a chunk of change on 128 acres of heaven in East Montpelier, forever known to us since as "The Land." How did we do it? Dear old dad had a collapse in judgment and lent us $10,000. The Milton could just not stop being a generous, sympathetic, loving father. He knew better, but he couldn't help himself or resist us. Maybe he understood the pain of our uprootedness and our obsession with being at home again. Or maybe it was Mom pulling the strings behind the scenes. This moment was the end of an eight-year quest. (I continue to live on The Land, now more than thirty years later.)

The relevance of buying land to the Earth's Best story was the entrenched resistance that now lived deep in our bones to leaving this long-sought-after home. There was such a strong emotional attachment in play, tied to our childhood, that skewed our judgments and perceptions and led to rationalizations about where to locate or not locate the company. This dynamic may have ultimately sealed the fate we eventually met in our Earth's Best lives. We'll never know, but the question lives on for me.

Arnie and I set off into the woods that winter of 1978 to fell the trees for his post-and-beam house. Generally when tackling trees sixty feet in height and twenty inches in diameter, you use a chainsaw. Arnie and I chose differently. We pulled out our trusty five-foot-long, two-person crosscut saw, bought an antique block and tackle, a peavey, and some chains, and walked into the silent woods. "Arnie, this tree is too beautiful to cut. What about that one to your right?" "I think we should take it Ronnie. No wait a minute. Doesn't this smaller one look like the daughter? We can't take the mother away, can we?"

We were such novices. We had no teachers and no experience. Our dad came back from his two years (1943–45) in the infantry in North Africa and Sicily hating the outdoors. To him the outdoors spelled danger, malaria, and loss, and the only mentoring we received regarding the outdoors was to be afraid of it. The closest we ever got to the woods with our dad was a picnic table along the side of a Catskill mountain road.

So as young men, Arnie and I shared the same ignorance and naïveté. It was a given. We took turns at making mistakes, laughing hysterically at our folly, and screaming at each other from time to time in the numbing cold. But one by one those logs added up. We were becoming the men we wanted to be and reclaiming in part what our father lost in World War II and what we had desperately wanted him to give to us. With all of our might and youth we dragged the heavy green logs through the deep snow to the building site. Dad, the world is safe again, the woods are beautiful, the mosquitoes are asleep.

It seems almost like Arnie and I had made a pre-incarnating agreement to make the task as difficult as possible. No power equipment, no experience, deep snow, and freezing cold. Why? To cultivate single-mindedness; to learn to be present with feelings, opinions, ideas, and love; to discover that with a unified purpose, we both could lead at the same time by situationally taking our lead from each other; and to experience the surrender of our egos for that unified purpose.

Arnie's experience of success and satisfaction was as important, if not more important, than my own, and vice versa. Imagine the trust, commitment, and synergy that then follow in such a dynamic. Why have it any other way in business or in any relationship? All for one and one for all. It worked for us.

Nonetheless, I grew restless. I turned twenty-eight in March 1979, feeling pretty disappointed with my post-swivel-chair progress in life. The faraway future was becoming the present. What was I waiting for? I guess I still had some time to bide and youth to expend.

I fell in love. It was far easier to commit to a woman than a career track. I directed and projected all of my pent-up longing for an object of desire to fulfill me in life onto Carley. Of course I was unconscious of this at the time and felt completely smitten by this beautiful, smart, spunky, and independent woman. My center of gravity began to shift. I imagined spending the rest of my life with Carley.

With a new raison d'être, I made a bold move to throw off my Hamlet-like yoke of indecision. The question was no longer "to be, or not to be." The answer was "to be!" My dad used to say "shit or get off the pot." I'm not sure which I was doing when I enrolled at the University of Vermont to take premed classes for a four-year naturopathic medical program, but I did feel relief.

I jumped into my studies with the full force of my old perfectionist student self. I got my As, but I was always obsessively studying, just like I did at SUNY at Albany before I got enlightenment through marketing. Before I knew it, I felt like I was fighting for my life. I was being suffocated by the inner experience of constantly fending off failure. Organic chemistry knocked me out, and not because I wasn't doing well. I had an A in the class, but the stress of falling back into my old ways and the separation from my vitality proved to be too much.

Why was I wired this way to self-destruct when I had the ability to do so well in school? I know the answer, and it proved central both in my decision to start Earth's Best and how I approached each and every day on the production floor. I have to digress so you can appreciate the dynamic operating so powerfully within me.

Ouch! Ouch! Ouch!

Third grade was a tough year for me. School wasn't just a place to have fun anymore. There were also expectations and judgments. The warmth and cuddliness of the place just seemed to evaporate. I wasn't ready for this transition, being the late bloomer that I am. I felt lost, insecure, and miserable. My teacher introduced Roman numerals to us. I actually was pretty fond of just regular numbers, but the linking of letters with numerical values was just too much for me. A fog descended, the fog of school. I was there. I remember saying "present" during attendance. I was hearing because I remember the nurse once telling me I had great hearing, but there was no comprehension. I felt stupid.

"Ronald, what's XL?" Silence. What I remember is my teacher pulling me by the arm up to the blackboard. She seemed angry at me and was tapping her chalk at those two neatly written letters. Then she took my head and, at least as I remember it, hit it against the blackboard. She probably pushed my face into those letters, perhaps thinking that the problem was my vision. I do not remember feeling any physical pain, but the shame and confusion were cataclysmic.

That moment was "the" defining moment of my life, for better and for worse. In that moment I knew that I would dedicate my life to never feeling that pain again. I would compensate for my stupidity by always being overprepared. No matter what, I would protect that little boy who was devastated that third-grade day. Those who knew me in school (throughout high school) probably remember me as always studying. I was teased and taunted relentlessly by the name "Ronnie worry." That was also painful, but apparently not as painful as that third-grade moment of shame and wounding that has lived deep in my psyche.

Arnie has often thought of himself as less academically smart than me. I have never bought that lament. Arnie was not in my third-grade class and was not introduced to Roman numerals in the hands-on way that I was. We did not share this trauma. Despite any outward appearance of sameness, our worlds diverged from this point on. Arnie faced boredom and feelings of inadequacy every day at school. I knew every morning that I faced the possibility of annihilation.

Believe me, I also wanted to watch *Walt Disney* and *Star Trek*, but I forced myself to stay seated at my desk. My parents had no idea why I studied as I did. I never talked about what happened way back when. There were no bruises that day, just a different little boy returning home from school.

I discovered over time that with enough effort I could learn anything, even Roman numerals. Imagine the guy that lifts weights all day and trains for the Iron Man triathlon all year, doomed to applying the same intensity and dedication to school work. I had no chiseled physique to admire in the mirror, that's for sure, but I developed the stamina of a marathoner to go the distance, no matter what the challenge, and the confidence to lift any weight, no matter how heavy or unwieldy. I was a lean, mean, studying machine.

But the constant pressure to keep running year after year from that childhood humiliation deeply exhausted me. I felt such great relief when I dropped that organic chemistry class, but I also felt defeated by that inner demon who had taken over my life twenty years ago and who still wouldn't let me have my destiny. I imagined my grandfather, Dr. John, looking down from heaven disapprovingly. Fortunately, the wave of energy that followed the relief carried Carley and me forward to a job as codirectors of Morehaven Group Home in Morrisville, Vermont, in May 1980.

Many times people have asked me, "Ronnie, whatever made you think you could start a baby-food company?" First and most obvious, ignorance is bliss. I knew virtually nothing about baby food, other than who was supposed to eat it. Many entrepreneurs are hard-wired with a standard "turn off the mind" feature that blots out the density of reality. Although Arnie and I were both pre-selected with this feature, I do not attribute my leap into Earth's Best to genetic makeup. I was an elite athlete of sorts. I had bulging muscles of will and confidence that I could learn anything that I needed to. All that I didn't know, the idea of which should have been completely overwhelming, was really incidental to me. What weighed heaviest was the perfection that I knew making baby food would require. I was afraid to put myself in that place, where a mistake really could be cataclysmic and where perfection was not just my distorted expectation of myself, but that of every mother and father who would expect Earth's Best to be just that.

Morehaven gave me a legitimate claim to having some semblance of a career in human services. I did feel some satisfaction and accomplishment, but that was eclipsed in short order by the third greatest life-changing event of my life. I will return to the second momentarily.

The imprint of deep exhaustion and the stress of Morehaven brought me to my first panic attack in December 1980. The shortness of breath, the rush to the hospital, the EKG, and the anxious waiting proved to be the death of my youthful invincibility. The gigantic tear in the fabric of my sense of physical security would emerge to dominate my life in ways that were confounding and threatening to not only my life as an entrepreneur, but to the viability of Ron Koss as a functioning adult. This first attack came out of the blue, disorienting me and catching my attention big time. It didn't knock me off my feet, and I rebounded, but I wasn't the same guy. Once you've had a panic attack, you are always anticipating and dreading the next one. My dread was well founded, for the knockout punch would indeed come soon enough.

The fact that twins are compared mercilessly brings me back to that second life-changing circumstance. Countless people have studied our appearance and have concluded, "You guys look exactly alike. I'll never be able to tell you apart," or "You guys don't look like twins at all, maybe brothers." Do we look alike? I have always hoped so.

I remember being a little boy standing in a sea of giant adults. They were staring down. I was staring up. Even though their voices seemed far away, I heard every word: "Arnold is the good looking one, Ronald is not." If this had happened once, I probably would have forgotten about it, but it happened over and over and over. Adults are such clods. They had nothing to say to each other, so why not mindlessly yak about the twins? The insensitivity was staggering and the pain was excruciating. *R* stands for round and Ronald and ugly. *A* stands for angular and Arnold and handsome. These endless twin comparisons, especially as a young boy, formed this second great life-shaping dimension of my life.

I grew up feeling ugly. My poor eyesight and thick glasses added to my woes. This account of my physical appearance probably also made studying all weekend easier. The mythlike task of forever running from the grim reaper of humiliation and the dread of being compared and inevitably deemed as the ugly twin converged in my life to create both a fiercely determined and disciplined me and a me that reflexively tended to shrink back into the woodwork because he felt safer.

So the dynamic was set that governed the way Arnie and I met the world as twins, as men, and as business partners. We rarely competed with each other. Arnie was more comfortable socially. I was more confident academically and with learning in general. I appreciated his strengths and he appreciated mine. We needed each other to start Earth's Best and we knew it.

Arnie often got more of the limelight because he bravely put himself out there and deserved it. Sometimes my ego was bruised because Arnie represented my ideas or signed his name to a letter I had largely written, but it was a good deal for me and always my choice. He had to contend with pressures that I could not. The impact of the panic attacks ultimately dictated what I could do and what Arnie had to do as Earth's Best unfolded.

This is not a poor-me story. I've had my studly moments in life. In fact, most people I know would wonder who the hell I'm writing about because my overall effect in life has not been wallflower-ish or retiring. But who you are inside is seldom what people see on the outside. My inner psychological terrain has been dominated by the features described above. The person I present to the world reflects how I have reacted, compensated, and related to my life's circumstances. It's the same basic paradigm for each of us, and the infinite variety of circumstances and then choices are what make the world go round.

Some people suffer and conclude, "Why shouldn't others suffer as I did?" Others like me want the suffering to stop. I came to Earth's Best carrying both the wisdom that Donna and many other group-home kids taught me about being real, setting limits, and building trust, and the deep knowing that everyone should be loved, even if he struggles with Roman numerals and has a rounder face.

ARNIE:

I am the older brother by eight minutes. After my birth, the doctor and my parents thought that was it, they had a son. And then without warning, Ron, who was supposed to be my placenta, blindsided everyone in the delivery room. And then there were identical twin boys.

Of course, I knew there were two of us, but I wasn't talking much at the time and certainly didn't want to ruin Ron's surprise. So I just lay there patiently, waiting for the hubbub to die down. It didn't for a long time. Amazingly, I was already displaced. Ron was getting all of the attention. And Carolyn, our older sister by two years, had the Chutes and Ladders experience of falling completely off the family radar screen in order to make room for us. She's been a lifelong recovering sibling of identical twins.

In theory, my elder-statesman status of a whopping eight minutes should not have mattered much, in the grand scheme of things, but eight minutes' difference is a long time if you're soft-boiling eggs, and it has proved to be a long time if you're hatching twins. I'm the older brother. Ron is the younger, the baby. I have outwardly led. He has inwardly led. I have looked to him for help reconnecting to my inner life. He has looked to me for help meeting the stresses of the outer world. This dynamic, although certainly not an absolute one, has had a constant presence in our lives, especially in how we met Earth's Best and journeyed our way through that experience.

I suspect because twins are just so irresistibly cute and were supposed to have names (back in 1951) that were also cute and catchy, my parents did their duty and named us Arnold and Ronald. In retrospect, it could have been worse, like Silly and Dilly or Pinkie and Winkie, but being Arnold and Ronald attracted a certain attention that I was not fond of. It sounded like a package deal. We were two people, but we were often seen as one unit—Arnold and Ronald.

This reality did not define my childhood or scar me for life, but it did lead to the inevitable merciless and mindless comparing Ron has already discussed. It is true that I grew up often being related to as the less smart or dumb twin. I don't know how or why this happened, especially since I didn't have a problem with Roman numerals. It hurt. I felt inferior and insecure about my own abilities. But there was no competing with Ron. He was driven in a way that I was not. He had willpower that seemed superhuman to me. I didn't know about his horrendous blackboard experience. We had different teachers. He didn't talk about it, and there was no twin ESP working for this. I just knew I couldn't resist the *Little Rascals* and later *Star*

Trek, and he miraculously could. If I was facing the annihilation Ron describes, we would have been study partners also.

I learned along the way that I was smart enough. How dumb could I be? I was Ron's twin after all. But the same logic did not work for him. How ugly could he be if he was my twin?

Ron and I had a playathon childhood. We didn't know boredom. It was fantastic to always have someone to have a catch with, play Ping-Pong with, bowl in the hallway with, and of course fight with. We were like different letters on the same page in life. Maybe we were even different letters in the same word on the same page. I always had a buddy to take the edge off of new social situations, share the brunt of run-ins with Mom and Dad, or buzz through house chores with so we could go outside and play. We shared so much that was the same, but somehow we evolved to see the world differently.

The Koss-Twin Prototype: Dad, a.k.a. Milton Koss

Unlike Ron, my childhood did not lead me to the expectation that "nice guys finish first." It's not that I thought they necessarily finished last, but first place was out of the question. That particular bubble was burst for me while witnessing the disappointment and heart-ache my nice-guy father, Milton, encountered struggling to pave his own path through the entrepreneurial wastelands. As a kid, I didn't understand what was really going on between the adults, but I did understand the universal signs of distress and worry.

Because I found school to be mostly boring, I had to pay attention to something that did interest me, and that happened to be what my dad was scheming to do next. I don't use the word "scheming" in a negative sense, but rather in an innocent one. Through my eyes, my dad was like a big kid perpetually working on a fantastically large lemonade-stand idea. I'm not talking about Kool-Aid. I'm talking real lemons and ice. I sensed excitement and adventure. I felt pulled to the risk of the unknown and the possibility of success. I always hoped my dad would leap into some new darkness, so I could come along for the ride. Of course, I always felt safe and never imagined that any consequence could threaten that safety. And it never did.

I remember sitting around our white Formica-covered kitchen table watching my dad fill up the pages of his yellow legal pad with ideas, numbers, questions, and exclamation points. The pad was always yellow. It was magic. He seemed omniscient. Sometimes, we all sat around the table listening to my parents discuss the future that all those numbers represented. I was captivated by my dad, but now I think about my poor mom who also rode into that darkness, whether she liked it or not.

I was amazed at how my dad could change his life the way he did. I remember the wholesale candy and tobacco business. That was fun: lots of candy, baseball cards, toys, and a great big warehouse to run around in, play hide-and-seek in with Ron, and most importantly, watch my dad play businessman.

And then without warning, the warehouse was gone. No more baseball cards. And there was my dad with a wrench in his hand, in a new business, this time Koss Motors, a hole-in-the-wall garage, where he sold American Motors Ramblers, pumped gas, and fixed cars. When did he learn to do that? The year was 1964.

Ron and I used to walk to the garage after school to pump gas and hope for a quarter tip if we did an especially good job of washing someone's windows and headlights. I loved working the cash register and going through the oil-stained Koss Motors receipt books, looking at all the repair bills and the tons of money people were paying my father to fix their cars. We were rich. My dad knew this would be the case, because all those numbers on that yellow pad told him it would be so. Right? And if all of that wasn't true, there was at least the Dairy Queen a block away and the opportunity for me to become very familiar with hot-fudge sundaes. Ron always got the coffee thick shake.

How many Ramblers have to be sold and gallons of gas pumped and cars repaired to make a living? I remember my mom and dad talking at night and hearing blame and bitterness ooze from my dad, as his business began to betray his yellow pad numbers. Longtime friends were not buying gas or servicing their cars at Koss Motors. He counted on these loyalties. His projections reflected them and he felt betrayed. I'm certain he was raised to believe that "nice guys finish first." I saw firsthand that it wasn't true.

Before too long the garage was a wreck, and it was on to the next pad of paper and business start-up. We never owned another Rambler. And my dad never forgave or retreated from his anger.

Then came foam and plastics and automated accounting and quick hair-set curlers. And who knows what business I'm forgetting? From my perch as an observant kid, I also came to understand that partners could be trouble, that trust was at your own risk, and that money came with strings, many of which were exasperating, fickle, and shortsighted. My dad was pummeled out there on the business playground, and he was a good, honorable guy.

In 1968, I was a junior in high school. By the way, this was the year of the quick hair-set curler start-up. My guidance counselor, Mr. Percoco, met with me to discuss my plans for college. He inquired about my interests and what profession I was attracted to. I could have said, "I don't know" or "hair-curler executive" and have sounded like lots of kids who were clueless, but instead I threw us both a curve and said that "I wanted to be nothing." I didn't know what I meant by that strange response, I only knew that the answer surprised me too and came from a place deep within me that was unfamiliar. It was a truthful answer and one that I struggled to understand and accept for many years.

Beware of Cement Blocks

At the time, however, my fate was in my parents' hands. "Nothing" would not do. I was going to college and was going to stay in college, end of story. The Vietnam War was raging, and the only future worth having was going to come as the result of a college education. This is what I was indoctrinated to believe. This is what was expected of me.

I shipped out to Wilkes College, a small liberal arts institution nestled along the picturesque Susquehanna River in Wilkes Barre, Pennsylvania, in the fall of 1969. I thought that I might discover the wisdom of my parents' insistence, but strangely I soon found myself sitting buck naked on a block of ice. This was a cold and unexpected introduction to college. The next day I was standing dutifully at attention with a bag over my head, holding a cement block that was inconveniently attached by a string to my penis. The command that followed from the friendly upperclassmen greeters was, "Drop the block."

The separation anxiety from Ron, which could have been huge, was no big deal because I was preoccupied with trying to keep both my penis attached to the rest of me and the skin on my ass. It was a clever diversion. I didn't recall hazing being described in the Wilkes catalog, nor was it featured in my freshmen-orientation package.

I studied and studied that first semester at Wilkes because I knew I was supposed to. Ron would have been so proud. I don't think I watched one *Star Trek* episode. I was determined to bring home a stellar report card. The truth is, I put my time in, but I also daydreamed a lot. It was a battle. I stayed very busy and intended to be super conscientious, but I was plagued by a new noisy inner voice that was screaming at me to get the hell out of there and claim a different life of my own choosing.

My accounting teacher was no match for this inner voice. Debits and credits put me to sleep. All my classes did. My inner voice didn't. I met some great people, but Wilkes was like the desert for me. I felt like I was drying up and turning into dust there. Ron, on the other hand, seemed to be thriving at the State University in Albany.

For the first time, we weren't on the same page or even in the same book. There was this separation that I never could have anticipated. Something was happening to me that I couldn't resist, that I didn't want to resist, and Ron was not there feeling the same force. In fact, he was rejecting it because he was scared of losing me to Vietnam or to some unknown that was off any road map in Mr. Percoco's office or in that career book that sat year after year in our Ellenville bathroom.

In hindsight though, something huge was also happening to Ron. In his first week at SUNY, while I was being hazed, he dropped his physics, calculus, and biology classes and replaced them with liberal arts choices. He actually started turning his life upside down before I did. This not only reflected his burnt-out adrenals from all those years of beating back annihilation, but a deep interior fault line within him that was getting ready to rock his world.

Surprisingly, my official college drop-out point was not at Wilkes College. I delayed the moment by spending a semester at the University of Miami. My parents begged me to do this. I couldn't say no. It turned out to be a smart move, because I needed more time to prepare myself to be in the world on my own. (But it was a qualified smart in that you have to ignore the thousands of dollars that my parents flushed down the toilet.)

On the weekends, I would hitchhike down to the Florida Keys to try out my survival skills. I bought a backpack, a sleeping bag, pocketknife, rope, and a snakebite kit. I camped on the beach and lived under the stars, practicing celestial navigation. I tried my hand at snorkeling and free diving. This was my classroom, and the people I met were my teachers.

College just seemed like an anachronism to me. It was unbearable for my parents. Their son Arnold was on his way to points unknown, and there was no recipe for his success or recognizable path for him to follow. He would be lost for sure.

Arnie, Inc.

I was actually just following my entrepreneurial nature. My first adventure had to be the founding or the finding of Arnie, Inc.

According to the bylaws, the only investor allowed was me. Every day of delay was an unbearable one. There was only one looming hitch that threatened the venture and my reverie: the Vietnam War. My lottery number was still fair game, but I knew that somehow I wasn't and wouldn't be.

Ron mentioned our dad was a World War II vet. He enlisted when he was eighteen to defeat Hitler, and his youthful enthusiasm died somewhere in North Africa or maybe Italy. One thing is for certain: Vietnam was a war he didn't want to lose his son to.

Consequently, it infuriated him when I abandoned my student deferment. He was right. It was inconceivably stupid, but something compelled me to do it. I couldn't wait in college for my life to begin. And I couldn't lose my life in a war that I didn't believe in. I had to take a chance. My plan was to beat the odds down with determined preparation. I was fighting for my life, literally, and this was empowering and very scary. I had never been out on a limb before, although that string-and-cement-block experience at Wilkes was a close call.

It took many months to familiarize myself with how to best fight being drafted. I was counseled and directed to doctors and psychiatrists who were sympathetic to individuals opposed to the war. Eventually when I thought I was ready, I petitioned my draft board and requested to be given my physical exam for induction. I failed due to "synovial crunching of the right patella." I refused to do a deep knee bend in a room full of guys who did.

I know how polarizing and painful the Vietnam War was and remains today. Setting aside the politics and emotion of that time, if possible, for a moment, my approach and actions to beat the draft reflected my temperament and the way I was hardwired. Arnie, Inc. was a start-up with a mission of self-discovery and expression. The war was an obstacle in the way that threatened my venture, that being me, and I attacked that obstacle with the full force and fury of my personal will. If I wasn't a natural-born entrepreneur, I don't think I would have found my way through the challenges of that tumultuous time without graver consequences.

This also proved to be a very lonely time. Arnie, Inc. was now in business without a plan and no working capital or credit line. Ron was sequestered away in Albany. My parents were relieved about my deferment, but once that was resolved, disgust settled in for the long haul. And to top it all off, I began to look like a hippie. I had no idea that I had a dark brown afro in me, but that's what happened when I abandoned the barbershop. It grew six inches in six months. I think the sight of my head made my dad nauseous, and I know it blew Ron away.

What frustrated and alienated me from most everyone, long-haired and short, was this assumption that I was on an escapist, hippie, drug-saturated track. I was not. I was on the most important mission of life, but everyone saw the hair, and I was immediately guilty by association. That didn't make me want to get a haircut; it made me grow my hair longer. Nine inches in nine months!

I didn't face my induction physical so I could, at long last, be free to do drugs. College, very generously, afforded me that opportunity. I'm certain the pain I was in could have been sufficiently dulled by the drugs floating around in my dorm room. The truth is, I was bursting with life, because I was finally on the precarious edge, living it. I didn't need or want drugs.

But what I didn't expect was to be alone on this edge. Where were the "others" who felt the passion I did to search within and without for a better way to live and be in this world? I really didn't know what I was looking for, but I was certain I would know when I found it. It didn't take long before I was thinking that there were students, there were hippies, and there was Arnie.

I wandered. I visited Ron at SUNY sometime in 1971. He marveled at my "do," but the little devil was actually growing one of his own. I liked Ron's SUNY friends and had great times with them, playing, laughing, philosophizing, and loving. For me, the campus was an oasis, a safe place to gather my courage for points unknown. I even got to enjoy the SUNY meal plan thanks to Ron's meal card and similar appearance. But I could only hack so much of dorm life and being a dust ball on the floor.

I landed in Tucson for a spell and took up residence in an old abandoned tuberculosis hospital that treated "Indians" way back when. The $65 rent was a stretch, but I was well on my way to being a man of thrift. I knew I'd be fine if I found work. I did, working for Man Power as a day laborer, mowing lawns and installing doors for a building contractor.

Tucson was my first time really alone; no Ron, parents, or college structure—just strangers and a torrent of feelings that overwhelmed me. My idealism became strong and harsh. It was new and untested. Not surprisingly, this had a strangling effect. I became intolerant of weakness in others, escapism, and words that did not jibe with deeds.

This judgment was a projection of my own worst fears. Would I ever discover what I was passionate about and destined to be or do? I was angry at the world for forcing me into this lonely place. My parents had already judged, juried, and executed me. They told me I was wasting my life. Suddenly their love felt conditional. This infuriated me, but the anger was just a reflection of the deepest pain. My own self-condemnation wasn't that far behind, but if you had told me that, I would have simply said, "wrong." My anger was righteous. It was a phase. No one was spared.

I planted my first garden in Tucson, had my first enchilada, and tasted my first avocado. I could see that the further I got away from my head, the happier and softer I was. A dream started to take shape. I wanted "out" of careers, jobs, consumerism, and convention. I wanted "away" from our bankrupt society. And I wanted "in" to living with the rhythms of the seasons, the natural world, and a life of voluntary simplicity. Now I could tell Mr. Percoco that this was my "nothing."

But there was no beeline to finding this simplicity. I could find no path whatsoever. After a day of backbreaking work at Man Power or a day spent under the thumb of an obnoxious or mean boss, I would peruse the yellow pages to look at all the professions and vocations there were. I always found things I thought I could do, but didn't really want to do. The practical in-the-world part of my being seemed to be missing. Some part of me obviously wanted to fit, but not enough to trade my hopes and dreams for safety and security or my parents' acceptance.

I did not start my journey away from convention by wanting to make a difference in the world. I started out wanting to make a difference in *my* world. The venture was Arnie, Inc. I was self-absorbed. In order to have even a thought about organic baby food, let alone starting a company, I had to cross this divide from "me" to "we." I needed those junk jobs. I needed to get ripped off at that New Mexican commune of peace and love. I needed to be a butler and a houseman and a chauffeur, not once, but over and over for several years. I needed my rough idealistic edges smoothed by experience, humbled by mistakes, and tempered by self-reflection.

It was fitting that as the older twin I would first let go of all that was safe, all that was expected, and all that I thought mattered, to confront the anger and disappointment of my parents and to meet the unknown, including myself. I did so with all the innocence and beauty of youth.

When my parents heard that Ron was on the verge of dropping out of SUNY in early 1973, nine credits shy of graduating, I solidified my place as the black sheep of the family. I understood the logic. They figured my vagabonding influence, which could only be negative, was behind Ron's inexplicably stupid move. But I had no reason to feel sheepish. I didn't have that kind of influence on Ron. His interior fault line did its thing, but since it was invisible and I was not, I took the hit.

Yes, it's true that I was living on the floor in his five-man SUNY dorm suite during this period. And yes, I was ecstatic that it was happening. I knew there was no turning back for Ron. He had leapt and it wasn't so we could revert to being two peas in that very comfortable pod, because we were still going our separate ways. He wasn't ready to leave the Albany area, and I was. I was Arnie, Inc. He was Ronnie, Inc. Separate ventures, same mission.

There were umpteen numbers of trips across the country. I hitched everywhere, and when I had enough money, bought Greyhound bus tickets. There were months of travel in Europe and return trips to Florida to visit my parents (who, despite their displeasure with my lifestyle, always welcomed me home). Ron and I would rendezvous there to catch up and recharge, and to see our parents whom we loved and we knew were suffering witnesses to our questing. We did give those swivel chairs on South Ocean Drive a workout. Ron spun so fast one day that he flew out of the condo and landed at Empire State College.

My spinning flung me to a remote area outside of Ashland, Oregon. With my dear friend Jan, we built log bridges, hand-dug a well, planted an orchard, and constructed primitive living structures. I was especially proud of the roughly hewn but stylish outhouse we built and the solar oven that baked our bread and chocolate chip cookies. I loved this life of pioneering. It was filled with the present. I imagined it to be my future. Jan and I even got two mules for the work ahead. Their names? Ani-mule and Bartholo-mule.

But we got ahead of ourselves, as is often the case with start-up ventures. There were problems, the most glaring of which was our inability to find a way to make a living in this remote area. I was not a sawmill guy, though I really appreciated our closest neighbor, Dale, who ran one. The fastest way we found to gather a new supply of cash was to leave Oregon for domestic estate work in California. How strange it was to be living outdoors with no electricity or plumbing and then to suddenly be catapulted into the opulence and crass materialism of Beverly Hills. Although I wouldn't admit it at the time, there was something about the lap of luxury that I liked.

After several of these exodus cycles from Oregon to California, despair descended. I couldn't see my future there anymore. I was tiring of the nomadic lifestyle, and I knew it was just a matter of time before Jan and I were broke again. Our lives weren't sustainable. I hadn't found simplicity, even without running water and electricity.

More troubling was the realization that I was no longer inspired. I complained about all that was wrong with the world, but I began to sound like a broken record. I knew a big change was coming for

Arnie, Inc., but I had no idea what it was. One of the Florida swivel chairs tracked me down. I started spinning around and around again.

I was finally ready to take a step toward the world I was running away from. Readiness is a phenomenon. I never could have predicted this evolution. I didn't even know it was happening, when it was happening. Somehow all of the moving parts and pieces in my universe shuffled and shifted in this way.

I began to feel restless for the East Coast. The land in Butte Falls was too remote. Oregon was not home. Jan, my adventuresome sweetheart, and I parted ways. I missed Ron. He was also getting restless. Four years had passed since my exodus from Wilkes.

The separation was good for us. We were independent. We respected each other. We both longed for home. It was time to venture together, north to Vermont, where land was affordable, cows outnumbered people, and young social and political activists were gathering to make a difference.

The Fire

I remember well the huge pile of frozen green logs that Ron describes sitting in front of our "big" house in Plainfield. And although tempting to forget, the frozen pipes and toilet ice curiously remain a fond memory. No one aims for toilet ice, even if you're rugged and manly, but Ron and I pulled it off.

We never blamed the other for our stupid choice to rent the house. We knew we bit off more than we could chew, but we also had what we wanted. The choice was to either learn to work together or freeze—one way or the other. Bone-chilling cold has a way of streamlining pettiness and discouraging egoism. And so did our propane blow torch that blazed on a daily basis uncomfortably close to the bone-dry basement timbers supporting the frozen web of copper plumbing. All of our stupidities, rashness, and brashness added up to creating the perfect training grounds for entrepreneurial adventuring and impossibly steep learning-curve management. At least, that's one nonparental way of looking at it.

In retrospect, it seems fitting that our first test flight together as business partners was the Vermont Sprouting Family. For years we had been like two seeds soaking in the waters of life, absorbing lessons and experiences and now swelling with readiness. Ron and I were young sprouts. We were family, and it was time to get our show on the Vermont roads. We put it all on the line to that buyer at P&C. There was a lot more significance in that crumpled brown paper bag than alfalfa, mung bean, and lentil sprouts. Our sense of hope and possibility were also in that bag.

Unfortunately, after the thrill-of-victory moment in the buyer's office, it didn't take long for my enthusiasm for the sprouts to begin to wilt. That's what happens when you become cashless, and desperation prevails and takes over your brain. But the embers of hope and possibility reward a good breeze with a long-lasting glow. Ron and I had a taste of success and empowerment.

True to form, the thought of ever becoming an employee again was the most unappetizing of prospects. More than ever, I understood what my father had been feeling all those years he had been doodling in his yellow notepad, rather than filling out employment applications. It was both scary and empowering to be in a position to hold my fate in my own hands. I knew my life as an entrepreneur had just begun, even when we sold the sprout business and I shipped off to take another lucrative live-in estate job as an attendant to an elderly paraplegic man in Connecticut.

Like Ron, I also longed for home. The ache hadn't stopped when I left Oregon; it had intensified. I must have been a frustrated frontiersman in a former life with unfinished business. I had this drive to build my house using only hand tools. The purchase of The Land in 1978 afforded me that opportunity. The timber-frame building project became my obsession. I just knew what I wanted and lurched forward. Ready or not, here I come.

The logs piled up. I was so happy in the woods with Ron and so happy to be creating something that had the potential for permanence and commitment. Twenty-below-zero temperatures didn't faze me. I was through bouncing around.

Predictably, the errors came fast and furious. Fortunately, I had a lot of logs to practice on. I edged my way forward, learning to swing a broadax with an eight-inch unforgiving blade and finesse the swinging angle of the adze that I used to help square the logs. I devoured the opportunity to learn these skills and wondered aloud many times if I would have found my way through college if they had offered this type of education.

My youthful enthusiasm and ingrained entrepreneurial nature propelled me forward. Although I was being meticulous and diligent in my own mind, I was also by necessity winging it. I didn't have money, didn't have credit, and didn't have a job. It never occurred to me to wait and be patient, because I had no sense that I ever would have any meaningful access to those things. In fact this was that "edge" that I loved living on: the edge where the rewards always overwhelmed the risks, the edge where the meaning and fulfillment I longed for were possibilities.

The morning of the house raising came with a steady stream of butterflies. I didn't want to be the idiot who spent more than six months hand-hewing a huge pile of timbers for naught. Perhaps I should have had those butterflies six months before. I'm pretty sure that's what Ron was thinking, because he kept telling me to get help from someone who knew something about timber framing and carpentry. I was a stubborn Koss, so to speak.

The first wall section was raised without a glitch. Bravo, Arnie. Then came the cascade of misaligned walls, errant measurements, and suspect joinery. My carpenter friends saved my butt. Section by section the framing rested on those stone piers; piers that Ron and Carley actually helped build on their very first date in late 1978. It was a fantastically exhausting experience.

I sat quietly on the hillside above, staring in awe at the timber frame. There stood all those sticks of wood that Ron and I had hand-cut and hand-dragged out of the woods in the deep snow, now miraculously interconnected to be the home I longed for. Although I didn't fall on my face, I knew the day could have been a big bust. I did learn a valuable lesson about next time. Risk should be managed whenever it can. Climbing onto the "edge" doesn't mean you can't fall off. I was lucky to have succeeded.

But the frame of a house doesn't make a home. I was so fixated on the timber-framing challenge that I failed to adequately anticipate the magnitude of what remained after I cleared that obstacle. So many decisions and tasks lay ahead that were as demanding as everything else that preceded them. They just weren't as glamorous or adventuresome to me. What about water and septic and heating and windows? All of which tied into this vast area of avoidance for me: money.

The greater the gaps in conscious engagement, the greater are the risks to an entrepreneurial venture. The Land, as it turned out, proved to be the cause of a huge gap in conscious engagement for me and Ron. We were so emotionally attached to the nurturing it provided us, that we deliberately avoided California as the smartest place to launch Earth's Best. Vermont was the best place. We convinced ourselves and, in turn, many others along the way that this was true. As diligent and earnest as we were, we could not face the consequences of a truth that was potentially known to us. Later on, Ron and I would pay dearly for this indulgence.

Winter was now fast approaching. I hadn't earned a nickel in months and began to scout around Montpelier looking for a job. Deep down inside, I was hoping to find nothing. I would soon be twenty-nine years old, and a passion for something, anything, related to livelihood continued to painfully elude me.

My employment track record suggested that my next employ would be short-lived. Every job I had taken in my life at this juncture was a defensive move to avoid complete financial collapse. However, I didn't have an exit strategy when I started my new and improved position as assistant manager at the Aquarian Grocery Natural Food

Store. Inevitably, I guess, the cards were dealt otherwise. I left this employ within my customary six-month time frame, but not for the usual, "I hate this lousy job" reason I would have predicted.

The phone call came sometime in January 1980, while I was at work. It was my neighbor, Dave, who broke the bad news. The house was fully engulfed in flames. It would burn to the ground, obliterating a labor of love and a dream come true. I went into shock. My partner and I had lived in the house for less than three months.

The fire destroyed every possession that we had. Far worse was the discovery that our dog, Raz, was unable to get out of the house and perished in the inferno. It was devastating. Nothing remotely like this had ever touched my life. I went numb. Horrible things happened to other people, not me.

The fire catalyzed many changes. My relationship ended. I walked away from my job at the Aquarian Grocery. Depression, something I had never known before, followed. In my judgmental Tucson days, back at that old TB hospital, I had been intolerant of anyone who exhibited fragility and vulnerability. Depression was for weaklings. Now, fittingly, I was depressed. I was like the brazen M&M who was discovering that his hard outer shell was thin, easily dissolved under the right conditions, and hiding a world of softness and vulnerability that could not be willed away. I was a mess.

I found a small third-floor room to rent in an old Victorian house in Montpelier complete with four roommates. The winter darkness had its way with me. Where was the silver lining? I found it in discovering the love of writing. I wrote a screenplay, "The Last President," which provided a creative outlet that I desperately needed at that time.

I kept straining to see what to do next, but I could only clearly see what *not* to do, which happened to be almost everything I could think of. The same old swivel-chair tape was playing. It would have been a big yawn, if hadn't been my life. Was it a curse? It felt like it. Somewhere within me, I knew or wanted to believe that this enduring dilemma had a purpose. In the meantime, all that lay in front of me was another round of menial work—or so I thought.

While Ron and Carley were immersed in the drama of Morehaven Group Home, I went to work that summer of 1980 as a warehouseman for a start-up produce distribution company. Green Mountain Produce was one of the first companies in Vermont to distribute fresh organic fruits and vegetables, transported all the way from California, Oregon, and other distant locales. Unknowingly, serendipity gave me a front-row seat and an insider's view of an industry I would soon dedicate a decade to improving and expanding.

At 3:00 a.m., I was on the job, freezing my butt off in this big cooler, or even worse, in the freezer, picking orders to load on the delivery trucks. But I liked being around the produce. There was a vitality to it. I was intrigued by the grower names on the various boxes. I wanted to know these people. I wanted to be these people. But I quickly learned that there were problems inherent in the business that would prove to be overwhelming.

Before I loaded a case onto a pallet, I had to open it up to be sure the produce condition was tip-top. Too often, the citrus had mold, the apples were mush, and the greens had slime. I had a connection to Glen, the owner of Green Mountain, and I felt his angst as he struggled to overcome the never-ending deluge of dying produce and out-of-stocks. The future for organic produce proved to be bright, but not for Glen's business. It was painful to watch. He was a little too early on the scene.

Organic growers had not perfected their post-harvesting techniques and storage practices. Transport from the West Coast was not precisely coordinated yet, and far too much produce sat in truck terminals and on tarmacs throughout the country. Watching Glen in the trenches gave me an up close view of what it was like to be in the shoes of a real entrepreneur whose vision I identified with.

I learned that willpower has its limits, but since we don't know what those limits are until after the fact, we tend to keep pushing and adapting until someone taps us on the shoulder and says, "Excuse me, sir, you died, you failed; just thought you'd like to know." That's what happened to Glen. I admired him and learned a lot.

Predictably, my life in the freezer was not a sustainable one, but I had responded to this business energetically. Organic-food production resonated with me. Environmentalism resonated. It had to be the future. I was engaged in a way that I had never been. Green Mountain Produce was another building block in my expanding resume, leading me to I knew not where.

The spring of 1981 was fast approaching. I was grinding my teeth thinking about another "next." What would it be?

RON:

Morehaven Group Home unexpectedly closed in the dead of winter in February 1981, due to shifts in state funding and a new emphasis placed on foster care. There was a mad scramble to find foster homes for the kids. One by one, they left. Finally we left. Carley and I retreated to a fifteen-by-fifteen motel cabin that we purchased for $1,000 and had it moved onto The Land.

We ripped out the bathroom and put a bed in its place. We had no running water or electricity. Some women would have run for the hills (or rather from the hills). Not Carley. Every morning we'd hike down to the brook, break a hole in the ice and fill our water jugs. Giardia was a thing of the future. We had 128 acres to roam around for bathroom use. I loved putting on my snowshoes and walking into those woods (with my shovel). As far as I was concerned, we were living the good life. (As for Carley's point of view, you will have to read her forthcoming novella, which Arnie and I completely disavow, tentatively titled, "The REAL Earth's Best Story.")

You can probably imagine how hard my dad was kicking himself for contributing to the delinquency of a thirty-year-old. I think my parents began to lose hope. But I would not disappoint them with my next three moves.

First, Carley and I returned to civilization in the fall of 1981. We moved into Montpelier. Second, I got a job teaching algebra, geometry, and basic math in a small, no frills, alternative high school. And third, I enrolled in a graduate program (one weekend a month) at the University of Bridgeport in nutritional biochemistry. I served up a trifecta of triumph for Mom and Dad, albeit quite temporarily.

I really liked teaching, loved the kids, and begrudgingly appreciated the advantages of indoor plumbing. I tried so hard to manage the stress at Bridgeport to avoid another burnout, but I just couldn't do it. Now I had panic attacks to contend with. I remember carpooling down to class sometimes and finding that I couldn't drive. Basically, I was jumping out of my skin. Unfortunately, the person I was riding with was not very sympathetic, and I really suffered. I've observed time after time that if a person has never had a panic attack, they can't even begin to relate to the intensity of the experience. Even as close as Arnie is to me, he has never been able to grok the panic attack.

But, interestingly, it was not panic attacks that pushed my Bridgeport impulse off the tracks. I sat in my Vitamin and Mineral Metabolism class one day and listened to the minutiae the teacher was dishing out about the biochemistry of life. Science had delved so deeply into the mechanics of our miraculous being. Yet I wondered, what was the point of so much knowledge without consciousness or spiritual connection? What was the point of health without morality and compassion? There was a certain bleakness to the Bridgeport, Connecticut, area that set the mood for this existential reflection, and I was overwhelmed by it. Once again the idea of a career felt too small.

It seems like the more knowledge and information we collect, the more separated we become from an essential, whole, and integrated intelligence. How much more microscopic detail do we need to know about refined sugars before we jettison them from—at least—the foods targeted for children? How much more do we need to know about global warming before we get serious about mass transportation? Will knowledge ever bring humanity to the experience of joy, self-love, goodwill, and inner peace?

I just felt like I was about to sacrifice my life to the infinitesimal, and I knew it was 180 degrees counter to some deeper, although confounding calling. I finished my semester at the University of Bridgeport with three As and went back to the drawing board and back(wards) to our primitive cabin on The Land in the spring of 1982.

Swept Away

T-minus two years to Earth's Best.

In a billion years you would never guess my (our) next move.

Perhaps you remember watching a movie where the Olympic gods above, swirling about in the clouds, are playing a chess game with the lives of us down below. It's a grand time for them with their mischief making and petty squabbles. The mere mortals confront every imaginable good- and ill-spirited circumstance, some calamitous and others humorous, with unexpected twists and turns. In any case, keep that image in mind.

As a kid, one of my chores was to sweep the floor after dinner. We had an ordinary broom and a gray metal dustpan with a fine edge. Every night I swept up the few crumbs on the kitchen floor. And after I swept and left the table, my dad would often sweep the floor again. I use to marvel at this. Sometimes he would show me what I missed. It never was more than a thin pencil line of gray dust that probably fell out of the broom while he raked it over the floor. Our floor was never any fun to sweep, because there wasn't any dirt on it.

Well, in that spring of 1982, I was looking for my "next" and so was Arnie. Predictably, neither one us wanted a regular job. With that mind-set, strange things can happen. Arnie and I took note of a local Montpelier craftsperson making beautifully crafted Shaker-style woven brooms. I repeat, "beautifully crafted brooms." It was intriguing street theater, and there was something magical in seeing a utilitarian tool like a broom made on a nineteenth-century treadle machine. The wheels started turning, and I conjured up a romantic footloose and fancy-free lifestyle as a broom maker! I'm sure Carley was thinking "very scary," but I don't recall ever hearing her say so.

I also don't recall pondering broom making as a profession in that career book my parents left for us in the bathroom.

But it was perfect irony and karma. No doubt the gods took great joy in anticipating the moment when Arnie and I would announce to our parents that we were going into the broom-making business. "And so, Milton and Judith, what are your twin boys doing now that they are thirty-one?" "They are professionals . . . professional broom makers. They make "Koss Brother Brooms."

First we did our homework. Arnie and I traveled down to Sturbridge Village, a great place to see a nineteenth-century New England village at work. We spent a day watching a broom maker make broom after broom, and we grilled him like no tourist had probably ever done. I carefully sketched a detailed picture of the treadle machine, so that we could theoretically reproduce one when we got back to Vermont.

And we did just that, thanks to our talented woodworking friend, Fred, whom we met during our sprouting days in Plainfield. A bale of broomcorn arrived, along with the twine, handles, and small dowels that we used for pegs, and our apprenticeship began. Arnie and I read our step-by-step notes and took turns turning out some pretty pathetic brooms. We persisted. We discovered tricks and slowly evolved into the craftspeople we imagined becoming and needed to become to make a living. Our second machine was a little more sophisticated. Our total production capacity was four brooms per hour.

Of course, we didn't want to compete with the local Montpelier guy, so we decided to establish our presence at the Champlain Mill in Winooski (near Burlington). We set up this amazing space filled with broomcorn, display racks stocked with full-size brooms, hearth-style brooms, little whiskers (whisk brooms), and high-end brooms with walnut and bird's-eye maple handles. The treadle machine was center stage, and so were we.

Watching a broom being made is a novelty in this so-called modern age. People were always gathered around asking questions. Kids were mesmerized. But it was hard to sell and manufacture simultaneously. And, surprise, it was tedious work for ten hours a day. But it was all ours, and we were proud of our entrepreneurial independence and the buzz it was creating in the mall. Arnie and I were the broom guys. To gear up for the Thanksgiving and Christmas holidays, we needed to really boost production and build inventory.

Carley and I were pregnant with our first son (the Earth's Best original test baby) and we said goodbye again to our rustic-cabin lifestyle. We rented an apartment in Montpelier that had a little unheated space off the kitchen. That became my place of work, my broom-production space. It was cozy. As winter rolled along, it was freezing. I cranked out the brooms and drove them to the Champlain Mill. Koss Brother Brooms was a holiday home run.

The owner of that mall became the first Earth's Best investor. Don't ever underestimate the power of a good broom.

And then as the holidays waned, a major wrinkle surfaced—I became allergic to the broomcorn. That's the way it is in a start-up enterprise. You try to imagine all of the bugaboos and you don't. There was a lot of dust and seeds in the bales, and over time I developed a sensitivity to them. I was constantly sneezing and sniffling. I wore a dust mask, but I was always congested. Wearing the mask over my face all day imposed a sense of impending suffocation. I carried on, but I could see the handwriting on the wall. My life as a broom maker was going to be cut short.

The Knockout Punch

And then without warning that looming knockout punch came. In May of 1983, I was driving to Burlington to meet Carley at her baby shower. I had a major panic attack in the car on the interstate.

Imagine that you're flying at 40,000 feet and both engines drop off the plane. The nose points down and you have 40,000 feet to the end. If that situation doesn't elicit terror, I've always wanted to be you. I blasted the radio, opened the windows, bit my fingers, and screamed at the top of my lungs. I pushed the gas to the floor and hoped for the first time that a state trooper was waiting for me. I pulled into a rest area and interestingly pretended to be a normal person. The panic would not subside.

Miraculously, I made it to Burlington. I walked into a house full of happy and celebratory women. I was a complete wreck. Losing control of my persona and having to admit it was excruciating. Encroaching on Carley's baby shower with my needs was a nightmare and seemed pathetic. I was mortified at being me, and yet that was the presenting situation I was stuck with. Carley and a therapist friend at the shower helped me through the crisis moment. The panic receded, but the aftershocks did not.

It was like I had been hit by lightning that day, and all my circuits for living in this world were blown out. I became afraid to drive, to be alone, or to take a walk around the block. What a nightmare for a woman who was expecting her first child and counting on her husband to be there with support and comfort. It was also a nightmare for me.

Inch by inch I crawled out of a very dark and lonely hole. First I walked to the corner. I would drive with Carley in the car. I sat in the house alone while Carley ran an errand or anxiously waited for her to call me to check in. Each minute was an eternity. Every day I pushed the envelope a little more. I saw a psychologist who specialized in panic disorder and he introduced me to "sensible self-talk." "Ron, it may feel like you are dying, but you are probably not." It seemed like there was no sense to be found in me, but at least there was a straw to grasp. Driving alone became the greatest challenge of my life. What a colossal regression.

Looking back at this time as a fair-minded person, I can now see there were some extraordinary stresses accumulating in my life. My mom had ovarian cancer and was quite sick. My livelihood was swirling down the drain, and my job prospects seemed quite grim and unappetizing. Lastly and amazingly, I was about to become a father. I think all of those converging events should have qualified me for some measure of forgiveness and understanding, but it would not be me providing that kindness to myself.

Gabe

About two months after the attack, Carley went into labor. Fortunately, I had recouped some of my resilience. Our home-birth plans didn't pan out. After two days of labor and three hours of pushing, there was our unnamed son, a strapping nine-pound, five-ounce combo of Koss and Claghorn. All I can say about three hours of pushing is that I'm glad it wasn't me. Carley was amazing. Then everything happened so fast.

The baby's breathing was sluggish, and there were some frantic moments, and then Carley hemorrhaged. I stood and watched over the pediatrician and nurses as they worked on rallying our son, and kept looking over to Carley, wanting also to be there with her. That was a moment of hell. I was afraid that all that I loved was leaving me. I was alone in my own faltering and invisible to all of those people in the room, who were attending to my family. Time stood still. I couldn't watch any more. I felt my resilience deserting me. I was scared. I lay down on the floor at the foot of the bed and tried to gather myself. The coldness of the floor revived me a little and the reassurance of one of the midwives comforted me.

I rejoined the scene. Carley needed a transfusion. The nurses had removed our son to another room. When Doctor DiNicola returned, our son did not return with him. He told us that he had a hunch that something wasn't right and decided to proactively start an intravenous antibiotic. That something was group B Strep. I remember asking, "Is he going to be alright?" And there was a moment of awkward silence. "I don't know. He is a very sick little boy. The mortality rate for group B Strep is 75 percent. His size is a plus, and we've started the antibiotic." The room started spinning. Three out of four . . .

Our unnamed would have to be transported to Dartmouth-Hitchcock Medical Center in Hanover, New Hampshire. Carley could not travel because of the hemorrhage. I could not travel because I just could not. Need I say more? We would travel together in the morning, when Carley was discharged. Arnie followed the ambulance.

Although none of us knew it, Earth's Best now had its number-one tester on board. Gabe would prescreen all of Earth's Best earliest formulations before we dared offer them to other babies in a focus-group setting. He was not paid, although now I think he should have been paid big bucks, given the concoctions I tried on him. (He probably won't read this book, so I won't be expecting any requests for back pay.)

Gabe was not the inspiration for Earth's Best, although that is often the assumption, and perhaps it would make a better story line. Planet Earth was my inspiration. My travels throughout California in the early 1970s, after leaving SUNY at Albany, brought me face-to-face with huge pesticide spray rigs. Amidst all of the splendid beauty of California, I felt like a sinister or gravely misled force was killing the Earth. I wanted the world to be different, especially if I was going to have to join it. But how do you make the world a different place? If I could have made that question go away, I would have been free of that dizzying swivel chair paralysis. The question was a torment.

Organic baby food had flashed on my "big-idea screen" in that inspired moment in 1976. Those spray rigs made a deep impression on me. I always wanted to find a way to make them obsolete. Of course, it's not much of a stretch to go from the health of the earth to the health of Gabe and all children. The point, however, is I didn't just have a child and then wander through the baby-food aisle looking for organic baby food, saying, "It's not here. I better start an organic baby-food company, so Gabe has something to eat."

After ten days of hospitalization, we finally went home. I was expecting sleepless nights and all sorts of difficult adjustments and stresses. During the pregnancy, Carley and I had been warned, "Expect your world to be turned upside down"; "Enjoy your last few months together as a twosome, because it will never be the same." But I found the transition to be a piece of cake. There were no sleepless nights. Gabe fell into a routine, and he was a happy, smiley baby. I remember thinking that those cautions applied to mere mortals and not people of extraordinary togetherness, paragons of parental perfection, such as Carley and me.

Our "extraordinary togetherness" lasted four weeks, and then Carley and I dropped into an alternate universe that catapulted us into extraordinary exhaustion. Gabe suddenly started waking up every hour on the hour, starting at midnight, and he wasn't happy or smiley. And that's the way it was for the next year and a half. Like clockwork on the hour he woke up. Although we loved him dearly, Gabe knocked the stuffing out of us.

Many entrepreneurs share a similar type of experience as first-time parents: delusions of control and togetherness followed by a loss of stuffing.

Gabe's birth forced me to accelerate the picking up of the pieces of myself in the aftermath of the panic attack. My mom's grave illness did the same. I had to drive and I had to fly. I never considered pharmaceuticals, though they were often suggested. They probably would have helped, maybe a lot, but they were so contrary to my self-identity, and I was afraid of becoming dependent upon them to live life. I wanted myself back, the way I always had been. And when I know what I want, I'm pretty stubborn about it.

The broom business finally crashed for me in November 1983. Arnie kept it going and really developed Koss Brother Brooms into a "brooming" business. Even our dad took a peripheral interest, given, according to my hypothesis, his compulsive sweeping habit and the prospect of a better broom. I was prematurely faced with the "what's next" question, and the stakes had never been higher.

Like cats tossed from a (small) tree, Carley and I somehow miraculously landed on our feet as the first codirectors of the Ronald McDonald House (RMH) in Burlington in December 1983. We needed a home. We needed a job. We needed meaningful work and to feel of value. And we needed a way to be all together. The Ronald McDonald House was perfect. Eighty-four applicants and we were the ones. And as destiny would have it, I was now living just one block away from the "Tru-Vision" building on Cherry Street. The attic loft of that building would soon become the $25-a-month, office-space hatching ground for Earth's Best.

I was completely comfortable in the chaotic RMH start-up environment. Carley and I had managed two group-home houses when we were at Morehaven. My bachelor's degree is in human services. Carley had worked in a social service agency, and live-in work was familiar and preferred by both of us. Theoretically, we still should be at the Ronald McDonald House.

Go talk to the one who knocked the stuffing out of us. Our efficiency apartment was cozy in the beginning and then grew smaller and smaller as Gabe persisted in waking up, hour after hour, night after night. Sleep deprivation is a terrible thing. Chronic exhaustion overcame me.

Gabe was our little Yoda, although I didn't know it or appreciate his Jedi masterfulness at the time. First he qualified us for the RMH job. We had just been a family in crisis. Then through his all-night partying and insatiable appetite, he proceeded to push my weary bones away from the RMH and back into my restlessness and the existential void. Conveniently, he even had a plush swivel chair placed in the RMH living room for me to spin around.

Stop the Swivel Chair, I Want to Get Off!

The winter passed. In Vermont, once you make it through the winter, you can withstand just about anything that comes your way in the spring and summer. Even exhaustion looks pretty rosy when the lilacs are blooming, and you're surrounded everywhere by a bright dazzling green. But I knew change was coming, because I was unhappy, and I have an allergy to unhappiness. I was feeling claustrophobic at the Ronald McDonald House and also unchallenged.

One thing I've learned about myself is that I love the excitement and challenge of the steep learning curve that's inherent in a start-up environment. The dilemma is that I work madly to flatten the curve out, and as the slope diminishes, so does my interest. As the systems and routines became established in the RMH, the day-to-day operation just did not hold my interest.

This preference for high-octane action, creativity, birth, and dynamism versus routine and predictability deflates many entrepreneurs, who always seem to be casting their net for some new mischief. Getting to know your disposition and anticipating its optimal expression and location within the organization would reflect a degree of enlightenment that is bound to impress someone. Certainly investors like to see an entrepreneur who appears grounded and forward thinking, especially in relationship to his or her own strengths and weaknesses. This, of course, only proves to be true if the entrepreneur's self-assessment is aligned with the perceptions and judgments of the investors.

Deviations from this alignment may result in subterfuge leading to dis-ease, ultimatums, and eventually the plotting of coups and either the testing of golden parachutes or the longing for them. Remember, investors (especially institutional investors) often perceive entrepreneurs as absentminded professors, naïve idealists, and/or obsessed and unbalanced individuals. In other words, entrepreneurs are wild cards who provide vicarious thrills and entrées into new worlds of opportunity, otherwise hidden from non-entrepreneurs. But at the end of the day, entrepreneurs and investors, despite all outward appearances, a shared language, and remarkable overlaps (such as nine-digit social security numbers and the love of chocolate), are two different species.

September is an exquisite month in Vermont, but winter is in the rearview mirror, and it's in the passing lane. My restlessness resumed full throttle, and I felt this deep longing and lack of accomplishment. It was already 1984, and I was thirty-three. My youth was expended, and I was disappointed in myself. I had made a lot of starts and stops, but there was no follow-through. There was nothing grand. I was not making my mark, expressing my ideals, or living up to my potential.

My passion was lost, and I yearned for it. I was up against the wall, trapped in my mind's inability to know how to flower and bear some fruit in this world.

ARNIE:
Next, after my life in the cooler at Green Mountain Produce, I had the strong itch to start a business of my own again. A new vision emerged from the ashes of my timber-frame house. "Village Renaissance Tools and Musical Instruments" was born in the spring of 1981.

I loved working with hand tools, especially the old ones like the broadax and adze that I had used to build my house. The know-how to use these tools was fast disappearing. The idea that they were all being relegated to mere antiques or snubbed as impractical by busy trades-people seemed like such a loss and felt so wrong to me. I was determined to recapture and bring to life another time, when tools were functional, hand-powered, and of incomparable quality and beauty.

My plan for Village Renaissance was simple. I would scour all of New England, attending auctions and garage sales with the objective of buying not only old tools, but any hand tool, be it a shovel, screw driver, or hacksaw, that was repairable and of quality. I would clean these tools, sharpen the blades, replace the handles when needed, and creatively display them in my retail shop in Montpelier. My new partner, Kate, was the musical end of the business, and, with her help, we would begin to buy used violins, banjos, and guitars that we would clean, repair, and restring for resale.

I spent every penny I had and then some buying the inventory to stock the store. Of course, the learning curve was steep, and there were multiple slopes. I had a lot to learn about so many types of tools, bidding at auctions, figuring the value of a tool, and how to negotiate with garage-sale entrepreneurs. I also had to learn how to repair tools I had foolishly purchased. In no time, I was working seven days a week, from morning till night, hunting down tools, getting them ready for sale, and finally selling them for enough profit to keep the venture going.

Our retail shop had the feel of a hybrid museum and tinker's shop, complete with the rich smell of linseed oil and turpentine. On every wall, in about 1,000 square feet of space, there were tools for carpenters, blacksmiths, barrel makers, machinists, leather workers, boat builders, and gardeners. There were old wooden chests, treadle sewing machines, and instruments hanging everywhere. The place was one of a kind, and I could not imagine doing anything else.

Where was Ron? He was on his own path. Sometimes our paths intersected and intertwined, and sometimes they diverged. Ron did not share the same connection to tools that I did, but he visited the store all the time and pitched in to help when I needed it. He was about to try his hand at teaching math and was captivated by these fascinating tapes by a nutritional biochemist named Jeff Bland. There seemed to be a natural ebb and flow to our working together. Village Renaissance was an ebb time for us.

From the beginning sales were erratic. This was contrary to the numbers on my yellow legal pad. Some days there were no sales, and other days some guy would walk in and spend hundreds of dollars. It was scary when things were slow, but I figured it would take time to build a clientele. I'm sure my dad was thinking the same way during the first months of Koss Motors. It certainly would have been helpful if there had been more blacksmiths and barrel makers roaming around Montpelier.

My expertise grew, and I became a shrewder buyer and seller. But I was still barely making ends meet. Disconcerting thoughts started to whirl around as I endlessly sanded handles and sharpened blades. It didn't make sense to work this hard and still be broke.

Used hand tools were a very small niche market. I could see that clearly now, as the romantic infatuation that impaired my start-up vision wore off. Nonetheless, my love for hand tools did not diminish. My passion for them actually grew as I got to know them, their histories, and their makers.

Besides a natural-born aversion to practicality, this passion is exactly why I couldn't give way to the dark side and include power tools in the store. I had no interest in them, even if they were going to make Village Renaissance a more viable business. My priorities were clear. I was in business to express my values and myself. Money did not define success. It accompanied it . . . or not. I could see that my sales were unlikely to jump. I had no more hours or days to give. I could hear the winds of change rustling in the distance.

Ding-Dong

In early March 1982, one of my best customers approached me to see if I might have an interest in selling Village Renaissance to him. I didn't think long and casually said "sure," assuming we could reach agreement on a price.

It seemed crazy to sell Village Renaissance, but an offer to buy my business presented an opportunity to answer the next question in my life. Could I become a serious toolmaker? I had the perfect tool in mind: a Shaker broom. I know that sounds crazy at best and more likely weird. But it was my destiny. These brooms were functional and beautiful, didn't require electricity to make, and the broomcorn could be grown locally.

It was an exciting and logical next chapter, a beginning that I had high hopes for. I was graduating from tools to toolmaking. There was something magical about watching a woven broom made. Ron and I were there together. I knew it would allow me to satisfy my new craving to be a craftsman and maintain my self-employed independence. Strangely, broom crafting had an irresistible allure for me.

On the other hand, I think Ron was on the rebound from his departure from the University of Bridgeport and needed a landing and a resting place. I really wasn't taking in his panic-attack problem. My outer shell had dissolved in places, but his somehow got obliterated. Our twin-ness didn't help me grasp the devastation of his experience. The truth is, Ron needed to be a broom maker at this moment. He needed to retreat. I wanted to be a broom maker, but needed help flattening the learning curve. Ron was such a good student of broom making.

Koss Brother Brooms had a ring to it, but you can imagine what my poor parents were thinking: Some ring, more like ding-dong. I cannot blame them. We were thirty-one and didn't make a stitch of sense to them, or to anyone for that matter. Carley sure was a good sport. I'm sure broom making was not what she had in mind when she signed on for a life with Ron.

As fate would have it, Ron's allergy to broomcorn eventually showed up. He hung in there as long as he could, but his time was up probably because, in his story line, the Ronald McDonald House would soon be calling. The broom business was up and running. I was determined to carry on and build on what we had accomplished together.

For more than a year, I devoted myself to making brooms and selling them at craft fairs all over New England. I would show up at a three-day event with a 150 brooms of all descriptions stuffed in my cargo van. Before a crowd of onlookers, I would craft a Shaker-style broom, and, like a showman storyteller, weave a tale about the art of broom making and the value and durability behind each broom they were staring at. I could sell and I did, often selling every broom I brought to these fairs.

It was during these broom-making days that I met Anne and her four-year-old daughter, Cora, at a New England contra dance. Somehow Anne and I ended up in a waltz, and, after stepping on my toes a few times, she revealed that she practiced waltzing at home with her kitchen broom as a partner. Destiny? I was impressed. The woman obviously understood the value of a broom. I soon would make Anne a Shaker broom with a walnut handle that I hand-carved from a walnut stave. It was my Mercedes, the fit-for-royalty model, for the woman who would, years later, become my wife and life partner.

Compost Happens

It was a Sunday morning in September 1984. I was making brooms on the front porch of an old Vermont farmhouse Anne and I had just moved into. The porch looked like a cocoon. It was wrapped in clear plastic to help keep the chill out, and for the time being it would suffice as my shop.

I started to think about the discussions Ron and I had been periodically having for almost eight years about organic baby food. The idea was so ripe; I could see the sweet juice dripping from it. I just shook my head in disbelief and marveled that no one was running with it.

I continued to carefully wrap the broom with the taut linen cord that was pressed against my fingers and mused. How could "I" start a baby-food company? I was a broom maker, now a craftsman. I was surrounded by a mountain of golden broomcorn and probably fifty brooms in various stages of completion. I could not bring my mind to leap the chasm between where I stood in my little broom-room cocoon to baby food.

But I was overripe for a change. The sweet juice was also dripping from me. Broom making wasn't my destination. It was another stop along the way, serving to sharpen and expand my understanding of entrepreneurship and myself. I always wanted to make a difference in the world, but always felt so small and thwarted. Suddenly I saw that organic baby food was the canvas. Suddenly, at age thirty-three, I knew I was ready to leverage the richness of my life's journey. The hodgepodge of jobs, businesses, travels, and experiences that on the one hand seemed so unimpressive and unaccomplished had by this point transformed into a rich composted soil, ready for a seed that would not only sprout, but grow deep roots and flower as Earth's Best Baby Foods.

I didn't know this composting or transformation process had been happening within me. When you throw sprouts, broomcorn clippings, banana peels, apple cores, and Vermont cow shit into a compost pile and add a mishmash of other life ingredients like dock-worker, houseman, store clerk, and homesteader, it's hard to imagine that the slimy, stinky mess will ever amount to anything. It's an act of faith to keep throwing things on the pile. Why bother? Now I know the answer: because there's so much happening beyond our perceptions that we can't see or sense.

I walked into my shop that day following my routine as a broom maker. And then a light turned on announcing that I was done—I had made enough brooms. I walked out of my shop and into the house where Anne was cooking a pancake breakfast. I told her I was going up to Burlington to tell Ron I was going to start an organic baby-food company. Anne was polite, and she asked the obvious question: "How, Arnie?" "I don't know," I said, "but I am not waiting any longer. It's time."

I gobbled down my breakfast and was on my way to the Ronald McDonald House to tell Ron.

— PART TWO —

The Earth's Best Start-Up Begins

What If?

RON:

Arnie drove into the Ronald McDonald House parking lot on September 16, 1984. I remember his fire-engine-red broomcorn-mobile van. It was a beautiful day, late in the afternoon. I wasn't expecting to see him, and he didn't waste any time getting down to business. "I've decided to do the baby-food business. We've talked about it for years. It's still a great idea. No one else has done it. Why not us? I'm doing it with you or without you."

In an instant I was at a decision point about starting a baby-food company. Give me a break! I wanted change, and yet I felt my heels digging in. The enormity of the commitment was thankfully an abstraction, but the responsibility of making baby food was not. I immediately connected with my fear of that responsibility (which somehow I knew would be mine), and the weight of that burden isolated the wind that was filling my brother's sails from my own.

Arnie's determination and enthusiasm was a done deal. He had leapt, but I had to wrestle with this deep-seated fear before I could join him. I wasn't sure if that was possible. He left the parking lot, and I was left in turmoil.

Two things happened then: a greater fear emerged, and I made a solemn promise to myself. First came the fear. What if I lived my life and never "went for it" and never stuck with something through thick and thin, no matter what? What if I had to look back on my life and face all of the reasons why my dreams didn't come true and my ideals were never expressed? What if I knew that I only got my toes in the water of life, but never submerged myself, never swam to the other side because, through my toes, I anticipated the current to be impossible or the other side undesirable or falling short of my expectations?

The fear of such a life overwhelmed my fear of making a mistake that might hurt a baby. I knew that food was made safely all of the time, and I trusted, despite the urgings of my supersized worry gene, that with the kind of attentiveness I would devote, food safety would not be a reason to say no to organic baby food.

Then came the promise. You know that feeling when you've started a diet and then an evil cookie presents itself or a pint of ice cream mysteriously appears in your freezer and then inexplicably in a bowl, your bowl. After the affair and those moments of self-hatred and despair, there is the swell of renewed determination and hope. "Never again will that cookie have its way with me. I will prevail. I must prevail." That's the way I was feeling when the decision to leap into Earth's Best materialized. No matter what, there will be no giving up. There will be no loss of focus. No matter how sweet the dessert, no matter how seductive the sirens' call to "forget about it," I promised myself that I would not be the one to knock myself out of the box. I would not quit. They would have to carry me away.

The sprout business was cut short. So was the broom business, at least for me. I started and abruptly stopped my aspirations to become a naturopath. Ditto for my clinical-nutrition career track. I was a math teacher for just one year. I dropped in and out of group homes, and I knew the Ronald McDonald House would be the same. Even if all my zigs and zags were perfect decisions, I was bothered by the question, "What if?"

Apart from my connection to the idea of organic baby food and all that I envisioned for what would become Earth's Best, I had formed a very clear and personal goal. This time, I would take myself to the limit, never look back, and never have to ask or wonder, "What if?"

All of this intention coalesced and crystallized around Arnie's visit. Carley breathed a sigh of relief. "Get that guy out of the house." Swivel chairs around the world sang hallelujah. I may not have found my life purpose but I had a destination, a dream, and a steep learning curve that would resist flattening in ways far beyond my imagination.

Consider This Question

How do you start an organic baby-food company with no money, no food-processing experience (except for sprout growing), no expertise in infant nutrition, and no organic-foods industry to speak of? There was no Google in 1984, there were no fax machines, and although there were computers, Arnie and I did not have one or even know of anyone who did.

If our focus had been on what we didn't have in place, Arnie and I would have been instantly swept away by a tidal wave of ignorance and more ignorance. But all an entrepreneur really needs to get started is that dream and destination. Arnie and I had already checked off those top two items on our "to do" list.

Item number three was to find a place to ponder the details. Just across the street (diagonally) from the Ronald McDonald House was the Tru-Vision building. An optician had his office on the street level, hence the name. There was a For Rent sign in the attic loft, and Arnie and I checked it out. The price was right: $25 a month for about 120 square feet. Clearly it was a sign from the universe—or so we thought: Organic baby food was an idea of true vision.

The location allowed me to run back and forth to the Ronald McDonald House. Arnie had a short driving commute. It was perfect. We set up a plywood desk, found a couple of non-ergonomically designed chairs, bought a pad of large paper for brainstorming, installed a phone, and borrowed an electric typewriter that unfortunately did not have a working q key. As it turns out, we proved you really don't need a q to get into business. What you need is low overhead that affords you both the time to find your way and the focus necessary to move forward.

All we did in those earliest of days was brainstorm madly and hang up the brainstorm on the wall. Then we'd lie down on the floor, talk, reflect, rest, and think. The pillar that all of our intention and orientation was anchored to was simple: Whatever we did in the realm of baby food, we wanted it to be the "best." Otherwise, what would be the point?

Mediocrity, in our opinion, had already been accomplished by Gerber, Beech-Nut, and Heinz. Added sugars, modified starch fillers, overcooked foods, foods grown with pesticides, and meat and dairy products derived from animals routinely exposed to antibiotics still plagued some commercial baby foods back in 1984. Amazingly to us, convention had established baby food as a cheap commodity.

Why would the first foods for children conform to the pressures required to drive costs down to next to nothing? Why would the most vulnerable and precious population of consumers be subjected to just ordinary and sometimes even the cheapest of foods, rather than the best of foods? Why did dog food and pet food in general have value-added brands well before baby food? Imagine organic dog food before organic baby food! Why was the "walk" about baby food and quality so inferior to the "talk"?

Our answer: Because of a failure in leadership, imagination, and lost or misplaced values. Gerber, Beech-Nut, and Heinz were all doing the same thing, more or less. Their focus was on market share, price point, margins, and the related pitched battles to either get the upper hand or fend off the invading forces. The actual baby food seemed incidental to their success; hence generally the same products across the board. In 1984 there were value-added consumer choices for just about everything, from cars, TV dinners, concrete sealer, and toilet paper to chocolate. But not baby foods. The Big Three had a lock on the product category and the category to us was stale and inferior.

Arnie and I came at the idea of baby food from a completely different angle. Our goal was to make the world a better place, nothing less. This is how we would define "success." This was our bottom line. The status quo was a farce, and perpetuating it was— and remains—indefensible.

What's the point of putting pureed peaches in a jar, if in the course of doing so, the pesticides used on or around the peaches pollute the ground, ground water, and air, and even sometimes migrate into the finished baby food? What's the point of putting food in a jar to nourish babies while simultaneously applying chemicals to the earth that does not? The fact is, children have the least developed and most vulnerable immune systems. This information was not top secret. The fact is, mother's milk is contaminated by chemicals representing our so-called modernity. Does such information suggest that we stay the course or change it? Arnie and I were hell-bent on change.

To back up a step and to be clear, the mediocrity that in our view defined the "Big Three" is not intended to be a knock on the thousands of people who were in the production rooms making these commercial baby foods. The people who are in the trenches inspecting carrots, running the fillers, cleaning the equipment, and doing myriad other production-related tasks are typically the salt of the earth. They are the "little engines that could" that do the hard work that most of America never sees. They form the backbone of this country. This was certainly the case at Earth's Best, and I have no doubt the same is true for the other three baby-food companies.

Let the Games Begin!

I tackled the infant-nutrition and food-processing learning curves. Arnie started to explore the undeveloped organic-foods-supply side. We intuitively believed that the idea of an organic baby-food company had to be a viable business concept. It had to. Would God create a universe otherwise? But would a four-ounce jar of our "ideal," driven by a "best" ethos, cost three bucks or fifty cents?

Somehow we needed to answer that question, but we knew so little about everything. It was a complete act of faith to move forward. Another view was our dad's. It was a complete act of stupidity to waste our time on such nonsense. This belligerent attitude came from a guy who inexplicably ventured way out on a limb to create the first quick hair-set (QHS) roller in the late 1960s.

But of course we needed money to move forward. Even though we believed our dad had to secretly admire our entrepreneurial pluck, it was pride and the fear that he would lose his money that kept us from going to him. There was no one else in the family to really turn to. At the time we bemoaned our fate because it seemed like such a great disadvantage to have no one in the family to bankroll us. Surprisingly, it proved to be a great advantage (this, of course, is written now with twenty-plus years of hindsight).

Our mom and dad or a family member might have "invested" in us out of love and/or guilt, but an acquaintance or complete stranger would need to see something cogent and convincing to justify an investment. By necessity then, piecing together a convincing business plan became an early focus. Arnie and I were dead in the water unless we were able to capture the imagination, inspire, and demonstrate to anyone who might listen that we had more than a good idea in hand, that we had a great business opportunity as well.

We scrambled to understand the business we were starting so we could not only build a business plan (which we had never done) to raise capital, but also reassure ourselves that our leap of faith was not into outer space, but to the other side of convention and the ordinary.

I tracked down Lavon Bartel, a Ph.D. nutritionist at the University of Vermont, in the late fall of 1984. Lavon specialized in infant nutrition. She listened to our concept of bringing wholesome organic foods to babies and agreed that commercial baby food could be a lot better. As obvious as that perspective might sound today, Dr. Bartel's enthusiasm for our idea was the first confirmation from the "real" world that we were not crazy. It was a relief; just how to translate our enthusiasm for the "best" nutrition for babies into reality would take two years of diligent literature research and product development.

Lavon was central to this effort. She was, as they say, the "consummate professional," and Arnie and I moved forward into the world of business and baby food with confidence, knowing that her expertise stood behind us.

I started brainstorming menu ideas, and it was fun. Arnie was always ready with input and feedback, but our determined strategy to get our arms around the business was "divide and conquer," and the food was my focus. Of course it was clear that we would plan to sell the organic equivalents of applesauce and pureed carrots, but what else? This is where poor Gabe stepped up to the plate.

I remember going through an almond-butter-and-millet phase. Then there was the buckwheat, tahini, and tofu and tofu and tofu obsession. And Gabe, forgive me, there was the seaweed phase. Fortunately, Lavon was always there to shed light on the nutritional and infant-health perspective, and Gabe was there to spit out many of the concoctions and bring me back to Earth.

In the beginning my product concepts were just too "complexicated." My earnestness and passion for the "best" required me to first overshoot the target of what was possible or desirable. I think overzealousness is a necessary chapter in most entrepreneurial tales. It may be even hardwired into the paradigm. The big question is: "How long does it take the entrepreneur's feet to find the ground?"

In this regard, I regret to say that I tend to have an excess of helium in my makeup, or conversely, a resistance to gravity. I'm prone to seeing what I believe and to push the envelope until I see with my own eyes or discover by some other energetic revelation that the envelope actually disintegrated some time ago. The way I have compensated for this proclivity is through intense concentration, incessant thinking, and long hours, the foundation of which might be due to my genetic makeup or karmic journey, but which I attribute to Roman numerals and my third-grade teacher.

The net result, however, has proved to be a plus in my entrepreneurial life. I went down many roads looking for innovation and excellence in baby food and infant nutrition. Whenever I changed course, it was because I was ready to and had taken ownership of the facts on the ground. This is how I became an expert in product innovation that has now extended well beyond baby foods.

"Operator, Do You Have a Listing for a Mr. Pecos Bill?"

Arnie focused on the supply side. One of the biggest questions we faced in developing our first (of countless) business plan(s) was whether the organic-food supply was established enough to support our organic baby-food idea. We expected the answer to be yes, but we knew our wishful thinking would not convince and reassure prospective investors. Would the food show up if the company did? Our business plan had to address this fundamental question.

Remember, the natural-foods marketplace was just beginning to take off in 1984. Organic sales had virtually no presence. In our minds, the perfect solution to mainstream organic was baby food. It would finally give growers a financial return for their perfect peaches, apples, carrots, etc., that just happened to be too small or blemished for sale into the fresh market. Arnie and I knew the industry would be perpetually hobbled unless it found a market for its processing-grade fruits and vegetables. Without that market, much of a crop would be composted or totally undervalued.

Our passion was not simply to create organic baby food; it was to find the most effective means to expand the organic-foods industry (and reduce pesticide use) in as diverse a way as possible. We determined that means to be baby food.

And, of course, not only did it make perfect sense for an emerging industry; it made perfect sense for babies. Our objective from the start was to go head-to-head with Gerber, Beech-Nut, and Heinz. We had no intention of being an obscure natural-foods brand, because we knew we needed the volume of the mainstream supermarket universe to give the organic growers a large enough marketplace to grow into.

Earth's Best proved to be the first and most prominent natural/organic-foods brand to be nationally distributed in mainstream U.S. supermarkets. This is because organic baby food, as a product category, could break down barriers in the marketplace that apple juice or frozen peas could not. Grocery buyers quickly understood that

Earth's Best would speak to one of their most important customers: young parents, especially mothers. Interestingly, and unexpectedly, the natural-foods marketplace was much slower in understanding the value of finally having a value-added baby food to bring new customers (mothers) into their stores.

One of the conundrums we faced from the outset was that we did not want to reveal our idea to anyone already established in the organic-foods business. I remember the first natural-foods show we attended in October 1984. Arnie and I were the mystery twins. We introduced ourselves to the key players in the organic-foods trade and asked lots of questions, but we kept our cards close to our vests. We knew we had a great idea and we weren't giving it away, especially to strangers.

Organic Farms was the lead pioneering organic-foods distribution company back then. Located in Beltsville, Maryland, and run by two visionary guys, Joseph and Richard, Organic Farms filled a major hole, at least on paper, in our business plan. Everything was theoretical. We had no projected volumes of fruits and vegetables needed. We didn't know how we wanted to take delivery of the raw materials. We didn't know who would make our baby food, and there was no time frame. Fortunately, Joseph and Richard were men on a mission. They were on a crazy ride of uniting farmers, processors, entrepreneurs, and certification organizations to bring organic foods into the mainstream. Arnie and I apparently presented a tantalizing and irresistible challenge/opportunity to them. They should have run, but they had enough Pecos Bill in them to climb aboard with us. And we didn't disappoint. We gave them the ride of their lives and then some.

Business *Not* as Usual

Arnie and I didn't stop with Organic Farms. We didn't know who we could ultimately count on. The bottom line is that we felt we needed to be hands-on everywhere to assure the quality and integrity of our venture. We were determined to establish our own quality-control standards and relationships with growers. We could see early on that the "business as usual" paradigm in play was like an unbalanced seesaw. Buyers beat the growers into the ground on price when they could, and growers reciprocated and gouged back when *they* could. Our dream, however, was to partner with the growers and succeed together. We would be there for them, and we wanted them to be there for us.

Many so-called business people scoff at such an approach. They think it's naïve, weak, and threatening. Arnie and I believed (and still do) that the planet and our collective futures depend on it.

First, we took the time to understand the growers and their situation. Then, Arnie and I explained our situation, including our dream and vision for Earth's Best. Over time, growers came to believe that we were for real, and the life of Earth's Best became an important part of their lives as well. Yes, we paid growers more, and yes, this ultimately made Earth's Best more expensive, but this was the price of a fair reality built upon what we valued most and wanted Earth's Best to stand for: "relationship," relationship to the earth, to children, to growers, to employees, to investors, and to ourselves.

There would have been little satisfaction in having achieved our goal of introducing organic baby food knowing that strewn behind us were growers that we beat a penny or two or three out of because we could. Our success was tied to theirs and vice versa.

Management teams (including those of both nonprofits and political entities) that sacrifice relatedness are, in effect, doomed no matter how big their bottom lines might be or how prestigious their positions. In our view, they've missed the point of existence, and eventually they rot from the inside out. That's of course little consolation for those who are left in the wake of the devastation and havoc they typically wreak.

Organic Farms arrived on the scene just in time to help us with our first business-plan story. There were others such as Marc Schwartz of

Little Bear in Minnesota. His grain mill and wonderful heart assured us that organic baby cereals were just around the corner. Also, on our first all-star team was Joe Smillie, today a certification legend for Quality Assurance International. Back then in 1984, Joe was a freelancer, a wild man who traveled the countryside visiting organic farms and helping us identify the best growers.

With Dr. Bartel (our UVM nutritionist) on board and the supply side appearing to have some legs underneath it, Arnie and I needed to articulate the marketplace opportunity to convince potential investors that the stars were truly aligned for organic baby food. The natural-foods industry was our logical entry point. We accessed the various trend surveys (that were free), and they were all screaming yes. It was undeniable that baby food was a missing product category in the entire niche. And it seemed a no-brainer that the first to market would have a preeminent position, assuming one of the "big boys" didn't blow us out of the water.

We believed that Gerber, Beech-Nut, and Heinz would watch us, and if we were successful, acquire us. It was hard to imagine that they would do the pioneering work of building the first organic baby-food company in the United States. Most investors who looked at our plan thought this rationale was plausible, but it didn't stop most of them from worrying and passing on the investment.

Price point appeared to be one of our biggest potential stumbling blocks. Baby food was a loss leader in the mass market. Sell it dirt cheap (at a loss) and get that mom into the store to buy the rest of her groceries. In the fledgling natural-foods industry, the loss leader, as a sales and marketing tool, was yet to be discovered.

Given the hefty margins taken by natural-foods' distributors and retailers, organic baby food threatened to be three to five times more expensive per jar than the twenty cents a jar that Gerber carrots cost in the supermarket. Would that fly in the real world? Would the natural-foods industry get behind us and discover the benefit of a lower margin leader, if not a loss leader? Ever the optimists, Arnie and I believed so.

What we were most convinced of was that new parents wanted the best for their babies, and that intention would create a degree of price elasticity seldom seen in a consumer commodity-like product.

Page by page, our first business plan took shape. I did my best to shed any words with *q*, but it was tough when the raison d'être for our effort was quality.

Deep Cover

There remained a few gaping holes in the plan. Where would we make our baby food? Who would make it? And what else could we do to make it the best for babies? One of our first field trips was to Walnut Acres in Penns Creek, Pennsylvania. Often referred to as the first organic-foods company (founded in 1946) in the United States, Walnut Acres had an idyllic aura about it for Arnie and me. Somewhat vertically integrated with a farm, bakery, and small food-processing facility, Walnut Acres' founders Paul and Betty Keene created one of the earliest oases for organic-food enthusiasts with a widely distributed mail-order catalogue and home farm store.

Arnie and I went to Pennsylvania under cover. Neither one of us liked being this way, but we just felt too vulnerable to lay our cards on the table. Walnut Acres was so inspiring. We were greeted like family and got the VIP tour of their operation. They were canning vegetable soup that day, and I remember how labor-intensive the operation was and also how sweet and wholesome it felt. This was my first production-room experience. I inhaled the smells, sounds, camaraderie of employees, and the whole flow of the process. I loved the environment. It was symphonic and miraculous how all the parts and pieces fit together and worked to produce beautifully labeled cans of organic Walnut Acres soup.

Of course the production manager was probably pulling his hair out because the boiler pressure was dropping or because he knew all too well that some other looming disaster was being propelled his way by mischievous gremlins. But, while I appreciated in a more concrete way the magnitude of my ignorance and the steep slope of the learning curve ahead, I was oblivious to such problems that day. I left Walnut Acres knowing that I wanted to learn how to make that music. And I knew that Arnie shared the identical aspiration.

Preliminarily, Arnie and I concluded that we would find a co-packer to make our baby food. Walnut Acres' production line was designed for cans and not glass, and it was too slow for baby food, but we saw and appreciated its great flexibility. Somewhere (over the rainbow), there was a production facility suitable and compatible for the Koss brothers' vision. We just had to track it down.

As I reflect now, I realize that the handwriting was probably already on the wall, even in these earliest of days. No food plant was going to be good enough for either one of us. But Arnie and I knew that investing in bricks and mortar was a no-no. It would dramatically increase the capitalization requirements and drive the perceived risk and complexity of the project through the stratosphere. It would also delay us, if not derail us, and we feared someone would beat us to the punch and get into the organic baby-food business before us.

Simultaneously, we were fiercely protective and controlling prospective "parents" and were prone to seeing insurmountable problems as we visited various food plants in the course of the next year. The chance of a match was improbable. We thought we were hot stuff and a potential bonanza for the perfect co-packer. We were wrong. As leery as we were of a given co-pack situation, most co-packers wouldn't touch us with a ten-foot pole bean. Why get into bed with a start-up that required lots of special equipment, segregation of all organic raw materials from any conventional foods, and extraordinary quality-control procedures? Besides, we had no track record, and the category (organic baby food) was unproven. It just wasn't going to happen, but we didn't know it.

What's That Smell?

Our early business plans conveyed the intention that Earth's Best would be manufactured by a co-packer. Any romantic vision of our own shiny, state-of-the-art food-processing plant thankfully collapsed or imploded upon itself. The notion was too big even for our bulging eyes.

Our first plan's financials included a cost-of-goods assumption, "Co-packer Charge." That's it, one line and one number. Imagine a business plan that had to convey building a complete baby-food manufacturing facility. Who would believe such a thing was possible—by sprout growers, broom makers, social workers, or health-food store clerks? Take your pick. The odds of finding a needle in a haystack looked pretty good when stacked up against the odds of Ronnie and Arnie Koss securing funds to build a baby-food plant. We had to find another way.

The last piece of our first business plan, before we could crack the champagne over it and launch our quest for investors, was building a three-year projection. There were so many unknowns and so many assumptions to make. Arnie and I had collected numerous bits and pieces of information. Now we had to tie it together into sales assumptions, cost-of-goods estimates, product-development costs, and administrative and marketing expenses. We needed help. Fortunately we found our way to Don Miller, a man of many disguises, including Lotus (software) operator and pro forma builder.

Arnie and I used to stand behind Don and his mysterious and magical computer. We fed him numbers. He wrote formulas, moved his hands very fast, and did a lot of clicking with something called a mouse. Arnie and I waited expectantly for him to push the F-8 button, or maybe it was F-5? Or F-7? All of the numbers changed on the screen, and our eyes focused in on some key number like gross profit or cases produced. Arnie would say, "Something's wrong." He just had a feel for how hundreds of changes spread out all over would affect the projection. And then the search began for the missing parentheses, misplaced decimal, or overlooked step. We massaged those numbers until we believed they were foolproof (or proof that we were fools, depending upon your perspective). They represented our best guess and posited an imagined reality that we grew to have more faith and trust in each day, as we conspired in ways to conquer the unfamiliar.

Arnie and I wanted the projections to show a viable and attractive business. There's no shame in that. That was the point of the exercise. As such, however, business projections should always be considered suspect, especially those generated for a pure start-up. We didn't want to fool ourselves or anyone else, but if there were ever a time for blind spots to rear their ugly heads, the business-plan projections would be their showcase.

And maybe on a certain (unconscious) level we did want to fool ourselves. That's a question for each entrepreneur to ask him- or herself, usually in hindsight. The business plan is supposed to convincingly bring to life and demonstrate how the entrepreneur will wrestle the rubber down from the ethers to meet the road. In the case of Earth's Best, the rubber had a long way to travel. I think the greater the distance, the more potential blind spots and the more places for those blind spots to hide and embed themselves in the entrepreneur's story. The more times the story is told, the more invisible the blind spot. Unless an investor, banker, spouse, or prospective key employee breaks the spell and uncloaks the booby trap(s) in waiting, the only hope is for the entrepreneur to attune him- or herself to the stink engendered by a story line that's worn thin, and ask "What's that smell?"

A mature and savvy entrepreneur might know to ask other good questions such as, "Where are the icebergs?" However, they may be as resistant to seeing them as the novice. That's the beauty of blind spots. They're egalitarian. They're for everyone.

Our first business plan had Louvre stamped all over it. That's where it would soon belong, under glass. It was like an epic masterpiece—or so we thought. Realistically, Arnie and I expected that we would need to make some minor revisions here and there as new information showed up and numbers became harder. We never foresaw that to move forward we would have to get into the business-plan-manufacturing business.

In a nutshell, banks typically wanted conservative numbers, and potential investors wanted more aggressive numbers. And the interests, biases, and demands of prospective investors presented a world unto itself that kept Arnie and me running back and forth with the latest and greatest plan models, always with new features and always presented with our highest hopes for approval.

Guardian Angels Come in All Disguises

I think, at the end of the day, there was so much focus on the plan numbers because Arnie and I did not have the résumés or the requisite panache to make those people looking at our venture comfortable with us. We were mutts. In the world of small business, mutts are welcomed. They're hardy, practical, sometimes strange looking, and definitely necessary. But the world of big business tends to be a more exclusive club. You need the proper pedigree to gain easy or easier access. A Harvard MBA or a big-name company in the résumé goes a long way.

I'm a golden-retriever owner. I understand the appeal of pedigree. I wanted something predictable and with papers proving its authenticity and reliability. I didn't want a mutt. That was my bias. Of course, pedigree also has its disadvantages. Certain weaknesses are prone to develop owing to (for example) inbreeding.

Since the investors weren't comfortable with us, the comfort had to be derived from numbers that were built upon numerous speculative assumptions. That's akin to getting comfortable going to sleep in a house built on quicksand. There was just no comfort to be found. We were slow to realize this. This is why the universe created angel investors.

Angel investors respond to entrepreneurial character, freshness, and vision. They're imaginative, optimistic, and more prone to responding to what their gut says rather than convention. They're the ultimate risk takers and typically the unsung heroes of innovation and discovery, including Earth's Best Baby Foods.

Arnie and I were so earnest in our striving. We recognized early on the catch-22 created by the contrasting needs of investors and bankers. We thought our mythic-sized task was to find the perfect pro forma, the perfect set of numbers that would finally bring contentment to all. What a colossal misperception on our part.

One crystallizing moment was during a presentation to a potential investor group in the Washington, D.C., area. Arnie and I thought we were going to be preaching to the choir. Right out of the chute, we heard someone blurt out, "Who the hell do you think you are proposing to start a baby-food company? You've done nothing. You're not qualified. If organic baby food is such a great idea, why hasn't Gerber done it?" The guy seemed like he was about to explode.

I remember the shock of that attack. It was so blunt. Like it or not, the gentleman did put his finger on why it took Arnie and I three years to pull the financing together to start Earth's Best. The roadblock wasn't about the numbers, it was about us.

Arnie and I fought back hard. We knew Earth's Best was a great idea. We knew our partnership was powerful. We knew we could do it. And we knew conventional wisdom and those wedded to it were not going to cheer us on.

No matter how hard the punch, Arnie and I were not going away. But when we bounced back, we were always better, smarter, and more prepared. It's not stubbornness that wins the day, it's evolution and adaptation. It's listening and being in relationship to the reality you're playing in. Arnie and I didn't like what that prospective investor said, but we heard him. In the moment he appeared to be a jerk, but I think now "guardian angel" is more like it.

With great anticipation, plan number one rolled off the production line in December 1984. We didn't have many places to take it.

Our family was out. Friends of the family were out. We had already invested most of our shekels. The landscape actually looked pretty bleak.

Arnie sat down with Ray Pecor, the owner of the Champlain Mill, where we had done our broom-making theater. Ray was a very successful Vermont entrepreneur, and we held high hopes that he would see the opportunity we were seeing or at least steer us in the right direction.

ARNIE:

Success has to start somewhere, and it is inertia that must be overcome. There's no way to predict what will unfold once you've taken the first step. This is one of the miracles of entrepreneuring. As your life's energy is given over to the endeavor, the endeavor takes on a life of its own. The idea also starts to mingle and percolate within the psyches of others. Joe Smillie, Marc at Little Bear, Joseph at Organic Farms, Dr. Bartel, and Don Miller, to name a few, were all envisioning and thinking about organic baby food. Gabe was spitting out Ron's millet concoctions. Energetically, Earth's Best was already born. And in that sense "it" became a player and a presence separate from Ron and me. Perhaps this is one of the occult reasons that the law considers a corporation a "person."

Every entrepreneur hopes for a straight line to the money. As it turned out, our journey made the zigzag look like a straight line. But that's part of the juiciness of the story. Very few investors want to be the first one into a new deal. No one wants to get burned or feel stupid. Everyone wants to feel reassured, and reassurance means being surrounded by lots of other smart, savvy, and successful people. We were asking Ray to be the first, the icebreaker.

People of wealth are hit up for money all of the time. Ray was no doubt an old hand at fielding such propositions and reading any given situation. This just happens to be the way reality is set up. It's awkward to ask, and as I have been told, it can be awkward being asked. Although the body of our due diligence was becoming formidable, and we were beginning to build our association with professionals to support the project's development, Ron and I were, relatively speaking, still babes in the wood. We were a long way off from having a viable business investment for someone like Ray to consider. True, all of the potential for our Earth's Best idea was palpable, but there really wasn't anything concrete in place to invest in, and there was no measurable outcome or return on that investment in sight.

If you've ever thrown a carrot seed into the ground, you know that it's hard to imagine that it won't get lost or suffocated by the mass of soil when you cover it. And if somehow the tiny seed sprouts and emerges, how could a bright orange carrot be its ultimate expression? Seed-money investors take gardening to another level. While carrot seeds have a successful track record, "idea seeds" do not. The chances of any speculative, high-risk-idea seed sprouting are modest. The chances then of that sprout expressing its full potential are remote. This is why seed money or early investors tend to be either angels— or demons.

Every entrepreneur should be alert to this. The angel connects to the entrepreneur's vision and the entrepreneur, sharing some moral and/or sociocultural value and aspiration. Angels like money; they're not above it all. They're inclined to be relational and allied with the entrepreneur. It's a simpatico thing. Demons are greedy, but typically hide their darkness very well. They may grok the entrepreneur's vision, but definitely not the entrepreneur. When the illusion falls away, demons are about themselves and their insatiable appetites. Fortunately, most are averse to the earliest start-up risks, but they are out there, even in the seed-money stage, so beware. Listen to what you don't want to hear, if you're lucky enough to hear anything.

Ray wisely advised me to go to family members for the first $25,000 in seed money. I knew there was no place to go, but thanked Ray for the meeting and advice and that was it.

Two weeks later, after much gnashing of teeth trying to figure out what to do, I set up another meeting and laid it on the line. "Ray, we have no family out there who could assume this kind of risk." The beauty about Ray is that he was businesslike, measured, and clear. He wasn't overly receptive to our plight, yet he probably remembered well his own humble beginnings and entrepreneurial initiation. Ray saw the spark in us. I think he recognized my chutzpah as I sat there in his office at the ferry dock on Lake Champlain. The ice broke, but not exactly how we had imagined it.

Ray offered to cosign a $25,000 note. It would be our debt with his name standing behind it. Just when you think that there's no possible way you could go into more debt, you find a way. Ron and I never envisioned our personal debt as the first money in. Ray was smart. He understood how important it was to have our own tushes on the line. Sure we were pouring in the sweat equity, but being at risk financially ourselves added another dimension of reality and gravity to our risk taking. It's easier to leap with other people's money. Ray made sure we started out with something to lose, besides our time and energy.

Prospective investors want entrepreneurs to have their own money at risk; the more, the better. There may be a limit, but you'll have to find another book by an entrepreneur who experienced it. Money in is part of the comfort equation. It's what makes an entrepreneur a bona fide player and more of an equal. Sweat equity, however, may be all you have. It really was all Ron and I had beyond several thousand dollars. Although sweat equity equates to your actual life, money at risk carries a lot more weight and qualifies you as an investor. Otherwise, you remain *just* an entrepreneur. We were asked many times over the three years of trying to finance Earth's Best how much money we were investing ourselves. I think our answer always fell flat, and it hurt us.

The Chittenden Bank wouldn't have given us the time of day without Ray's guarantee. He was in effect in the deal and behind the project and us. Instantly, we had a degree of credibility and standing that put us on the map in the Burlington, Vermont, financial community. Although this did not automatically translate into other doors opening for us, we had taken our first major step forward. Relative to our destination, it was a baby step. One baby step, however, was heavenly compared to one rotation of a swivel chair.

The Birth of Best

RON:

Twenty-five thousand dollars was a drop in the bucket, and it was a fortune. Arnie and I started drawing a small salary. We didn't need a morale boost, but getting paid definitely boosted our morale. The nutritional research with Dr. Bartel intensified. Should we do a beet puree "first" food? There was a concern about nitrates. Spinach was good for Popeye, but what about Sweet Pea? Oxalic acid was our concern. I liked working with sesame butter, but what about phytates and their impact on mineral absorption? We researched salt, modified food starches, and the digestibility of numerous grains and legumes. The stability of oils (oxidative rancidity) was a front-burner question. We assumed nothing and researched everything.

Earth's Best was not a marketing concoction. Arnie, Lavon, and I were committed to its foundation. We were preparing for the day when we would stand in front of a group of pediatricians, moms, dads, and of course, babies. There were no shortcuts, assumptions, or personal ideologies that would trump our sound and determined research. Our goal was to bring the best to babies, and that did not necessarily mean what Arnie and I thought was best for us.

We knew "best" meant organic, whole, and natural. We knew that "best" had to encompass improving nutrient retention during processing. We knew that "best" would mean instituting comprehensive pesticide testing of all Earth's Best ingredients. And we knew that to be credible and to have peace of mind, we needed to offer dietary choice and diversity, even if a given choice did not conform to our strongly held vegetarian philosophy (at the time). We were trying to start a business, not build a shrine to ourselves.

Arnie and I located a food-processing consultant in Pennsylvania and completely latched on to him. We knew virtually nothing. Les Allen knew everything. He understood exactly what kind of co-packer we needed and was networked to find it, if it existed.

Arnie and I learned that most food-production facilities were not small, cozy, and multifaceted like Walnut Acres. Typically they have a specialization to maximize efficiency and realize cost-saving economies of scale. One might exclusively bottle juice. Another may can just asparagus and green beans. A Dannon facility does yogurt. But who could do it all? Who could make the juice, process the vegetables and fruits, cook the grains and legumes, and incorporate meat and dairy ingredients into little glass jars?

We needed a miracle. Any food plant that was going to take us on would have to be a partner. Significant investment dollars would be necessary to adapt their facility to baby-food production. Would those be our dollars going into their facility or their dollars going into our business? Putting that deal-killer type of question aside, any given food plant would have to twist itself like a pretzel to accommodate the ordinary needs of baby-food production. Add another layer of extraordinary needs such as our 100%-certified-organic standard and we became absolutely indigestible.

One facility we visited processed sweet potatoes. Their production capacity was so large that in one hour they could produce our entire sweet-potato-puree needs for a year. Everything we looked at with Les was an unwieldy mismatch like this in one way or the other. Our own bricks and mortar seemed inevitable if we were ever going to get into business. It was an alarming realization. Yet Arnie and I preferred a seemingly unscalable mountain that was our very own to a life of endless worry and no sleep. That's what our lives would have been reduced to if we had tried to shoehorn Earth's Best into that sweet-potato facility or any other food plant that came our way at the time. They tended to be too ugly and industrial and just not what we had in mind for our baby.

Of course, now we were really asking for it. Everything about us smelled like "high risk," tasted like "high risk" (according to Gabe), and sounded like "high risk." Some would even say Arnie and I looked like "high risk." But that's where the big river of entrepreneurial life was taking us. We didn't know where we were going, but we wanted to go there. It was crazy, but Les, a food-industry veteran of impeccable credentials, confirmed our fate and affirmed our pronouncement that the only way forward was through the doors of our own manufacturing operation.

If Only Ben & Jerry Had Failed

One of the most confounding, exasperating, and smart questions Arnie and I heard from this point on was, "Why don't you start Earth's Best like Ben and Jerry's did, in a garage?"

If only Ben and Jerry had failed, we would have been spared the endless comparisons and attempts to overlay ice cream and baby-food production on top of each other. Some food making accommodates itself to kitchen- or cottage-scale production, and some does not. Ice cream does. Bread making does. Applesauce does. Strawberry jam does. Baby food *does not*.

Arnie and I did not set out to make thirty flavors of pureed applesauce for babies. If that was our target, we probably could have, at least from a production standpoint, made Earth's Best at the local cooperative cannery in Montpelier. But we weren't shooting for an applesauce product line. We were aiming to create an organic baby-food company that offered a complete and balanced diet for children, from their first foods all the way though toddlerhood and beyond.

Once Arnie and I took the seemingly small step from pureed apples to pureed carrots or green peas and brown rice, the complexity of our enterprise jumped orders of magnitude, especially as it pertains to governmental regulation and food safety. Carrots, for example, are known as a low-acid food. The canning or jarring of low-acid foods requires pressure-cooker temperatures (approximately 250°F) and exact cooking times, as determined by a certified, USDA-approved thermal-processing authority. The stakes are very high when you undertake low-acid food processing. Get it wrong and botulism, catastrophe, and tragedy stand by ready to turn personal worlds upside down.

Arnie and I could not capture the quaint, homemade, Vermonty, two-real-guys-making-baby-food mystique that Ben and Jerry did with ice cream. Maybe there was a way, and we just didn't find it. At the very outset, Ben and Jerry could make 5 or 10 or 20 gallons of ice cream a day from their retail business outlet on St. Paul Street in Burlington. Try to imagine a retail outlet for baby food with moms and dads waiting on line for a dollop of sweet-potato puree at $1 or $2 a pop. Imagine the noise, the mess, and the home videos.

Even if such an approach was a viable business concept, Arnie and I would have never touched it. Selling 10 pounds of sweet-potato puree a day and 15 pounds of apple-plum sauce would not have had the impact on the organic-foods industry that we were contemplating. Of course, we could have set sail to launch a nationwide chain of stores to boost the ingredient volumes. But there is only so much that you can pioneer. Organic baby food in glass jars was a big enough bite for us.

Actually that's almost true. Early on we got the bright idea to minimize the degradation of light-sensitive vitamins, such as riboflavin, by using tinted glass (green or brown). I really wanted to do this and pushed hard to see if we could navigate our way through the glass-supply obstacles. We certainly would have had a distinctive look, and standing out seemed logical. The tinted-glass idea had a lot of early momentum, but there were good reasons to think otherwise. Did we really want to start out financing the purchase of a gazillion brown jars? Some friends expressed concerns that mainstream consumers might perceive Earth's Best (in colored glass) as medicinal or just too different or strange to risk purchasing for their children. This notion had never crossed our minds.

The entrepreneur's bubble is so comfortable. Why bother stepping out of it just to hear naysayers and people who just don't get it? If you're an entrepreneur and this general train of thought characterizes your mind-set, think train wreck.

The status quo meant nothing to Arnie and me, because it was more ordinary than extraordinary. Maybe clear glass was passé; if so, then bye-bye. If we were going to perpetuate the present, it would have to reaudition itself to have any part in our future. We of course consulted with Lavon. When we finally crunched the various bits and pieces of input, we concluded that since a baby-food jar was quite small, and the label covered much of the jar's surface, the food's exposure to light and any related nutrient degradation would be inconsequential. Arnie and I could move forward in peace with clear glass jars. This should be noted as a rare moment in the Earth's Best story. Arnie and Ron voluntarily made a choice to simplify their entrepreneurial lives. Bravo.

The business-plan writing and pro forma development took a radical turn once we framed our fate as both manufacturers and marketers of baby food. We could have analyzed and calculated our diminished chances of ever getting into business now, but Arnie and I felt more empowered than ever. If we were going to fail, we would fail trying to fulfill the dream we envisioned. And if we were going to succeed, it would be success as we defined it and no one else's idea of success. Whatever the outcome, we knew we were going to have to live with it. And we didn't want to have any regrets.

Baseball Meets Baby Food

I remember standing in center field in Monticello, New York. I was eighteen, a senior on the Ellenville High School 1969 varsity baseball team. During the previous game in Chatham, I had dropped a routine pop fly. True, the wind was really blowing, but that ball should have been mine. Given my issues with shame and perfectionism, you can probably imagine how I beat myself up for that mistake. Why was I standing in center field again, subjecting myself to another chance at failure?

I held my breath and prayed for that ball to stay away from me. And the pitch. . . . A high fly ball was hit to short right center field. Our second baseman, Steve, backpedaled. I started jogging toward the play, but believe me I had no intention of being in it. My movement reflected a combination of reflex and just going through the motions to make sure I looked normal. Steve gave up on the ball. He had no chance. My speed picked up. The field must have been slightly sloped. As I ran, the ball came into focus. My fear fell away. I don't know how that happened.

I was now running as fast as I could. There never was a thought about stopping and pulling up short. There never was *any* thought. I slid my glove down my wrist for maximum extension and stretched my arm as far as I could reach. That ball fell into the tip of the web, just before it would have hit the ground. I remember my coach's comment as I entered the dugout at end of the inning: "They'd never believe you could make a catch like that in Chatham."

Somehow, without any understanding of how, I was transformed from a neurotic mess into a Zen ballplayer. It was a moment of grace. It was impossible. For ten seconds I broke free of that poor soul suffering in center field. It actually felt timeless.

That same suffering soul swiveled in my parents' chair for years. When organic baby food came back into focus in 1984, I started running toward it almost out of desperation for change and meaning. As I ran in its direction, all of the entrenched inner babble and fruitless noise started to leave. Earth's Best became that baseball. Although the company was years away from manifesting, I was already one with it. When the manufacturing issue came into focus, Arnie and I were already running for the Earth's Best ball with abandon. There would be no stopping or slowing until that moment in time in which the ball hit the ground . . . or not. We had no fear that it would hit because "now" it was in the air. And there was only now for us, just as there was only now for me during those miraculous ten seconds in 1969. What a treat to share this kind of experience simultaneously with someone else. Arnie and I felt tremendous joy running together, yelling, as good ballplayers are taught to do from Little League on, "I've got it."

All of this might sound corny or New Agey. From the perspective of that suffering soul in center field, I hear you. From the perspective of that same soul who experienced a ten-second never-to-be-forgotten reprieve from that suffering, I hope you hear me.

Wisdom You Won't Find in a Book

When Arnie and I sat down with prospective seed-money investors, they no doubt saw the formidable risks and the daunting landscape that we would have to traverse to succeed. Rationally, logically, and prudently, everyone we encountered should have walked away and wished us well. But that's not what happened.

First, our business plan started to have some shine to it. There was more and more substance, and our authority grew. The legion of consultants and their pedigree was becoming impressive. The idea of organic baby food was hard not to love and root for. And Arnie and I were putting on the table a tangible way to help reduce toxic pesticides and destructive agricultural practices on a potentially grand scale. The whole thing was driven by our shared focus, unity, and determination, which was really a unique force and wonder unto itself. Even our greatest skeptics and doubters eventually marveled at our tenacity.

Arnie and I networked and followed every lead and suggestion. The angels descended, one by one. There was Tim, a very friendly, easygoing guy who just understood where we were trying to get and wanted to be part of it. David was an entrepreneur and author who saw the mountain in front of us and urged us on. Jon was a gem: a great heart filled with hope and enthusiasm. Angels do what ordinary mortals will not. They don't show their wings to everyone. Angels have to want to be discovered.

Maybe $100,000, the total of which we had raised by the spring of 1985, sounds like a lot of seed money, but as conservative as we were with our spending, the money burned. We needed an attorney to make sure that we were soliciting money legally and not violating any of the blue-sky security laws. We needed an accountant to make sure that our projections and pro forma statements could withstand anyone's scrutiny. Our infant-nutrition research was ongoing. The development of a manufacturing facility was a huge project completely dependent upon consultants. We started to envision the graphic identity of Earth's Best and retained expertise to help us there. Arnie and I were each drawing an annual salary of $20,000. There were car rentals, hotels, and incidental expenses as the scope of our outreach expanded beyond the Burlington, Vermont, area. In order to keep going, we needed to keep raising money.

How much money did we actually need to blast off? This turned out to be a very loaded question. Arnie and I made our best guesstimates on sales, costs, and expenses over time (five years). We had no idea what would actually happen, and neither did anyone else. Everyone had an opinion. Here's what we learned about entrepreneuring and ourselves.

Novice entrepreneurs think (typically) that the more money they need, the less desirable they are and the less likely they are to succeed in raising those funds. The mistake here is that these entrepreneurs carry their generalized fears and anxieties about the risks and dangers of debt and assume that since more debt looks bad, more capital to start something probably must look bad as well. This is akin to a platform diver thinking that it would be less risky or safer to do his 3-somersaults-and-2½-twists dive from the 10-foot platform rather than the 20-foot height he actually needs, because the 10-foot board is not as far to fall from. So the earnest diver assumes that he can do his flips and twists faster if he tucks tighter. He figures that since he is only 5'5" he can rotate faster, and if he cuts his hair short there will be less air resistance, and he'll have that extra millisecond he needs . . . to go *splat*.

The novice reflex causes the entrepreneur, despite the best of intentions, to make financial assumptions that are rosier than Murphy and all of his sadistic pals will ever allow. Early on (and the emphasis here is "early on"), our thinking went something like this: "God, Arnie, these numbers show we need $800,000 in working capital before we even break even." "I know, Ron, this isn't right. We can't have numbers looking this bad. After all they're only guesses, so why guess and knock ourselves out of the box?"

It took so much effort to raise $100K in seed money. The thought of finding $800K or more was unfathomable. And if we really needed this much, we were doomed. So the natural response was to find a way to need less. And no one could build better rationales and defenses for supporting their assumptions than Arnie and me.

As it turns out, God made not only novice entrepreneurs, but unsophisticated investors as well. Together they have the potential to represent both sides of the same mistake, miracle, or combination thereof. The unsophisticated investor may also think that the bigger the equity requirement, the riskier the entrepreneurial venture and investment. Bigger is scarier. It's autonomic. The water appears deeper and darker, and the creatures swimming around don't look like koi fish, although they might be. As such, the investor's comfort zone dictates the preference for seeing smaller dollars needed, rather than larger, and is prone to accepting or wanting to see and believe an entrepreneur's attempt to beat the odds with financial assumptions that won't.

Although the term "unsophisticated" has become by today's conventions a negative or judgmental inference, it is not intended to be so in this context. "Unsophisticated" describes investors that are relatively fresh and untested in the particular sphere of entrepreneurial initiative that they are cannonballing into. They may be quite sophisticated and wiser in other realms of investment and/or life, but not so in the one in question that has caught their imagination, for whatever reason. Angels may be sophisticated or unsophisticated in this sense. In either case they are angels.

The reason that God created the universe this way is because the combination of novice and unsophisticated, expressed in its infinite shades of color and degree, and despite any perceived imperfections, is often filled with heart, trust, and brilliance. Those are especially potent ingredients capable of synergizing magical, unpredictable, and inspiring outcomes in business. Unpredictable may also mean disastrous. When such cross-pollination occurs, the fruits can be nutty. They are often one of a kind. Each one, no doubt, has an amazing story with great lessons for serious contemplation. In the case of a venture like Earth's Best, the fruiting process came at great cost to the entrepreneurs and the earliest investors.

There was a lot of converging tumultuousness during this time. Arnie and I were caught in a place that Dante would have called "raising seed money hell." We wanted to get into business before someone beat us there. We had come a long way in a short time. It was time to take a crack at raising the equity. Of course, the seed-money effort had to keep going as did our research and development. But we had to pick up the equity ball and see what we could do with it.

Our first thought was to locate Earth's Best in Vermont and therefore finance it there. After all, Vermont was already famous for its year-round perfect growing season and vast acreage of organic agriculture. Wasn't it?

Remember those blind spots, red flags, and quiet whisperings you (should) hope you hear, see, or sense? Remember those gaps of conscious engagement Arnie wrote about? I loved living in Vermont. I loved The Land. I didn't want to move to California where organic agriculture was most advanced and the climate most friendly for just about every ingredient we needed and were going to need.

Arnie and I sold ourselves on the notion that organic-foods production was just as viable on the East Coast as the West. And given the population density in the Northeast, Mid-Atlantic region, and southern United States, a Vermont location was strategically defensible. Also, the Midwest and its population centers were arguably more accessible from Vermont than California.

Add to the equation the fact that Beech-Nut was located in Canajoharie, New York, H.J. Heinz was in Pittsburgh, Pennsylvania, and Gerber was in Fremont, Michigan. Why not Earth's Best in Vermont? Theoretically and on paper it could have—and should have—worked.

Arnie and I wanted to bring the promise of the organic-foods industry to Vermont—and more broadly to the East. This prospect was very exciting to us. Dairy farms were disappearing left and right, and the future of Vermont's farmland was in serious doubt. The thought of productive land being carved up into two-acre lots was sickening to us. Growing organic apples, peas, green beans, corn, blueberries, carrots, raspberries, pears, yogurt, cheese, chicken, and beef all seemed possible right here in the Green Mountain State. And there was plenty of neighborly backup.

Sweet potatoes, peaches, and just about every other baby-food ingredient we were thinking about could have been grown on the rich farmlands of New York, Massachusetts, New Jersey, Pennsylvania, Maryland, Virginia, and right down the eastern seaboard. Organic rice was growing in Louisiana. Bananas were everywhere in Central America. Wild blueberries were abundant in Canada, as were apples and organic cereal grains. Who needed California with all of this organic-production potential sitting right here in Vermont and the greater East Coast environs?

Armed with the conviction that we didn't have to move to California, Arnie and I made a compelling case that Vermont would not only work, it was the right place. The Vermont name connoted then and still connotes quality and purity, and that's what Earth's Best was all about.

Think about managing risk. Yes, everything directly above is true. There was great "potential," but the factors necessary to realize that potential were numerous and complex, especially in the time frame we were building our business plan around. Arnie and I latched on to the grand Vermont vision and were inflated by it. Important grounding opportunities were lost to us. And there were warning signs that could have—and should have—penetrated our entrepreneurial hides, but didn't.

Deep Root, for example, was an organic grower's co-op in Hardwick, Vermont. Their focus at the time was root vegetables like carrots. Earth's Best was going to need a lot of carrots. It seemed like a match. The snags showed up in a hurry. The amount of carrots needed for our start-up far exceeded their production and harvesting capability at the time. The price that we could afford to pay was a premium price out West, but a drop in the bucket for local Vermont growers selling directly to customers at farmers markets and retail accounts like co-ops and natural-food stores. And the kicker finally was that a particular variety of carrots grown in Idaho soils, which we loved, tasted completely different when grown in Vermont. Not even close.

That's a level of detail that's hard to anticipate when you're making your way everywhere on a steep learning curve that encompasses 360 degrees of your life. It's also information that's easy to ignore when you're inflated, attached, and wanting to see what you want to see because the alternative does not fit at all into the idealized picture you are painting.

Of course, these revelations did not obliterate the "potential" for Vermont carrots. It just showed that there was a very long road to travel before Earth's Best babies would be eating Vermont carrots. That is, if there was a road. Sometimes an entrepreneur is smitten by "potential" and then counts on it almost as if it were already money in the bank. But you can't write a check on that deposit.

Arnie and I identified an amazing organic apple orchard in Quebec. The volume was there. We needed sixteen forty-foot-trailer loads of apples that first year. The potential for more volume was there. The apples were beautiful. The varieties were perfect, and the pricing was in the ballpark. This sounds like a home run, doesn't it? But building a plan that aimed to meet our demand around one orchard, even though there were other potential prospects in Virginia, was in hindsight (and as you will see) a big mistake.

When you have colossal willpower as Arnie and I did, you think that if you apply enough of it, any presenting obstacle will eventually give way or go away. We were mobilized around Vermont, but we were also blinded by our vision and personal needs. And don't forget our appetite for "big." Some people feel most alive when they are on the edge of possibility. Maybe it's the edge of a ski or snowboard or mountain. Those edges paralyze me with fear, but not the edge of reason. The variables and vagaries that were out of our control here in Vermont and throughout the East dwarfed us. No contest. Even with our aligned tenacity, there are limits and there are consequences. There are consequences. It's humbling.

Arnie and I had no hindsight yet. Foresight was our preoccupation.

ARNIE:

Ron and I crunched and tamed the pro forma numbers and decided to try to raise $400,000 of equity and $400,000 of debt. Because we were novices at this scale of business, we no doubt were aiming lower than we should have for the reasons stated above. Naturally our assumptions supported the proposed $800K financing. The numbers made sense and hung together. Ron and I were enthused and wholeheartedly believed we were ready for showtime. But it wasn't so simple.

There are security laws in place to protect people from scam artists who are trying to sell the "blue sky" to people like you and me. You can't just knock on people's doors, wow them with a dog and pony show, promise them stock, and take their check for $10K. There are prescribed ways to raise equity, and you had better do it right. If your venture turns sour and you were lax in your obeisance to these security laws, you're facing heartache, maybe even jail time.

This security-law stuff was completely unfamiliar to us. Although we understood it was necessary, the closer we got to it, the less we liked it. Why does everything important seem to run through the doors of a law firm? And too bad weight isn't as easily lost as pockets are lightened when exiting those doors.

Ron and I can be well-behaving boys when we sense thin ice or danger. The notion of a "blue sky" now seemed quite threatening to us. We decided to head to Boston and work with lawyers who did security law in their sleep. When you think you've picked the best, it's easier to trust and easier to follow. Just get me through this—fast and painlessly.

Slick, Melon & Sputz, a prestigious firm, was the horse we chose to ride to victory. I remember walking through their doors and feeling a sense of security. The plan was to raise the $400K of equity, soliciting twenty-five or fewer "qualified" investors via what's called a "private placement memorandum." This so-called memorandum is a legal document that encompasses much of the business-plan information and a distressing laundry list of all the risks and the reasons for individuals not to invest. The risks are highlighted in nauseating detail and repeated over and over. Would you invest in the Titanic if you knew it was going down? I can't recall if the potential rewards ever made it into the document. Probably not, because they were too close to the blue sky.

Slick told us that the memorandum would cost approximately 10 percent of the $400,000, or $40,000 in legal fees. This was sickening. Ron and I should have stopped there and at least said we better raise $444,444 so we could net the $400,000 our plan called for, but we didn't. I'm not sure why. Paralysis of a sort, I guess. Instead of adapting to change and facing reality, we opted for the status quo. And it's so easy to do that with computers and spreadsheets that transform themselves instantaneously. We ran back to our pro forma, massaged the numbers, and voila, everything was fixed. The business worked now with $360,000 of equity.

You can always hope for the law of unintended consequences to spare you from such foolish choices, but there is a better chance that you're going to take it on the chin for indulging your wishful thinking. Of course, if you're one of those people who have always wondered if they can "take a punch," rest assured, even if you can, it's going to hurt.

An "accredited" or qualified investor is an individual that has a significant net worth (greater than $1 million) and is not at risk for financial calamity should the investment fail. The law really makes the effort to protect people who may have the appetite for risk, but not the means to handle it. This is a good thing. We knew that our venture posed great risk and didn't want anyone to get hurt.

Ron and I worked closely with Peter, the Slick attorney. Unfortunately, we weren't three happy peas in a pod. He seemed somewhat aloof, arrogant, and too busy, and Ron and I figured for $40K we should be the center of his attention. But we weren't, and a certain tension hovered about as the memorandum developed.

Much of the document could be extracted from the business plan that Ron and I wrote. Some of the language was boilerplate or standard legalese, ready to be inserted into any private placement using a word-processing program. Yes, there was legal work to be done in properly presenting the proposed organic baby-food company as a high-risk securities investment. And down the road, if good fortune shined upon us, time would be spent qualifying investors and then making sure the security-law requirements of the various states represented were met.

No matter what, the feeling of being ripped off lingered. Perhaps if the chemistry had been more collegial with Peter, the edges would have been softer, and we would have felt less polarized. Unfortunately the relationship only became more pressurized as time went on. Ron and I, however, were not turning back. If it was just a matter of grinning and bearing it, that's exactly what we would do. Or would we?

Although I find it quite easy to fault Peter (and find myself almost nostalgically content doing so), I also think Ron and I carried a bit of an entitlement chip on our shoulders. I think we felt entitled to a break in what we perceived as extravagant legal fees. We weren't a big company with deep pockets. We thought that organic baby food was so meritorious that it deserved some accommodation and reprieve from the business-as-usual mind-set that we encountered at Slick. It would have been nice.

Maybe that sounds spoiled, naïve, and presumptuous, but when you're starting a venture from scratch and desperately trying to bring it to life, expectations of others grow (perhaps unfairly) and attitudes happen.

Our agreement with Slick required that Peter provide us with a computerized accounting of his time on the project, so at least we could compare his sixty-minute clock to ours. Ultimately, the only thing Ron and I could do is to keep our phone calls with Peter as short as possible and plug in to help wherever we could. We wanted to be the exception to this 10 percent rule of thumb and were dedicated to doing so.

Real Is Scary

Ron and I were simultaneously hot on the trail of finding a home for Earth's Best in Vermont. We approached the Central Vermont Economic Development Corporation in Montpelier and introduced our project to them. When you go out into the community and start talking to the regional development people about the prospect of one hundred new jobs, they get excited, and you become quite important. You can never get enough of the feeling of being embraced, believed, and wanted. The gentleman we interfaced with, Don Rowan, was a can-do and seasoned type of guy. He listened to us, sized us up, and got on board as a collaborator and ally. Much like the feeling when Dr. Bartel first affirmed our organic baby-food concept, it was a marvel and incredibly uplifting to be taken seriously by these economic-development people. Suddenly our feet seemed to be touching the ground. We could smell success.

Just outside of Montpelier in East Barre sat the Wilson Industrial Park and an empty 20,000-square-foot steel Butler building. I don't remember what its sad story was. It was pretty plain and ugly, to be honest, but nonetheless it was patiently sitting there waiting for us. The park was situated at the top of a long and steep hill. The exquisite panoramic views were a plus. I was already imagining my afternoon walks. It was definitely off the beaten path, but then so were we. I imagined trucks filled with apples lumbering up the hill and baby-food jars filled with organic applesauce flying down the slope on the way to Interstate 89 and points south. The peg may have been square, but Ron and I could see enough round, or the potential for round, to venture forward. It was in our backyard. I don't think we would have seen a square peg if it had hit us between the eyes.

The Vermont Economic Development programs seemed on top of everything. We learned that there was a low-interest-loan source from the Vermont Industrial Development Authority (VIDA), whose purpose we understood was to support manufacturing initiatives such as ours aimed at underutilized industrial parks such as Wilson. The ducks were lining up. It seemed too good to be true.

Ron and I enthusiastically walked through the doors of the VIDA office in Montpelier to present our business plan to the VIDA director, Barry Mann, and several associates. We thought we had found the $400K for our plant and equipment. We were dead wrong.

Ron and I encountered not only resistance and skepticism, but also a hostile and cynical arrogance that was downright unfriendly. Skepticism, sure, but the antagonistic and adversarial attitude? Why? Why was the light so green when we were with Don and so bloody red with this Barry?

Lenders of money are risk averse. They don't want to make mistakes. As a start-up and as novices in the baby-food industry, we were dead on arrival when we walked through the VIDA door. I believe there was nothing we could have said or done that would have revived our chances. The assets that theoretically could have secured the loan, such as the equipment and projected accounts receivable, carried no weight. If we went belly-up, how much value would a carrot washer have? And we had no receivables to our name because we did not yet have sales and an ongoing business. The bottom line was that in VIDA's view we didn't have any assets with which to secure a loan. We were worthless.

This was the beginning of being stymied by a confounding catch-22 reality that would undermine us for years. Lenders of money see all of those risks that the private placement document spells out in grisly detail—and not much more. Unless they value the assets in a given deal, a loan will be tough to secure. No one at VIDA and no bank officer that we ever encountered had any familiarity with the baby-food business. This circumstance created a huge obstacle for us, because Ron and I then became the sole experts and interpreters of a vast foreign landscape. And we had no baby-food experience ourselves, so what kind of credibility did we really have?

In the case of VIDA, Ron and I accepted the skepticism and resistance. We weren't expecting a VIP pass. But we naïvely thought that because Don and the economic-development people were behind us, we just needed to persevere, address the concerns, and refine our presentation. The logic was that the Central Vermont Economic Development enterprise and VIDA were a team of public servants collaborating on behalf of the Vermont economy. Perhaps they were sometimes, but not in our case.

We met VIDA's death ray with all the life force we could muster. Months went by, and many meetings fell underneath our belt. We were still actively looking for seed money to keep us going. Les (our food-processing consultant) was busy sketching out a compact and versatile production room for the Wilson Park building. Lavon's research on optimizing baby food was growing into a treatise. Ron and I became aware of this advanced rotating European pressure-cooking equipment (Rotomats) that minimized the nutritional losses during thermal processing by reducing the cook times. This was the kind of innovation we were looking for and what gave us resolve to tolerate the condescension of the banking and quasi-public funding world.

At the time a used Rotomat cost $90K and we would need two. In contrast, a conventional still retort (no agitation) cost around $17K. How could we be Earth's Best and not opt for superior quality? Some answered, "Because you don't have the money." Some said, "Get started and introduce the Rotomat later." Ron and I always appreciated practical advice, but would not follow it if it meant submitting to mediocrity. We were not on this planet breathing just to get into business. It had to be the business we wanted to get into. For us the Rotomat decision was a principled one. If it really delivered the quality for babies, we would find a way.

With some digging we learned that Rutgers University had both a lab-size Rotomat unit and a still retort. Certain nutrients, like thiamin (vitamin B1) are particularly sensitive to heat, and so we tested for those. The results showed that the Rotomat delivered significant nutrient retention compared to the older technology. And so it became part of our story. We were compelling because we were for real. Who wanted a piece of real?

Real is scary. Ron and I were scary. Convention aims to whittle you down until you're conventional. We both see convention as a doomed lemming stampede. Why perpetuate it? This planet needs leadership, and you know the reasons why. If Ron and I were also unwitting lemmings, we were determined to carve our own path and find our own cliff.

We were at a critical stage in the homestretch of the private placement memorandum's development when Peter unexpectedly announced that he was taking a two-week vacation. Ron and I were shocked. We had been essentially on hold for months with our equity-raising efforts, trying to blot out the blue sky, and now our attorney was going to disappear for weeks! Flabbergasting! Peter assured us that he had brought his Slick associate entirely up to speed, and then basically he was gone. Ron and I traveled to Boston to sit down with the associate, and it was ridiculous. We spent hours backtracking and the feeling of abandonment grew, as did our anger.

We went nowhere for two weeks, and it was exasperating. Ron and I returned to Boston to meet with Peter to pick up the pieces. Historically, I have been the twin more quick to express his anger when wronged. If anyone were going to shish-kebab Peter, the Vegas odds would have picked me. In fact, as we rode up the elevator to our meeting, Ron was anxious that I was going to blow us all out of the water and really set our project back. He urged me to keep my cool.

RON:

Well, I was the one who exploded. KABOOM! I can't remember what inane comment set me off, but I just ripped into Peter, a torrent of unexpressed feelings unleashed. I had in mind to do one thing and did the opposite. When I feel violated, the childish temper-tantrum thrower rises up to annihilate the transgressor. "I'm mad as hell and am not going to take it anymore." Arnie and Peter maintained their professional demeanor, but not me. The meeting survived the explosion, but the relationship was irredeemable from then on. I remember Arnie staring at me in disbelief as we rode the elevator down. He had taken the brunt of my childhood tantrums and probably was glad it was Peter on the receiving end this time and not him.

We finally got a document from Peter, and predictably a $40K invoice or thereabouts. I remember that day in our little office. We were deflated. Our foray into central Vermont was failing. We didn't have $40K, and we didn't even need the memorandum because there was no deal to solicit funds for. We were dead in the water. All the yakking in Vermont about being pro-growth and pro-development didn't translate into financial support for a pioneering business like Earth's Best. We were too much of a start-up and just too big for comfort. VIDA rejected us and we rejected VIDA. Believe it or not, some money is more trouble than it is worth.

Interestingly, the Slick bill did not detail Peter's computerized time charges. I remember typing a letter requesting, as per our agreement, this level of detail. Arnie and Peter spoke a few times. A bill showed up every month from Slick and every month I dutifully (and smugly) sent out my letter explaining the problem with payment. Periodically, accounting would call us to induce payment, but they never delivered the computerized time charges. Amazingly, we never paid the bulk of this bill. There really must have been a screwup at Slick.

Rock bottom is a lot deeper than you think, and so is your well of capacity. Arnie and I felt stranded in the middle of nowhere; if not Vermont, then where? We probably should have made a beeline for California, but we didn't. When all of the poles seem greased, don't forget your entrepreneurial initiative has a life of its own, and it's working for you in ways you can't imagine. Of course, there are no guarantees, but the dynamics in play are bigger and more complex than you. Suspend disbelief and pretend that you just caught a break. In hindsight, the Wilson Industrial Park was not only the wrong place for Earth's Best, but also Arnie and I were not ready to be in business. The hill was wrong. The Butler building was wrong. The amount of equity was wrong. The organic-food supply was still too early-stage, and our overall learning curve still way too steep.

Also be aware that because your business does have a life of its own, you could become superfluous to it, a virtual footnote. This may be hard to imagine when you think "you" are the business. Trust me, there are many entrepreneurs out there who are licking their wounds and know exactly what I'm talking about.

"One Size Fits All" Does Not Apply to Angel Wings

Somewhere on a crumpled slip of paper in our Tru-Vision office was the name and Boston phone number of Jeff Coolidge. An organic-grower friend had mentioned his name as a possible seed-money investor months ago. Arnie and I had set it aside. It was such a cold call. But now everything felt cold and unlikely. We were scrambling for a toehold, and Mr. Coolidge was it.

Arnie made the call. I remember lying on the floor and holding my breath. I didn't have a lot of hope. Arnie was so articulate and did such a great job presenting Earth's Best. There's no better guy to have with you in a clutch situation than my brother. Amazingly, the call progressed to planning a meeting in Boston. There was suddenly new life. We celebrated and instantly mobilized to get ready to be our absolute best.

We overhauled the business plan, scrubbing out all of the references to Vermont. We knew by now that management or the lack thereof was a red flag and tried to shore it up by making Les, Lavon, and our accountant Bruce Towne more prominent. We also tightened up our projections and decided to show a bigger business with more aggressive growth and profitability.

This did not address the standing conundrum we encountered with VIDA and other prospective lenders, who preferred conservative numbers and modest growth, versus prospective investors, typically turned off by the same. The middle ground made everyone unhappy. Out of necessity we became flip-floppers. Our gut inclination was to go small and decrease the need for the business to hit a home run in its first few at bats. However, small numbers translated into pushing the break-even point further out into the future, which then necessitated more equity to cover working capital. And the killer was that when we went small, we couldn't show the bigger return on investment numbers until year five or thereabouts.

As we set sail for Jeff Coolidge's office in late August 1985, a dramatic change was already well in motion that forever changed entrepreneuring and affected greatly the start up of Earth's Best. The time horizon that investors used to gauge an opportunity and weigh a potential return on investment (ROI) had typically been around five to seven years. Instantaneous enrichment was not expected, and projections to deliver it were usually met with skepticism. Now, however, with the boom of the high-tech sector, the ROI outlook was suddenly changing because the patience to earn a return was no longer necessary. Any start-up that you couldn't pop in the microwave to deliver instantaneous gratification was being viewed like a dinosaur. Why tie up your money in an enterprise that showed a 40 percent return in five years when there were hot prospects that promised so much more in half the time or less?

The result was that in order to compete there were pressures to show a pro forma that performed better and delivered results faster. We weren't high-tech, so we really couldn't compete. We could just look less bad and hope that was good enough. The net result, however, hurt us because these pressures kept pushing us to make assumptions about market penetration, margins, price point, and inventory turns that were not conservative and would sink us if we missed the mark by very much.

This was one of the reasons Jeff was such a unique and curious person. He was willing to give us the time of day when it really didn't make any compelling financial sense to do so. The herd was running away from deals and opportunities like Earth's Best. Jeff, a very modest man, still valued the long view and although a moneyed person, was not defined by money. Arnie and I were about to meet the angel who almost single-handedly helped us go the rest of the distance.

Rest assured, however, that the process to yield this result, while always amicable, was not easy, at least for us. Jeff would not be rushed in his evaluation of our business plan. Countless trips to Boston followed, and numerous plan revisions were necessary. Arnie and I kept anticipating his decision to become a seed-money investor. As it turned out, we left the city time after time wondering if we would ever see that day.

Arnie and I were hanging by a thread. Money was very tight. We had already invested a year in the project, and Jeff was our only prospect. We began to compulsively look in our rearview mirror, anticipating being eclipsed by some established natural-foods company or some entrepreneur with family connections to deep pockets who could fast-track the development work without being consumed and delayed by raising money. When we felt overwhelmed by such anxieties, Arnie and I often defaulted to our grandfather John's maxim, "More time has been wasted waiting for the rain than anything else." We weren't going to wait or slow down in fear of what we could not control. If the sky fell, we would be under it.

In December of 1985, four months or so into our negotiations, Jeff made his decision. He committed up to $100,000 in seed money to be distributed in $25,000 increments. There was no guarantee we would receive the full amount. He would evaluate our progress and decide whether to invest the next $25K at the time of our request. We were ecstatic to have a moment in time where there was a tangible reward for our hard work and perseverance. It was so dearly needed. We no longer had to invest our energies into raising seed money. It was the elusive equity nut that we still had to crack.

But not so fast. What did Jeff want in exchange for this money? Many an ecstatic entrepreneurial moment has been drawn and quartered in the last-minute details of a supposedly "done" deal. There were actually a few killer ones coming up for us. Fortunately, with Jeff, he was always eminently fair and professional. We took a field trip over to the law offices of Fine & Ambrogne and were introduced to his attorney, Cathy Stone, and an associate, Larry Kletter. Everything clicked. Cathy, the widow of Supreme Court justice William O. Douglas, represented Jeff, but I believe quickly formed a warmth and affinity for what Arnie and I were championing, and maybe even us. It felt like we were all on the same side, engaged in making the deal work for Jeff, but also with an eye toward the future equity deal and the perceptions of those yet-to-be-identified investors.

Suddenly, where there had been desert, shiny steel tracks appeared as far as the eye could see. Now we just needed to find twenty-five or fewer passengers who wanted to get on board and take the ride with us. Earth's Best was rolling toward Massachusetts. As we drove back to Vermont, Arnie and I were already counting on the presence of Jeff and Cathy to catapult us forward the rest of the way. We were the happiest car on the highway.

Sounds Like a Dirt Company

Our momentum kept building. Arnie and I were introduced to Gus Schumacher, the Massachusetts commissioner of agriculture at the time. He was dynamic and bullish on Earth's Best and its potential impact on the declining fortunes of Massachusetts' agricultural lands. Where did the future lie? Gus saw it the way we did, with organic agriculture, and he wanted us planted in Massachusetts.

Organic foods are a mainstream phenomenon today, but in 1985 they and their proponents were still very much on the fringe, swimming upstream and flailing about in what the mainstream judged was a fruitless and impractical hippie pursuit. However, the handwriting was on the wall, clear as day for anyone willing to pick his head up and look out from his spray rig. The Environmental Protection Agency (EPA) reported that pesticides were the third-worst environmentally related cancer risk. Some crops required a virtual treadmill of twenty applications of agricultural sprays. The number of insects and mites resistant to insecticides was growing exponentially. Children of farm workers, typically subject to the heaviest doses of sprays, had deformed limbs at a rate thirteen times the rate of the general population.

And what about the prevalence of pesticide contamination in foods? My research in the late 1980s showed that contamination was commonplace. Not necessarily in excess of established EPA tolerance levels, but nonetheless present in detectable levels. For example, one survey showed pesticide residues in 48 percent of domestic samples of apples; 52 percent of lettuce; 61 percent of strawberries; 52 percent of peaches; and 47 percent of carrots.

Fortunately, beyond all of that depressing news, we collectively saw the opportunity to be a pivotal player in establishing a value-added market niche that supported the historic small-scale farm and values of New England agriculture and beyond. Family farms would have a future. Industrial-scale farming requiring mega acres of pancake-flat farmland was not necessarily the only way forward. With a smidge of imagination, the prospect of Earth's Best was much bigger than organic baby food. As such, Gus Schumacher opened every door he could to introduce us to public monies and support to get the deal done in his Massachusetts.

The I-91 Industrial Park in Greenfield, Massachusetts, came into view. Arnie and I jumped on it. It wasn't Vermont, but close enough (only fifteen miles from the state line) and appealing enough. We would be in the upper part of the fertile Pioneer Valley. We were on Jeff and Cathy's home turf. It was hard to imagine that we had not crossed the divide. We were in good hands. People who were players in important places socioeconomically, culturally, and politically were behind us. The dominoes leading to getting into business would now certainly fall in rapid succession.

The only nagging hitch floating about was that Gus hated the name Earth's Best. "Too hard to pronounce; sounds like you're a dirt company." And he was serious about us changing it. Arnie and I laughed it off publicly, but privately we were worried about the kinds of pressures we were going to be subjected to and where we might have to ultimately bend to get into business. Gus wasn't the only one who hated the name Earth's Best. Prospective investors and even some bankers urged us to change the name. Were they right? If we changed the name to "Loving Spoonfuls" or "Baby's Best" would all the gatekeepers lying in front of us spontaneously push their OPEN buttons and let us through? Was that the key? Even though it was hard to repeat five times fast—Earth's Best, Earth's Best, Earth's Best, Earth's Best, Earth's Best—the name resonated with us. Arnie and I were already it. If Smucker's worked, why not Earth's Best?

"Everyone Gets Squashed"

What about bending? I remember a smug, worldly, and perhaps well-meaning businessman telling me assuredly that Arnie and I wouldn't even recognize our idealism by the time the Earth's Best experience was through with us. We would be completely riddled by compromise and eclipsed by the necessity to surrender to practicality. "Everyone gets squashed." I thought to myself, this guy doesn't have a clue to whom he is talking, and he didn't. At the same time, I didn't have a clue about the pressures that he was talking about.

It is a battle. Any value or ethic that is not deeply held will be subject to the auction block. And even the deeply held ones are in jeopardy. The pressures to sell out are great, and the power to rationalize and co-opt personal values is extraordinary. What will you sacrifice to be competitive? At the outset of our venture, Arnie and I were already completely disillusioned with the repercussions of "business as usual" in the world. Of course it's not a black or white story, but for us, the overall impact of conventional bottom-line-driven thinking was sufficiently gray, and the long-term global prognosis problematic enough to warrant serious contemplation and soul searching for another way.

The name Earth's Best Baby Foods reminded us every moment of every day of what we stood for and why we were standing for it. It was a mirror that was ever present for reflecting our actions. Arnie and I knew who we wanted to be and the change we wanted to see. Our upbringing and nature did not allow us to avert our eyes from that intention.

Without this reinforcing convergence of nurture and nature, the standard we set for Earth's Best would have not been 100% certified organic. The supply-side unknowns and pressures did not support an absolute and inflexible number such as 100. Our all-or-nothing approach increased the risk of falling victim to a short crop, unanticipated competition for the available supply, certification irregularities, or just poor quality due to crop variety, poor weather, or poor harvesting. The cost of goods and the ultimate retail price to the consumer might prove to be a death knell. Who would take such a risk?

And to then magnify this risk exponentially, Arnie and I decided to create a pesticide-testing program and standard that disqualified any certified organic food that had any detectable pesticide residue whatsoever. The California organic standard at the time allowed for residues on organic food up to 10 percent of that allowed by EPA. The Earth's Best standard would allow zero.

Was it even possible for such a standard to practically exist in our polluted world? Arnie and I didn't know, but we did know that we wanted Earth's Best to stand for something extraordinary. We wanted the world to be perfect for babies. But this quest for perfection may have appeared irrationally rigid and scary to many looking for a way into our venture. Arnie and I knew it could be no other way. "Why not 50 percent organic? How about 90 percent?"

There was never a temptation to compromise our 100 percent standard. The organic farmers that we were meeting were inspiring people. It was possible. The zero-detectable-residues standard, however, felt much more precarious because it was factoring in environmental conditions that may have nothing to do with the grower and crop in question. Spray drift from neighboring farms, pollutants from distant regions, and/or persistent chemicals (such as DDT) used generations ago might contribute to a detectable residue on a given carrot or apricot. You could say we resisted practicality.

We would not be able to test for every chemical, so we understood the perfection we were aiming for was a relative one. But Arnie and I knew our standard would be unbeatable.

If Not the Golden Rule, Then What?

The search for equity began again in earnest. Arnie and I ran hither and thither, following every lead. To Oklahoma to chase oil money, to Virginia to sit in front of doctors, to New York City to ride around in a limousine with someone connected to Doan's pills. We were endlessly optimistic and gave each presentation every bit of our life's energy we could gather. Unfortunately, Arnie and I had found a way to go nowhere fast. There were simply plenty of reasons not to invest, and we could not overcome them. Although often admired, our glass was always perceived as half empty—or less.

I used to hope that if prospective investors would only taste Earth's Best, their resistance would melt, and the business potential and our mission would dominate the foreground, rather than all of the unknowns and uncertainty. But try asking someone in a three-piece suit if he would like to taste your baby food and see how many takers you get. I observed when carrying "live" baby food that people quickly scattered away, as if I was threatening a tooth extraction. The thought now occurs that maybe Gabe was calling in advance and warning everyone. He was very talkative back then, but not yet quick enough to escape from my fast-approaching tofu-hiziki gourmet treat resting on his spoon.

We kept our happy faces on for Jeff, updating him regularly with a list of prospects and a summary of all of the progress we were making on the supply side and with menu research and our quest for public monies in Massachusetts. At the same time we were wondering why Jeff didn't put us out of our misery and put the deal together himself with the people in his network. And what about Cathy (whom we imagined had magic powers and a wand in hand to manifest anything she wanted to see happen)? Why did we still feel stuck and alone in the middle of the wilderness, when we had landed by all appearances in the middle of high society?

The grind and rejections took their toll. Why did babies have to wait another day for their birthright? What could be more compelling and fulfilling than building the organic-foods industry and stopping the poisoning of our planet? But then for some confounding reason one plus one has trouble adding up to two in this world. Why are so many children malnourished in the United States and starving and dying throughout much of the world for lack of the most rudimentary public health-care infrastructures and safety nets? Where are the adults? Where is the outrage? The nightmare is that too many important things are ass backwards. Might makes right; game, set, match.

For Arnie and me, Earth's Best represented a journey to prove that "right could make might" without righteousness or fundamentalist fervor. Earth's Best would show that the bottom line is not antithetical to the values and feelings held and yearned for at the bottom of most hearts. If not the Golden Rule, then what?

Arnie and I did not want to abandon the values we were taught as children and taught to reject as adults. Getting into business scratched the surface of what we longed for. We were looking for the ground under our feet. We were looking for confirmation that the world we wanted to live in was really out there. This is why we were able to persist despite rejection after rejection. How could we give up on that hope? The hope that there was, I guess, a God who could do the arithmetic and set the world straight.

"So Boys, Where Is Vermont?"

The private-investor strategy persisted in being a dead end, but there always seemed to be another promising road waiting for us to venture down. Through a Jeff contact (as I recall), we were granted a private audience with a prestigious Boston bank president who, as we understood, had taken a real fancy to our project. This was exciting. Arnie and I meticulously planned for this meeting. Our business plan, which we sent in advance, was in tip-top shape. We bought new three-piece suits and spiffed ourselves up as much as we could. The trip down to Boston was full of expectation because we would be in the presence of a person who had a genuine interest in us and the power to "make it so."

I had butterflies as we rode up the elevator. I remember a huge mahogany desk and a gentleman, probably in his mid-sixties, sitting behind it. He was kind of grandfatherly. Arnie and I sat down completely ready to meet this man and engage him wherever he was at.

His first question to us was, "So boys, where is Vermont?" Did he say "boys"? I wish you could have been there listening to Arnie trying to explain where Vermont is. It was surreal. "You know sir; it is west of Boston, bordering New Hampshire, Lake Champlain, and Massachusetts. Montpelier is the capital, but Burlington is the largest city." The banker conceded that he had heard of Burlington. What a guy! Once again Arnie's earnestness astounded me. My head was spinning. When Arnie and I were anticipating where this gentleman might engage, we weren't thinking about describing the location of Vermont.

The meeting went nowhere. I can't remember anything beyond his opening question, because it set the tone for everything that followed. His point was that we were nothing. We came from a nowhere backwater. We had nothing. Why did he bother meeting us? Probably it was a favor or perhaps he was a serial sadist. It really hurt to be toyed with like that. I felt violated. There are a lot of sad, small, pathetic people in power. They are the nothings from nowhere that must be overcome and maneuvered around to change this world.

The elevator ride down and the four-hour trip back to Burlington was silent. The meeting knocked me off my horse. I landed on my solar plexus. It was a new low point. Arnie deserved so much better. I worried about how he would process such an unexpectedly mean-spirited experience. But it was also so bizarre that reflecting upon the meeting helped us to view it (in part) comically. Arnie and I had a good laugh reliving his ponderous attempt to explain where Vermont was to a person who probably had never heard of New Hampshire either.

The quest for the equity hogged most of our psychic space from 1984 to 1987. However, in between presentations and business-plan revisions, Arnie and I were also consumed with the daunting prospect of what if we were actually successful and had to start making baby food. Even though the money was not in sight as spring dawned in 1986, we were running as hard as we could to be ready just in case.

There was this ongoing insecurity about the readiness of the organic-food supply and a great deal of uncertainty as to what standards would prevail that defined certified organic agriculture. There was chaos back then as entrepreneurs, growers, certification organizations, and established companies jockeyed for position and control of a dream that would soon become an industry.

Arnie and I kept pestering Joseph and Richard at Organic Farms, assuring them that we would become good customers some day.

They were good-natured eyeball rollers, despite hearing the same tape over and over about the imminence of our start-up. We regaled them with the travails of our fantastic investor stories and probably scored some points for entertainment value.

I worried incessantly about how we would manufacture and make Earth's Best the best. Les was pretty much at a standstill with the manufacturing-plant design at this point. He needed a real building in order to take the next step and real money in order to shop around for equipment. Arnie and I had a sketch layout and a projected equipment list and budget in hand, which added substance and gravitas to our presentations, but did not ease my worrying. I had the sense that there was no margin for error, and saw, as far as my eyes could see, trapdoors and blind spots lurking everywhere.

As I became more familiar with the world of food processing, my questions to Les became more precise and probing. I no longer submissively deferred to his experience and expertise, but engaged and took more ownership. My product-development work in the kitchen and at the University of Vermont food-science lab caused me to think that our vision for product innovation and the use of whole and natural foods might not be so easily applied to a larger-scale manufacturing scenario. Sometimes I felt that Les was not fully taking in our ambitions and that we were headed for disaster one way or the other. All I could do was politely push for more depth and rephrase my concerns in every conceivable permutation of word combinations. Ultimately, without knowing it, I was pushing us toward Les's discomfort zone. I didn't even know that he had one.

I felt fed and satisfied by the process of flattening the manufacturing-process learning curve. I loved the learning, yet energetically I was tied up and threatened by the slipperiness of the slope. I had this impending sense that my life was on the line. Do or die. The familiar inner experience that obliterated me in school was also consuming me here. This time, however, Arnie was in the thick of it with me, and his support and our unified presence would not allow me to self-destruct.

We Should Have Been in That Room

ARNIE:

Next up was Abe Ackerman.

Abe came to us through our connection to Cathy and her associate Larry Kletter. He owned a fat-rendering plant just outside of Boston. Ron and I didn't know exactly what a fat-rendering plant was, and frankly we didn't care. Mr. Ackerman had the capacity and the interest to invest $500,000, and that would get us into business. Getting a deal done with one investor was cause for ecstatic anticipation.

Ron and I traveled to meet Abe at his production facility. The meeting went well. No bumps, no bruises, and no geography lessons needed. He seemed comfortable with our plan and inexplicably started out serious and ready to take us to the next level. Maybe it was Cathy's and Larry's recommendation, or maybe it was destiny finally showing up to give us a break. Ron and I sat in Abe's office feeling the same thing: the joy of finally finding a watering hole with water and a spigot that worked.

The meeting concluded. I asked Mr. Ackerman if we could see the rendering facility. He warned us that the smell was bad and might taint our clothes and even our hair. I wanted in. I was completely curious and assured him that we wouldn't miss the opportunity to see fat rendered for the world.

I remember the handle to the door. It was greasy and hard to turn. I didn't expect that. I didn't even know how that was possible. The door opened. The stench cannot be described. The ceilings were low and covered with grime. The lighting was dim and yellow and the air suffocating. Inconceivably, there were a few people inside working. It really shouldn't have qualified as a place of work. It was a nightmare, and it cast a shadow on any comfort I had felt minutes ago sitting in that office with Abe.

I tried to push away the confusion and doubt. It never had occurred to me so clearly that Ron and I should be as equally intent on interviewing and screening investors as they were on screening our credentials and business-plan assumptions. It was easy to forget or discount the fact that we also had a huge investment of time and energy at risk. Our future depended upon Abe's acceptance. We needed him. He did not need us. The balance of power was heavily skewed in favor of Abe, and the conditions therefore were preset to favor some version of the ostrich syndrome (heads in sand) or up-front compromise on our part, just to get into business.

Abe was another grandfatherly figure. It was hard to reconcile the working conditions we just witnessed with the ideal Ron and I held for grandfatherliness. There was such a disconnect. There always seemed to be some wrinkle waiting around the corner to undo us. Would we ever know smooth sailing?

The tour ended at the loading dock where all of the slaughtered animal waste was dropped off for processing. Abe suggested lunch. He took us to a nearby Howard Johnson restaurant. We stunk, and there was no hiding. In this regard, we were all equals. Ron and I set the odor aside and focused on answering one question. Was Abe really on board with our vision for Earth's Best? We concluded that he was. There was no more socializing that day. I still remember the long hot shower I took when I got home.

Finally all systems were go. Larry and Cathy advised us that we had done our job, and it was time to let them take the reins and finalize the deal details with Abe. We happily did so.

And that was the end of Abe. The deal fell apart, and it wasn't a lingering death. What happened? Ron and I don't know or have forgotten the details. Maybe Abe wanted too much ownership for his investment. Maybe the seed-money investors that were already in the deal (like Jeff) presented a conflict. Maybe Abe had a problem with us that never came to light. Whatever it was, Ron and I learned never to surrender the reins and stand outside of the loop of a negotiation again. Smart attorneys and wonderful people do not by definition make good businesspeople or deal makers. The outcome may well have been the same if we had been involved in the negotiation, but maybe not. I regret surrendering our power and deferring so absolutely to Cathy's and Larry's judgment, because I will always wonder what would have happened if Ron and I had been in that meeting with Abe. We should have been in that room.

Remember, investors mean a lot more to an entrepreneurial initiative than the money they hand over. Once in your business, they are in your life, in ways that you cannot imagine until something goes wrong.

The Brothers, Flotsam and Jetsam

During this time, Ron and I were also jumping through all of the hoops and over all of the hurdles necessary to secure the quasi-public financing dollars Gus (commissioner of agriculture) rhapsodized about in our early Massachusetts days. We trudged to Boston meetings many times, believing that if we could just demonstrate to prospective investors that the commonwealth was behind us with substantial dollars, then our credibility would be enhanced and a deal more likely. Ron and I were like two greyhounds chasing that mechanical rabbit at a dog track.

To dear old dad, our efforts looked futile and the results a foregone conclusion. "Dummies, the dog never gets the rabbit!" But every dog thinks he will. "Dad, that rabbit is going down."

Ron and I devotedly continued to try to make Greenfield work. Risk is just not very appetizing, and whatever reward we were able to convey, it apparently wasn't a big enough or ripe enough plum to match up to the risk. It's a terrible feeling to have all of your potential sitting in wait for others to say yes to.

There were many very capable people in our expanding universe who saw the potential of Earth's Best, but sadly just didn't mobilize on our behalf. They stayed spectators, cheering us on and filling our calendar with meetings and expectant but unrealized breakthroughs. Amazingly and impossibly to us, the prospect of Greenfield, Massachusetts, was growing dim.

Before this chapter of futility concluded, Don Timmons would offer us one last bit of excitement, the last ray of light at sunset that Ron and I were ready to follow the curvature of the earth to hang on to. Don was a mover-and-shaker attorney in Northampton who had a no-nonsense, edgy, irreverent style. Don was refreshing and fun, and he gave us hope that the nonsense was going to stop. He knew how to deal and get a deal done, and Ron and I were way beyond ready.

During this time, I remember a friend pleading with me to face up to reality. "It's over Arnie. There's no shame in a technical knockout after twenty rounds or so." But the message back to him and everyone, including the universe, was that along with that damn rabbit, "defeat" was going down as well, not us. Don was our new corner/cut man. He gave us a little respite from the pummeling, but unfortunately not the promised result.

What happened? Good question. Things got murky. What remains in my memory seems so unlikely that I hesitate to say. Don introduced us to his partner, who seemed like a nice enough guy. A deal of some sort seemed to be materializing out of the woodwork, but something felt a little off, a little too hocus-pocus. Ron and I never got comfortable enough.

Maybe we got scared or maybe we got smart. Maybe it was an opportune moment that would have led to headlines declaring the Koss brothers' brilliant financing strategy and success, rather than the future that did materialize, that was plagued with venture capitalists. The chemistry was there with Don, and that's why the question lingers. I guess we'll have to hope that he eventually writes his own book (probably titled "Those Idiots").

Suddenly the stage was empty again, except for us. Everyone had fallen off. What more could we possibly do to get Earth's Best started? We had Jeff, Cathy, Larry, Gus, the community of Greenfield, and the Commonwealth of Massachusetts in or near our corner. Something must have been wrong with us, because everything else was right or right enough. And there *was* something wrong with us: wrong pedigree, wrong experience, wrong haircuts, wrong start-up scale, wrong competitors, and wrong amount of inherent risk.

Things felt dark, and success felt so far away. It was the spring of 1986. Soon Ron and I would be out two years on our journey. Were we in some endless circular loop, where there was always possibility, but the catch was it could not be fulfilled by us?

Ron and I waited listlessly in the doldrums. We spent our days lying on the Tru-Vision office floor staring up at the ceiling and hoping for a phone call or a sign. The silence served us, because we needed a pause in our pursuit. We reflected and talked about our experience, second-guessed ourselves, contemplated failure, and wondered what could possibly be next.

One day there was a breeze. Way back when we were hot on the trail of locating Earth's Best in the Wilson Industrial Park near Montpelier, we had met with a real live wire, a fellow named Jerry Breyez. Jerry, at the time, was working for the state of Vermont to promote its agricultural products and the "Made in Vermont" label. The prospect of Earth's Best as a Vermont company had engaged his interest, and we had had some great conversations. He had seen the potential and the promise. Unfortunately, not everyone in Vermont was as savvy as Jerry. While Ron and I were doing our Massachusetts thing, Jerry left his Vermont employ and was reestablishing a relationship with a businessman in New York City by the name of Leo Woolsey. Leo was interested in Earth's Best—all of it.

There we were, in one moment stuck, and splattered on the floor, the brothers Flotsam and Jetsam, and the next, out of nowhere, our engines were running near the red line, preparing for the most important meeting of our lives. By this time, Ron and I were well practiced in making presentations, but we were both nervous as we walked into Leo's Manhattan office.

This Really Happened

It was amazing. Mr. Woolsey, a gentleman in his late sixties (I'm guessing), was a straight shooter and really had a plan outlined to move forward, pretty much right there on the spot. He was ready to invest $1 million, and we would locate Earth's Best in Geneva, New York, where there were great economic-development incentives. It was Ron's and my show to run.

Ron and I left the meeting kind of in shock. We had prayed for this moment, but it was completely disorienting to be meeting it so suddenly in the flesh. We knew little about Leo and nothing about Geneva. It all seemed so random and unlikely. I imagined the gods above moving their chess pieces and having a good laugh as they admired their last move and watched us process the events of the day.

It was hard to make the whole thing feel real and grasp what the impact would be on our personal lives. What would Anne and Carley think?

When Ron and I leapt to start Earth's Best, we had no idea that we were embarking on an odyssey. We thought we were initiating all of the action and doing the creating, but we did not foresee or comprehend the forces that would be acting upon us and re-creating our lives. We were strangers in a strange land. Questions such as "Where am I?" and "Who am I?" intensified, and fears surfaced even though success appeared more imminent than ever.

Subsequent meetings followed and all went well. Ron and I traveled to Geneva. The Finger Lakes Region of New York is beautiful, and the agricultural soils are outstanding. The community support was solid and engaged. Ron and I began to think it could work, and the momentum built. Earth's Best would start in Geneva, New York, and the local newspaper started to write about our prospective arrival. I felt like our lives in Geneva had already begun. We all began to plan our move. It was a scary and exciting time.

Someone had finally believed in both Earth's Best and the Koss brothers. It turned out to be a guy named Leo Woolsey. That was the story. Ron and I returned to Manhattan to button up the remaining loose financial ends and finalize the deal. There were no big surprises, but there was a wrinkle.

In the course of trying to get Earth's Best started, Ron and I had accumulated around $20,000 in payables, owed, for example, to Cathy Stone's firm in Boston and our accountant, Bruce Towne, in Burlington. The sum was relatively small, and the goodwill and generosity expressed by Cathy, Bruce, and others over time was something we deeply appreciated and would never forget. As we sat around the conference table reviewing the various documents, Leo made a fairly blunt comment regarding the payables: that in effect, the past was the past and what happened prior to his involvement was not his concern.

Of course Ron and I understood this position, but we were talking about only $20K accumulated over a two-year stretch of time. We were talking about potential allies and resources going forward, and most importantly we were talking about values and doing what was right, not necessarily what was easy or expedient. The sacrifices and goodwill of others had enabled us to make it to Leo's door with a strong business plan, financials, manufacturing-plant design, and an increasingly sophisticated supply-side resource base. Who would discount that to zero?

We took a breath and emphasized to Leo that it was very important to us to make a clean break from those who were so integral to our effort to date. Surely he had to expect some outstanding obligations. Leo reiterated that what happened prior to his involvement was not his concern. There was no give, no softness, and no willingness to discuss the matter.

It is a moment forever frozen in time. Ron and I glanced at each other and we both knew we were done with this deal. Our future would not be built on a foundation of compromised or abandoned personal values. There would be no rationalizations concocted to justify the sacrifice of friendships or previous agreements and commitments. It was that simple. Once again we had a lot more to lose than failing to get into business.

There it was, a million dollars and our ticket to finally get started, and there it went. But there was no angst or uncertainty. For Ron and me, everything was interconnected. The values reflecting our commitment to organic baby food were not separate from those related to the payables in question or the opportunities we hoped and intended to provide to future employees. There was an energetic whole that we were in relationship to, and any Earth's Best that we were going to be a part of had to reflect it.

On the other hand, it seemed so crazy to my left brain to walk away from our dream over $20K, owed to people who would not be hurt by our delinquency. Wasn't it crazy not to get into business to protect the money already invested to support our research and development? But what if Leo decided on day five that he didn't like the 100%-organic standard or balked at spending the money necessary to implement the pesticide-residue testing? Would there be no give, no softness, and no willingness to discuss the matter, when the heart of our enterprise was on the line? Ron and I could not and would not take this kind of chance.

RON:

I remember the elevator ride down. The familiar shock was setting in even before we got to the ground floor. It seemed impossible that we were dropping away from Geneva. Everything was about to come to a dead stop again. The comfort level with Leo had evaporated in an instant, and it was not retrievable.

It was empowering to know that we could say no even with $1 million dangling right in front of our noses. We would not have to regret being weak or desperate enough to knowingly place in harm's way the essence of the impulse that filled our dreams and imagination. We knew it was better to pull the plug now than after we moved to Geneva, built a production facility, and had a hundred people depending upon us for their livelihoods.

Leo did not take the news well. As I recall, he threatened to start the company without us. Could he do that? Arnie and I knew that we were the heart and soul of Earth's Best. Even with the money in hand, starting an organic baby-food company would not be a slam dunk for anyone, no matter what. We did worry about what might happen in Geneva without us, but what could we do?

The clarity helped us be decisive, but it did not diminish our disappointment and sense of loss. Arnie and I retreated back to the Tru-Vision floor. We began to seriously discuss the end days. The dots wouldn't connect or stay connected. Either the doors of opportunity closed on us or we closed on them.

Destiny

Sometimes I sensed that there were invisible forces working against us, standing in our way. In my imagination, I linked one to the karma Arnie and I were carrying forward from our dad and his dad and who knows how many generations of Kosses or Cohoses or whatever our last name was ten generations ago. Basically the Koss story was one of heartbreak, being screwed by a partner, being cast in the shadows by a large company, innovating too early, and relying heavily on others for the money to get into business. The deeply held emotional result and pattern in the Koss lineage then became a certain unresolved, unexpressed, and entrenched bitterness and anger. In my dad, I had seen a creeping calcification that encrusted his good and very generous inherent nature. He had become invested in resentment and defined by his disappointment in others.

It was amazing to glean an insight into comprehending that Arnie and I were in the midst of potentially repeating and reproducing many of the same dynamics that set us on a direct path to follow in our ancestors' footsteps and fulfill that path's unfulfillment. Would we, could we, break the chain of feeling victimized and embittered in business such that it defined how we greeted the rest of life each day? What story would we tell to ourselves and our children about what happened when it was our turn to be entrepreneurs? This is it, the Earth's Best story; our opportunity and attempt not only to start an organic baby-food company, but to resolve an encoded family trait already set in motion, that if not transformed, would cause us to relive our father's, father's, father's separation from a more joyful life.

At this point I became convinced there was another more sinister force present that was furiously working against us. I saw it as a dark force that attempted at every turn to thwart our heartfelt enthusiasm and unselfish intention. It wasn't a force especially created to honor the particularly threatening nature of organic baby food. Rather, it was more like a universal dark force, usually cloaked and unseen, but occasionally visible or sensed by me as an intense, swirling, dark, disruptive vortex of energy.

I used to mumble to myself, "No you don't" when I sensed its presence or felt like it was trying to kill our momentum and the Earth's Best impulse itself. "No you don't. You can huff and puff all you want, but you picked the wrong entrepreneurs to blow down. We've got your number, so beat it." This probably sounds delusional, but it was the way I responded sometimes to what I perceived as impossibly bad luck or circumstances. Instead of conceding defeat in moments of confounding setbacks, this paradigm that acknowledged the presence of evil made me stronger and more resilient. Arnie and I might fail, but not because we let this dark force have its way with us.

As we stared at the ceiling in those raw post-Geneva days, we tried to sort out what was what. The days passed into August 1986, and we began a natural withdrawal from our pursuit. The bottom line was that there were no more cards to turn over in this ponderous game of solitaire that we had been playing for two years. There always had been another move to make if we turned the cards slowly enough or studied them long enough. What can you do when you've played every card and every angle? You mix up the cards and start a new game.

Arnie and I began to consider a new venture, completely unrelated to baby food. We learned of a German company (Auro) that was looking for a U.S. distributor for its all-natural, plant-based line of paints, finishes, and glues. The opportunity had appeal and posed some consolation to us because it was novel and environmentally and socially responsible. Clearly, however, we were meeting it on the rebound. We had a huge void to fill, and we arguably latched on to the first big fish that qualified to receive our attention. Guaranteed was a steep learning curve, a foreign language, and a completely untouched market and uninformed nationwide target audience. Earth's Best would soon be pushed to the background.

And this is how destiny, if you choose to see our story through that lens, worked. To our surprise, we discovered there was an established organic baby-food company in Germany near enough to the Auro office to combine a trip to visit both companies. Without the prospect of the natural-paint company descending from out of the blue and seemingly leading us toward an alternate future, there would have been no strand of continuity holding us to our Earth's Best lives. From out of the deck came a fifty-third card, a joker. Suddenly Arnie and I would be going to Germany to see a European version of our dream that had already come true.

There were now two blips on our radar screen. One was small, unfamiliar, and dimly lit (Auro). The other, representing two years of our lives, looked like a haggard, torn-up hurricane that had disappointedly fallen apart with no impact (Earth's Best). We knew every inch of *that* embattled blip.

There was one glitch in the plan. Carley was pregnant with our second son, and her due date was October 7. Arnie and I were scheduled to return to Vermont on October 1. I couldn't bear to think of missing the birth of my second child and of not being there to support Carley and Gabe. But neither could I bear to miss sharing this adventure to Germany with Arnie. Why did these two momentous events have to coincide?

In retrospect, I think Arnie and I needed a break from each other. We had been sharing everything for two years, and our energies and perspectives had become similarly flat and stale. The conditions for dynamism and chemistry had dissipated between us. We were talked

out and played out, which is why the Tru-Vision ceiling could enter-
tain us for hours.

In the end, I could not risk failing to be with my family, and so
Arnie ventured to Germany by himself. The separation proved to be
a wonderful tonic for us. Arnie had a fantastic trip, and he returned
bubbling with enthusiasm for anything and everything. Auro proved
to be fascinating, substantive, and certainly legit, and the baby-food
company encounter was both grounding and exhilarating to him.
What was more clear than ever was that the presence of organic baby
food in the United States was not a question of if, but when. What
remained a mystery was if Arnie and I would have any part in it and
when that might happen.

In the meantime, I was elated by the birth of Aaron, who fortunately did not present the drama and trauma of Gabe's birth. Aaron
was born on September 30, 1986. I would have missed his birth by
one day if I had traveled to Germany, and that loss would have left a
deep empty space in my heart forever.

I reflect back on that gray-haired businessman who had confidently declared, when we first set out on our Earth's Best journey,
that I wouldn't recognize my idealistic, highfalutin values-driven
self by the end of my Earth's Best experience. Missing Aaron's birth
would have been the fulfillment of this man's prophecy before my
Earth's Best experience even began. It's so easy to get lost and sadly
to lose touch with what is most important. I came very close.

As it was, the center of my world had shifted again, and the net
result for the Koss brothers was that Arnie and I both returned to
our office recharged and more determined than ever to get over the
hump—with something.

The universe had also conveniently placed in our midst the second
Earth's Best guinea-tester. Gabe was the pioneer, but had wised up
to my tricks at the age of three years and three months. Besides, he
was almost obsolete as a baby-food customer. Aaron represented the
future and would be standing by on an as-needed basis, for the next
chapter of Earth's Best.

Never Say Never

Although Arnie and I appeared to be standing still in our efforts to advance organic baby food in the United States, Earth's Best itself was still out there as a captivating and intriguing discussion item. Many people in the Burlington, Vermont, area knew first-, second-, or thirdhand of our determined pursuit to get the company started. We hadn't succeeded, but our grit and refusal to quit had taken on a life of its own. While our academic and business credentials didn't impress anyone, apparently our resiliency did. Also, as identical twins, Arnie and I were an interesting curiosity and presence in the community. While we were far removed from the fray in the Tru-Vision attic, taking in the ceiling, enduring attacks of melancholy, and contemplating the future, unbeknownst to us, people were talking about the idea of organic baby food and those two guys crusading for it. With us or without us, the life force of Earth's Best was percolating about and nipping at the heels of the energetic fabric of the Burlington, Vermont, community.

By now, Arnie and I had utilized almost $75,000 of Jeff's funds. We continued to keep our communication current, but there wasn't much to offer as a rationale for him to invest the last $25,000. You can only stretch optimism so far, and then the effort collapses on itself. We needed a breakthrough to make a credible request to Jeff. Otherwise in about thirty days we'd be out of cash. Arnie and I kept working on the Auro project, which basically just needed our decision to take the next step. Beyond that, there was nothing. We sat suspended in uncertainty and expectation.

Many possibilities had risen on the horizon during our odyssey of the past two years, and all had quietly set behind us. There had been a few spectacular sunrises and sunsets. They made for great storytelling, but they didn't get us into business. As an entrepreneur, you never know what the significance will be when someone appears on your horizon. You just have to be ready.

One day on that horizon rose the Rick Shays star. Arnie and I never expected our Earth's Best lives to return to Vermont, but we were thrilled with the possibility. Never say never rings so true.

The first meeting in the Belmont Building with Rick was our first meeting in Vermont in almost eighteen months. We only had one condition to prequalify a prospective investor at this point. He or she had to know where Vermont was. Rick passed with flying colors.

Arnie and I were pretty comfortable from the get-go. He wasn't our long-lost missing triplet, but he did make an impression as a capable, personable, and shrewd good guy. He had an easy smile, and, most importantly, he stood at the heart of Burlington's financial community. Arnie and I did carry one misconception into the meeting. We thought Rick was interested in being an investor. He was not.

We thought our starting point was obvious. We needed investors. So our knee-jerk reaction was one of frustration and disappointment. Here we go again: another person who thinks the idea of Earth's Best is great and that we've got the right stuff, but who wants to stay on the sideline. But this time Arnie and I were missing the barn door. What we really needed was one person to believe in our dream enough to put his reputation on the line by connecting us to his network of financially capable friends and associates. Rick was this person. He was not going to risk his own money, but he would champion Earth's Best on our behalf and stand as the deal maker.

And so began many introductions and presentations to businesspeople and professionals in the Burlington area. Rick became the center of our universe. We were aiming now to piece together $500K in equity and $400K in debt. Arnie and I once again presented a Vermont manufacturing scenario, although we still didn't know where or how it would manifest. Everything needed to be accomplished at once. Although battle weary and leery, we were full-steam-ahead once again on baby food. The Auro star set.

Baby Boom

ARNIE:

How likely is it that Hollywood would be making a movie about a Vermont baby-food start-up, just as we were closing in on getting financed to start up Earth's Best in Vermont? Very strange!

Sometime in early 1987, Ron and I were contacted by someone who had the merchandising rights to the name "Country Baby Foods." This was the brand name of the fictional Vermont baby-food company in the Diane Keaton movie *Baby Boom.*

Somehow these people heard about us and pitched the idea of leveraging the movie release with our launch of Earth's Best. The hitch being, of course, that we wouldn't be launching Earth's Best, but rather Country Baby Foods. And there would be a significant fee for doing so.

The idea was intriguing and inflating and a temptation. We were sent the script to help us decide whether we wanted to attach our fate to the movie. Unfortunately, the script was clever and well written, so we couldn't just dismiss the opportunity without torturing ourselves.

Ron and I loved the name Earth's Best, but suddenly it seemed like we had serendipity screaming in our face to march with her. The stars were aligning here, if ever there was an alignment of stars, including the Diane Keaton megastar! How do you turn away from this synchronicity without feeling stupid sooner than later? Was this finally our big break, the universal payoff for being good boys and not giving up?

We turned away and never felt stupid. Ron and I had no idea whether the fictional Country Baby Foods would approach the standards we were envisioning for Earth's Best; most likely, not. If not, why would we want to be Country Baby Foods? Also, how likely would we be nationally distributed in the marketplace in October, when *Baby Boom* was released, ready for the hoards of parents who just had to have Vermont gourmet baby food? The odds were zilch.

Baby Boom turned out to be a very cute movie, and Earth's Best unexpectedly benefited from it, just the same. The film brought to light the idea of a value-added, healthy baby food. No one remembers the name Country Baby, but everyone wonders if the movie was about Earth's Best or asks Ron and me if we got the idea for Earth's Best from the movie. We got all the mileage associated with what became a good-feeling movie memory for many people.

Entrepreneurs have to be careful about reading too much into serendipity. Clearly others were now seeing the alluring speck of light on that distant shore that Ron saw eleven years earlier. And clearly these people were smarter than us. They knew it was easier to make a movie about starting a Vermont baby-food company than it was to actually start one.

The timing however of Earth's Best and *Baby Boom* converging in 1987 never ceases to amaze.

Players At Last

RON:

It just must have been our time to break through. The pieces of the puzzle started to fall into place, one by one. We were introduced to Paul Carrera, a savvy, good-hearted, icon of a man who operated a successful concrete business in the Middlebury area. Paul owned property in an industrial park outside of Middlebury on Pond Lane, and he constructed concrete tilt-up buildings. And Middlebury had the septic capacity to handle the waste stream of a baby-food processing facility. Finding a town with septic capacity in an industrial park probably sounds like an obscure, mundane detail, but it was a giant hurdle for us to clear back in 1987.

In Vermont, the choices were few and far apart. Discover a willing and able developer/builder who just happened to specialize in manufacturing the exact type of building best suited for food processing, and you had a miracle.

The prospective investors that Arnie and I were introduced to actually wanted to taste the baby-food samples. This was definitely an encouraging sign, because it reflected a genuine interest in what Earth's Best really was intending to be and with what they as investors and people of standing in the community would be associating their good names.

Tasting baby food shoots you back in time. It was great to see those palates working on my oatmeal, yogurt, almond butter, and pureed raisin extravaganza. Gabe loved it. And so did Fred and Peter and many others who started to form the nucleus of the investor group that would go the distance with us.

I admit to getting a little carried away in the paragraph above. Fred and Peter and the others didn't actually *love* the gourmet baby-food samples. Adults don't generally love the texture of mush (more or less), and are accustomed to more sweetness and saltiness in their food. Also, adults like to know what they're eating, and most mush looks alike (more or less). So it wasn't love. It was more like interest, curiosity, and engagement. It was the kind of hands-on experience that they probably never could have anticipated having in their professional and personal lives, at least with baby food.

The tastings added both a dimension of tangibility to the "idea" of Earth's Best and one of capability to the "idea" of Arnie and me as entrepreneurs. We showed we could make baby food and present the nutritional rationale and benefits to children. We showed we could source the organic ingredients. We were indisputably for real. Jeff's last $25,000 came in. We were positioned again to keep on trucking.

By this time, Arnie and I had become seasoned showmen, in the most positive sense. We knew our stuff. The supply side was more solid, our recipes were simplified and fine-tuned, and the financials had been overhauled, reworked, massaged, and scrutinized to reflect a defensible operational scenario. In effect, thanks to our tenaciousness, we had finally established a presence of accomplishment and credibility. We had reached a turning point. Arnie and I were players at last.

The Dalai Cone

ARNIE:

One person we *didn't* impress was Ben Cohen of Ben & Jerry's. Ben had already attained guru status in Vermont when we sat down with him and a group of prospective investors in Rick's office, sometime during this whirlwind 1987 time frame. This was a gigantic meeting for us. His endorsement would have surely catapulted us into fat city, but Ben couldn't seem to favorably wrap his brain around the idea of organic baby food in jars. Now, frozen baby food was another story. Seriously.

Ron and I patiently tried to explain why convenience was so integral to the baby-food shopper, why it was essential for EB to sit next to the Big Three (Gerber, Beech-Nut, and Heinz), and why the added costs and logistics of frozen distribution and shelf-space availability were so problematic.

The Dalai Cone had spoken. None of our explanations penetrated his predispositions. Ben was stuck on frozen baby food as the only way forward for Earth's Best, and that was that.

If he had nailed us for starting with too little capital, it would have been brilliant. If he had suggested baby food with a chocolate swirl and Reese's, it would have made sense. But frozen baby food or bust?

Ben was so brilliant with ice cream and so wrong about baby food. His rejection could have hurt us, but it didn't, because frozen didn't make any sense to anyone else in the room.

Arnie, Did You Catch the Number of That Train?

RON:

We reengaged with Les (our trusty food-processing consultant), who was pretty much sitting on the sidelines as we gallivanted through Massachusetts and New York. Now it was Vermont again. Les must have thought we were crying wolf when we assured him that this time was for real—really. No more false alarms. We had to be ready with the plant design, infrastructure requirements, and equipment specifications. Actually, not just ready, we had to be as close to perfect as humanly possible because there wasn't going to be spare cash to burn. There would be no time to learn the ropes, or rather time that we could afford. And there was no room for error in delivering perfect baby food. We had to hit the production floor running. Arnie and I felt like "showtime" was just around the corner, and the expectations on Les began to intensify. We were completely leaning on him. Despite all appearances at the time (two rather skinny brothers), that was a lot of weight.

Meetings also began in earnest with the Chittenden Bank as well as with the Small Business Administration (SBA) and the Vermont Industrial Authority (VIDA). You might remember our fondness for VIDA back in the Wilson Industrial Park days (near Montpelier). But times do change, and wounds, while leaving scar tissue, do heal. We needed to raise equity and we needed to secure debt to finance the equipment purchases. Nothing was a slam dunk, but we were in three-point shooting range now, and scoring was possible. As the investor momentum gathered and a Paul Carrera building and a Middlebury location became possibilities, the financial institutions slowly settled in to figuring out just what they needed in the way of collateral to make the risk of lending to us acceptable.

As we moved into early 1987, it was conceivable that we could break ground in the spring. There would have to be a harmonic convergence of money, local and state permit approvals, engineered building and plant design, organic-food supplies, and the marketplace. Using our inherent entrepreneurial optimism, Arnie and I could see how the dots could connect. Complete the financing in March, break ground in April, order equipment in May, commit to food purchases in June, begin equipment installation in July, hire production employees in August, and start up manufacturing in September, just in time to introduce Earth's Best at the October Natural Foods Expo in Philadelphia.

If ever there was a crazy scramble, this was it. So many big pieces of "complexicated" reality had to fall into place, and the failure of one would lead to the failure of all. The thought, however, of not getting into business in the year 1987 was not only unbearable, it was unimaginable. As such, the pace was furious and the effort to control our destiny intense.

In this state of suspended tension Arnie and I were acutely sensitive to the subtlest hiccups that might slow us down. We tried to be out in front of every speed bump, so it wouldn't be there when we got there. It was fun to be so engaged and focused. At the same time, the experience also had the terrifying quality of life or death.

But unfortunately everything that came our way wasn't of the scale of a hiccup or a speed bump.

From the beginning of our venture, Arnie and I always worried about someone beating us into the market. We were as secretive as possible at the outset until that was impractical, and then we ran as fast as we could to get into business. So, each month, Arnie and I turned the pages of *The Natural Foods Merchandiser*, the natural-food industry's showcase trade publication, holding our breath, until there was relief at the end. It became somewhat of a ritual for us.

Over time, as nothing had shown up in the two and a half years prior, we naturally grew to expect that nothing would probably show up. Certainly by now we had accrued some insider-status credentials within the organic-foods community. We knew all of the key players, and unless there was a sinister conspiracy in play we would have heard another train coming before it smacked us. Our ears rested on the cold steel rails day and night. We were the only train on the track.

I vividly remember standing behind Arnie's Tru-Vision plywood president's desk as he slowly turned the *Merchandiser* page by page on that day in 1987. I'm pretty sure it was the January 1987 issue. Our trusty *q*-less typewriter was waiting at the ready to the right, rolls of white paper were tacked all over the walls, covered with mostly historical chicken scratches. A full-page advertisement settled down in front of us announcing the first all-natural baby food: "Baby's

Garden." There was an instant sense of panic and disorientation. Was our goose finally cooked? Arnie and I studied the ad and retreated to the floor. It was well done. Excellent name. "Arnie, did you catch the number of that train?" We were flattened like pancakes.

What other shape could we be in? Someone had beaten us to the punch. How did they do it? How could we have been completely blindsided? When the dust settled in the office, we could answer the questions ourselves.

Baby's Garden was targeting the natural-foods industry, but it wasn't organic. Not a peep about organic. Interestingly, they also chose to introduce their baby food in plastic aseptic containers, touting the benefits of the almost instantaneous cooking time and "freshness" that high-temperature, short-time thermal processing afforded. In effect, Baby's Garden decided to pioneer packaging and aseptic processing, while leveraging the attributes of natural and fresh. Arnie and I had decided to let go of our packaging-innovation temptations (brown or green glass) and focus on delivering 100%-organic, natural, and whole foods, while leveraging state-of-the-art thermal processing (rotary retorts) and enhanced nutrient retention.

Minus the "freshness" spin and the container, Baby's Garden's applesauce was essentially the same as that of Gerber, Beech-Nut, and Heinz. And because aseptic processing at the time was still perfecting the safe processing of low-acid foods like carrots and peas, the Baby's Garden product line was extremely limited (fruit flavors) and would probably remain so for some time.

It is only in a competing entrepreneur's mind that spin can so easily be reduced to nothing. Baby's Garden was taking direct aim at our backyard. There was no baby food a natural-foods store could offer their customers until Baby's Garden was introduced. "Natural" and "fresh" were all they needed to be embraced by the industry. Also, aseptic packaging, which connoted "future" and "upscale," initially helped showcase a difference between the stodgy, out-of-touch mass market and the up-and-coming value-added natural-foods industry.

As Arnie and I stared at the ad, we knew Baby's Garden was going to make a big splash. Would we survive it? It was so hard to feel displaced, even though we really didn't have a place yet. We believed we would be so much better, if we could just get started. Baby's Garden wasn't pioneering the organic-foods supply, so that wasn't an obstacle. They weren't dealing with low-acid foods, so they could probably find a co-packer. As such, they didn't have the burden of materializing bricks and mortar like we did. Basically, Baby's Garden was a marketing company. But so what?! They would soon be the darlings of the natural-foods industry. Arnie and I would still be stuck in the "close, but no cigar" phase.

In our stubborn, thick-skinned minds, the outstanding question regarding Baby's Garden was, "Why bother?" If someone had offered us the money to launch exactly what Baby's Garden was about to introduce at the Anaheim trade show in March 1987, Arnie and I would have passed. Our objective was to introduce a complete whole-foods diet for babies so parents could completely rely on Earth's Best—and it had to be 100% organic. The aseptic packaging provided Baby's Garden with a point of difference from the ho-hum glass of the mass-market brands, but it also put them in a straitjacket.

Aseptically processed low-acid foods, especially anything with texture and varying particle sizes like chunks, was not commercially viable at the time. In effect, the Baby's Garden product line could only advance as fast and as far as the advances in aseptic technology would allow. For Arnie and me, this would have been like placing our racing fire truck behind a big float in the Macy's parade. No matter how blaring our siren or urgent the call, we would have been stuck.

I have no idea why Baby's Garden didn't choose to start out with organic foods. It made no sense then and makes no sense today, in retrospect. They were a California company. Certainly by 1987 organic apples were readily available to them. Price may have been a factor, but if it was, it was a miscalculation by the entrepreneur(s). The willingness of consumers to pay a premium for organic was well on its way to being established. Also, strategically, going with organic would have given Earth's Best and any other starry-eyed baby-food initiative a lot less room to establish a compelling point of differentiation and identity. Baby's Garden could have—or might have—blotted us out right there.

When you're entrepreneuring, there's so much that you're seeing and doing, and there's so much that you're not seeing and not doing. Baby's Garden saw the same glaring market niche that Arnie and I did. It was the proverbial barn-door opportunity—invisible or unapproachable by most, but screaming to be fulfilled by those with an appetite for baby food. But there are so many choice points along the way, before you actually pass through that barn door. And your barn experience will reflect most of them.

In my view, Baby's Garden got caught up with the sizzle (aseptic packaging) and either lost sight of, or never had in sight, the steak (organic foods). But at the time, Baby's Garden felt like the center of a storm that was not supposed to be happening.

Maybe the Clampetts Were Right

ARNIE:

Ron and I had the presence of mind to keep our overreaction and any pervasive doom to ourselves. So far, Baby's Garden was only a slick full-page ad in a trade journal. Maybe they wouldn't even show up at the Natural Foods Expo in March. Stranger things have happened. All we could do was wait and see if they could pull it off in Anaheim. Ron and I pushed the panic aside and pushed Earth's Best forward. There was reason for us to have hope, and no matter what, "our reason to be" was not diminished. To be clear, we didn't hide this development from Rick or anyone else. We just didn't inflate it or give it more energy than it deserved. Baby's Garden wasn't 100% organic. Earth's Best was (or would be).

As it turned out, Baby's Garden was the talk of that Anaheim Natural Foods Show. Ron and I watched the big buzz around their booth with longing and envy. They really did it. Prospective distributors, retailers, moms, and babies overwhelmingly approved. Admittedly, it was hard for us to take. Ron and I were probably the only ones standing around straining to find flaws and perceive some disappointment from the crowd. But Baby's Garden was an impressive force and made that big, first splash we anticipated and dreaded.

I remember seeing from afar our counterpart, the entrepreneur who pulled it off. She seemed like a bright, energetic woman who was enjoying being in the spotlight. I could only imagine. I marveled at her success. Who were the investors? Maybe the Clampetts were right. Maybe Ron and I should have "loaded up our truck and moved to Beverly . . . Hills, that is," a long time ago. Aside from all of the reasons noted above that made our start-up so much larger a mountain to climb and so much more compelling (to us), it was impossible not to appreciate the accomplishment of this entrepreneur. Even if the money appeared magically through family connections, she had had to execute it, and she had done it in spades.

Who knows what personal and business-related obstacles she overcame that were unique to her world? Maybe for her, the money had also been an interminable mountain that seemingly refused to be scaled. Inside the swirl of our own survival-induced, adrenaline-saturated beings, Ron and I admired this woman and felt a kindred spirit with her. We didn't want her to fail. We wanted to succeed. It wasn't clear whether those were mutually exclusive outcomes or not. Baby's Garden was off to the races.

And so were Ron and I. We just kept pushing. The financing was taking form. The prospective equity investors were beginning to congregate around the table. They were not disappearing or turning weird the deeper they sank into the details and uncertainties of what was taking shape as Earth's Best. There was, I think, this growing sense of a wave that was about to form and grow into a big one—the kind that people looking for big waves would not want to miss. There was an undercurrent of excitement and possibility. Ron and I began to feel that the arduous pushing phase was about to shift and, amazingly, there was something scary about this.

When you're pushing something heavy up a steep hill, you know that the object is never going to go too fast. It might be hard and slow, but you control the speed by just taking the weekend off or going to sleep at night. You know where the object is going to be in the morning: where you left it. But when you're about to finally crest the hill, these new questions form: What's it going to be like to be pulled? Am I going to be dragged somewhere I don't want to go? Am I going to be moving so fast that I make poor decisions, miss critical road signs, and perhaps lose control?

Ron and I had enough practice counting our chickens before they hatched, so believe me, we were not obsessed with worry about the hillcrest. But when your experience is pretty much all about pushing, it's hard to grasp exactly what it means to be pulled and what the consequences might be.

In any case we were so ready for the downhill and completely willing to barrel down it. There was no time to waste, and we thought the breeze would be wonderful.

Gotcha Rabbit!

RON:

Encouragingly, the possibility of Paul Carrera developing a production facility for us at Pond Lane in Middlebury continued to move into the foreground, as did the planning work with Les. The plant started to take shape on paper. However, as we moved closer to the precipice of actually starting, Les began to hedge more and more about his certainty that what he was laying out on paper would deliver the Earth's Best baby food we were envisioning. This development was completely unexpected because Les had been such a rock, a constant of surety and professionalism. And it was professional of him to give us an honest, cautionary heads-up, but it was way late in the game.

How could Arnie and I go down the road, accept all of the investment money that was coalescing behind Rick, assume all of the bank and quasi-public debt, commit to $200,000 in equipment leases, and hire fifty or sixty people with that kind of doubt hanging over our heads? At the time, it felt like another variation of the rug being pulled out from underneath us. It was traumatizing. We were leaning so heavily on Les. I think the potential liability scared him. It all looked good on paper, but Les wouldn't guarantee the result. That was not good enough for Arnie and me.

It's in moments like this that you really have to face and experience your vulnerability. Arnie and I were so exposed. Even at this point, it seemed like at any moment years of work could just disappear beneath the waves and never be seen again. Would the end of the "Les era" cause a stampede? Would all of the investors decide to bail on us? Would this development throw an impossible wrench into our timetable for 1987?

No. Actually, the short circuit to moving Earth's Best forward in the spring of 1987 was our failure to identify the gray-haired, sage-like plant manager, who could give comfort to all who were about to put their financial necks on the line. Les was not that guy. He was always the consultant. And it certainly wasn't me. The suddenly "Les-less" world caused us to mobilize our focus to find a huge missing piece of the puzzle, the Earth's Best plant manager.

The catch-22 all along was that we didn't have the money in place to make such a key executive hire. At the same time, we had reached a point where we couldn't go the distance without solving this catch. We learned that there *is* a way to solve a catch-22: question your assumptions. Arnie and I assumed that an executive-level plant manager would never want to stick his head into the ring with a high-risk start-up. We had an underlying belief in play that pegged us as unappetizing and undesirable. This caused us to assume that we needed to look "prettier" before we could attract the caliber of plant manager that we needed. We thought we needed the money in hand to be credible.

Wrong assumption. Here's the other side of the coin, which was invisible to us at the time. To the "right" someone who has spent a lifetime working in the trenches of established food companies and playing it conservatively, there is a longing for adventure, challenge, and meaning. That would make the prospect of an Earth's Best–type start-up intriguing and filled with the thrill of possibility and potential. Arnie and I had become so conditioned to see the bleakness of being untested and unproven that the idea that Earth's Best could be viewed by such a person as the opportunity of a lifetime was outside of our box. A failure of imagination leads to assumptions that can breed the conundrum we call a catch-22.

Even the age-old question "Which came first, the chicken or the egg?" falls away. The failure of imagination starts with our acceptance of the question. The question assumes linearity: "Which came first?" Is everything compelled to follow a linear sequence? What about waves and particles? Assumptions define paradigms, shape stories, institute beliefs, and create confounding and often self-limiting situations and circumstances. Thanks to Les coming to terms with his own limitations, Arnie and I were forced to explore beyond what we thought we knew.

This quickly led us to the dissolution of the catch-22 and to a gray-haired, sweet guy named Bob Fielder, an engineer with forty years of experience in the food industry, who was ready and waiting for his opportunity of a lifetime.

I can't remember exactly the cause of Bob appearing from out of the blue. A gentleman in his late fifties, looking to retire in Vermont, but not quite ready, Bob definitely had some Pecos Bill lurking about in his inner recesses. All of our preliminary meetings pointed to a perfect match.

The chemistry was there. Bob had a sense of humor, an easygoing style, and plenty of reassuring confidence. He was more than Les. He seemed to know exactly what we needed to do and how to go about it. Arnie and I were so ready to finally have this sage manufacturing presence in place to comfort the bank and the investors. The relief I was anticipating in letting go of carrying the burden of being the manufacturing "expert" was monumental.

Arnie and I saw green lights in front of us, and apparently so did Bob. We struck a deal that included a modest salary and stock options. It was a very exciting moment for us all. The dark clouds, stormy skies, and courtroom battle that lay ahead were inconceivable.

Everything accelerated. It was February 1987. The equity pieces fell into place one by one. Rick Shays was totally on board, and the championing of Earth's Best became a little easier as other big pieces like landing Bob and the Pond Lane Industrial Park in Middlebury became for real—for real. We would soon have $500,000 in equity committed. And the $400,000 in debt that we were cobbling together through the Small Business Administration (SBA), VIDA, and the Chittenden Bank was in sight, waiting on the equity to close and the weight of their collective bureaucracies to shift gears.

Earth's Best would be a $900,000 start-up, the largest ever to that point in the state of Vermont. And there was an additional $260,000-plus of seed money already raised and working on our behalf to get us to that red-ribbon ground-breaking ceremony.

There we were, two and a half years out from the Ronald McDonald House parking-lot conversation, and we were finally about to catch that damn rabbit. Gotcha!

60/40

Arnie would always remind me that there were only so many hours in a day, whether you're running a small business or a large one, so why not a large one with a grand mission and a big upside? I could never argue with his logic. True, there were only so many hours in a day, no matter what. But there was a dimension to the equation that Arnie was totally missing or not appreciating, and that was "pressure."

When we were making brooms or selling tools or sprouting seeds, we did seem to work and worry all of the time, and we did have deadlines, constraints, and various pressures. But there's pressure and then there's PRESSURE. We had only known pressure. This was a huge gap in our understanding that was necessary in order to get into what we were getting ourselves into.

The days that followed were a blur. The timetable remained impossibly tight. And to move forward required leaps of faith of every stripe and color. We had to proceed as if everything would fall into place, like well-set-up dominoes. Paul Carrera was willing to invest his time and energy in working with us to design a building. Bob and his wife were arranging their move to Vermont. Arnie and Joe Smillie (our supply-side consultant) kept talking it up with the growers. I dreamed up production scenarios, made assumptions about waste, and projected tons of ingredients needed to fulfill imagined sales scenarios. Baby's Garden seemed to be a smashing success, and it just became part of the retail landscape that we were going to hopefully share. From time to time we also heard unsettling reports about a baby-food company that was going to be starting in Geneva, New York.

There was an ongoing effort to structure the equity financing that we had been chasing. How much ownership would Arnie and I have to give up to get Earth's Best started? There was something strange and abstract about giving up "ownership" before we even got started. And what did giving up ownership really mean? We knew it meant sharing the financial opportunity, which made perfect sense, but what about control of the business and its operation?

In our minds, Arnie and I were it. We were Earth's Best. What else could we think? And yet we knew we had to protect our control of the company, as the experience with Leo Woolsey had dramatically taught us. We didn't have a clue as to the myriad ways that we could be marginalized, but it was an instinctive reflex to armor ourselves as best we could.

We worked on an employment contract with our friend and lawyer Larry Kletter at Fine & Ambrogne in Boston. And we strategized how to retain control of the board of directors and the ultimate decision making. At the time, the whole exercise seemed like a necessary evil, even a distraction from our focus of getting into business. Arnie and I were in fact surrounded by unfamiliar territory. We leaned on Larry to help us negotiate the increasing preponderance of legal minutiae and defensive positioning, while being excruciatingly careful not to alienate those about to jump into a deal with us. He was a saint.

The numbers we settled on were 60/40. Arnie and I would sell 40 percent of the company for $500,000 and retain 60 percent. We would control the board of directors and any major decision making with our two votes. The 60/40 ratio did not reflect hard science or any semblance of rational number crunching. We simply tried the numbers on for size. Given the risks inherent in the start-up, ratios like 70/30 or 80/20 seemed like a very hard sell to the prospective investor pool. They weren't "rich" enough proportions, or at least that was our perception at the time, colored by our desperation to get into business.

Arnie and I had a great fear of not getting into business and failing to manifest Earth's Best. Although excellent at hardball, we were reluctant to play hardball and negotiate a more lucrative deal for ourselves. Selling 40 percent of the financial future of Earth's Best from day one was huge. We also wanted to reserve some percentage of ownership for all of the employees, and we knew key management hires would require ownership incentives. And we knew in our rare contemplative moments that it was probably inevitable, despite our break-even projections, that more equity would eventually be needed to carry the day-to-day operations and to finance growth.

But it was not money that was driving us. It was changing the world. It was our personal expression and fulfillment. It was our idealism. Would we risk getting into business to own 10 percent more of the company? Absolutely not. But control was another matter. We needed it to make Earth's Best *the* best. Control was not negotiable. It was everything.

Arnie and I had never been down this road. We took in a lot of the landscape along the way, but we also missed a lot. We also didn't know what to look for other than the billboard signs that said "Earth's Best Start-Up—Straight Ahead."

It happened. We closed on the equity in April 1987. Arnie and I were jubilant. We were scared, excited, worried, and redeemed. Against all odds of raising the money to start an organic baby-food company, we miraculously prevailed. We got what we had worked for and wished for, and it was a shock to have done so.

PART THREE

Crossing the Finish Line
but Just Beginning

"No, You Gambled."

ARNIE:

I can remember a meeting in Boston with the financial advisor of one of Earth's Best's largest early investors. The meeting took place after Ron and I had left the company. We first exchanged some pleasantries before the guy said to me, "You didn't have enough working capital when you launched." I agreed to the obvious, but explained that when it all began, we thought we saw a realistic way forward, although a very narrow one. He then said, "You should have never gone forward with the launch; you were reckless, even irresponsible to do so." I simmered for a moment and said, "More equity would have been great, but we started as big as we could. Ron and I thought we had enough to get off the runway." He smiled and said, "Then what?" I shot back, "We looked for midair refueling. If we had waited for everything to be just perfect, Earth's Best would have never happened. We took a calculated risk." He leaned forward and said, "No, you gambled."

We all gambled. We all were aware of the blue sky. Ron and I had a plan to succeed with this first equity round. But we were blinded by ignorance and innocence and had to slip the start-up through the eye of a needle on our first try. Naïvely or arrogantly, we thought we'd find a way to squeeze through. No one told us we were nuts, although, as you will see, a compelling case could be made that we were.

This Is Not a Test

Soon after the closing, I departed for a supply-side trip to the West Coast. I realized, with butterflies in tow, that we were no longer playing pretend. There was money in our account to back commitments to growers and sign contracts. The three years of wandering in the wilderness were already forgotten. I was so ripe to start Earth's Best.

As I drove toward Dinuba, California, thinking about plums

and peaches, I wondered if Paul Buxman and the Olsen Brothers were for real and whether they would think I was. To the best of my knowledge, they were the only organic stone-fruit growers out there. They had never sold their processing-grade fruit as organic, because there was no processor small enough or interested enough to segregate and handle their organic fruit. So even if they had organic fruit to sell, I had no way to turn it into frozen puree that we could ship to Vermont. I cruised south worrying and feeling that PRESSURE I had never felt before.

It didn't take long to figure out that Paul was for real. As I approached his orchard, I felt like I was driving into Eden. Planted in between the rows of peach trees were brightly colored flowers and herbs. The orchard ground was pancake flat, but there was a dimension and depth to his farm that was intriguing and inviting. It was a sanctuary, a forty-acre oasis in the middle of a vast, chemically dependent agricultural wasteland.

Paul was all enthusiasm. I learned that his move to grow organically came after his young son was diagnosed with leukemia, and his well water was found to be contaminated with the pesticides that he and his dad had been using for years. His farming paradigm changed instantly. It became Organic or bust!

It was a dream to feel Paul's support for our organic baby-food venture. He estimated the tonnage and gave me a fair price. No negotiation was necessary. That's how easy it was. But who would process the fruit? Paul suggested I go see the folks at J.R. Wood, a big local processor that might have an open mind to handle organic fruit, if there was enough volume. I left the Buxman farm feeling hopeful and thankful. I had met a great organic farmer. The Olsen brothers, Wayne and Richard, were next, and then, if someone would see me on short notice, J.R. Wood. I was having fun.

I can still see Wayne Olsen standing in his driveway, as I drove down the dirt road to his farm. Wayne was a striking presence, a tall blond man with a welcoming face. I can remember his farm-hardened hand swallowing mine. Sometimes handshakes mean nothing; sometimes they can tell you a lot. Wayne's was a gentle, almost humble shake, packed with power, and it meant something. The Olsens had already had their fair share of disappointment drive down their farm road. They liked the idea of organic baby food and were hopeful I was for real, because they needed a market for their processing-grade fruit.

This is what I longed for when I was stuck endlessly revising business plans: the opportunity to make a difference. In those early days, organic farmers were true pioneers with little support. The marketplace was, for the most part, undeveloped; distribution and effective handling and transport of fruit was still in its early stage; and processors paid little attention to them, because their scale of production was too small. Organic was still a fringe movement.

Farmers like the Olsens paid their dues, and it was their dedication, before organic was trendy, that I felt and appreciated as I toured their orchard. It was a privilege to be there. I left confident that they would deliver the plums I needed, assuming again that I could find someone to process them. A community of farmers was forming and rooting for us to succeed, not just for their own benefit, but for the planet's too. I didn't think it was possible for my determination to grow, but it did.

I found my way to the J.R. Wood processing plant. I sat outside the gate in my rental car, mesmerized by the size of the operation. The plant was so big and we were so small. How would this ever come together? I was very familiar with this size problem. It's why we ended up building our own production facility. Somehow I had to convince them to work with us. There had to be a way. I didn't want the Koss brothers to disappoint the Olsen brothers.

I introduced myself as a potential new customer. I was a little reluctant to use the "O" word for fear that "organic" would be polarizing, but of course I had to. As fate would have it, my tour guide was also the guy responsible for prospecting for new business. J.R. Wood was looking at organic as an opportunity, but had not yet found a way in. Prior to my arrival in Atwater, they had serendipitously been in discussions with Organic Farms. The convergence of interests invigorated and emboldened the collective creative process.

A plan was imagined to coordinate the simultaneous arrival of as much organic stone fruit as possible. The projected volumes were still small, but feasible for the plant's operation. Why would J.R. Wood bother if their equipment was going to be underutilized, if they had to go through the hassle of segregating the organic fruit, engage in the extra audit-trail work, and interrupt their conventional run and clean out their processing lines?

We offered to pay them a contract packing fee that was two or three times greater than what they were getting for processing conventional fruit. It was a good deal all around, if we could actually coordinate the fruit delivery with Organic Farms. This was a big if.

The fruit had to be picked ripe, but the ripening wasn't as simultaneous as it was in our imagination. Once you pick a peach and put it into a bin with a thousand pounds of other peaches, the clock is ticking before the fruit loses its quality or goes to mush. The weather also had to cooperate. Too hot, and the fruit waiting in bins would be compromised. Too cold, and fruit waiting to be picked would have to wait too long for fruit already picked. The days leading to this first processing event were very tense. Organic Farms did an amazing job of helping to bring it all together, and, in a move they would soon regret, financed the processing expense for us.

Ron and I wanted the fruit to be perfect for Earth's Best Baby Foods. We were very fortunate to clear these daunting hurdles.

PRESSURE

RON:

Arnie and I hit the ground running in every direction. I guess my youth wasn't expended, because to do so required inexhaustible energy. The task at hand was simple: Create a perfect convergence of building, equipment, ingredients, manufacturing, and marketing, and be ready for the Natural Foods Expo in October 1987.

If you've ever gotten into a taxi with only a twenty-dollar bill (or less) in hand, you know the feeling when the meter gets switched on. And you also know the feeling when you're stuck in traffic and you have plenty of time to read over and over the card on the dashboard declaring how much each forty-five seconds of waiting time will cost. That's the way it felt for Arnie and me the day after the closing. We had a twenty-dollar bill in hand and the meter was spinning.

Our sails were filled with enthusiasm and so were those of everyone around us. The cash was burning, but we weren't stuck in traffic. The concrete tilt-up building design was on the drawing board in earnest. All of the environmental permits were submitted. Bob began chasing down equipment. And we started making commitments to farmers and to Joseph and Richard at Organic Farms: 35,000 pounds of peaches, including early season 'Springcrest' and 'Raycrest' varieties and the later season 'O'Henry'; lots of plums like the deep purple 'Laroda' and 'Santa Rosa'; and Canadian apples to the tune of sixteen tractor-trailer loads. These commitments were of course a huge act of faith. There was no track record and no track to follow. We threw the proverbial dart, and it landed in the wilderness of a pure organic baby-food start-up. Everything was a guess.

We didn't know whether we were going to get from here to there or when or how the marketplace was going to respond. This was Bob's first baby-food plant. We had a shoestring equipment budget. Would peas and brown rice really work on a commercial scale with shoestring equipment? What about those $90,000 (each) Rotomats? Gulp! And what about that "sounds too good to be true" electronic liquid filler (ELF)? Uncertainty became the norm, and Arnie and I adapted to it.

The ground-breaking ceremony at Pond Lane happened in July with fanfare, shiny shovel, and red-ribbon cutting. It was surreal back then and remains surreal today. I remember worrying about the red-winged blackbirds that were nesting in the field that we were about to disturb. I felt conflicted and guilty about turning their world upside down, but was resigned to the necessity of their sacrifice. Maybe they were fine, but I remember a very protective mama bird perched on a long strand of timothy. She looked worried too. The project did not have a moment to spare. But I did uneasily recognize at the time that this was my first compromise.

Watching that building go up was exciting and satisfying. Concrete tilt-up buildings go up fast. The synchronizing of the many parts and pieces still seemed possible. There were challenges galore, but amazingly no roadblocks. So far, we had anticipated every step of the way sufficiently. Our confidence was bolstered, and our heads were probably a little swelled and giddy. Enjoy it while and when you can.

As the equipment arrived, I of course began to worry. The used equipment looked really used. Right away we were in the mode of rebuilding it or modifying it. Maybe for Bob this mode was old hat, but I didn't expect to shell out tens of thousands of dollars and then shell out more so the equipment was actually usable. Fortunately, Bob seemed to know how to respond to all of the twists and turns, and whatever was wrong became more right.

On the other hand, the new pieces of equipment—the apple juice press and ELF filler—were shiny and unsullied, and it made me feel secure and assured that at least something would run well. The Rotomats were used, but they were impressive hulks just the same. Piece by piece, everything showed up: the jar washer; capper; coders; conveyor belts; labeler; apple washer; steam cooker; jacketed kettles; and the numerous pumps. The six-hundred-horsepower boiler was gargantuan. Talk about excitement.

Now the task was to stitch it all together, so that when we flicked the proverbial switch, the Rube Goldberg hodgepodge would produce the best baby food in the world.

Bob found Kevin McGloughlin (a.k.a. "Red") to install the equipment. Kevin was a gem with all of the experience, confidence, and capability in the world, but he was not cheap. I guess I should say "fair enough," but when the stainless-steel welding, piping, and valving began in earnest, the meter also started spinning in earnest. Our budget number was way off, and life behind the eight ball became a way of life for us. It couldn't be helped.

Plus, there was all of the plumbing for steam lines, water lines, waste water, and cleanup. And there were so many motors that needed wiring and emergency shutoff switches. The enormity of building the manufacturing facility didn't hit me until the installation. In fact, why would it? I had never done this before. And I think (relatively speaking), too much of that enormity missed Bob as well, or at least the cost part.

Arnie and I scrambled to find money in the budget to make up for the installation overruns, and we did so by raiding the various "miscellaneous" line items we had included as protection against our ignorance and the unexpected. Of course, we were smart for learning how to spell "miscellaneous" and generously placing it throughout our projections, but not nearly smart enough, because, at the end of the day, actually early on—let's say by 10:00 a.m.—we had wiped out most of it. All we could do was spend and hope that somewhere down the line we would save.

My world became that production-room installation. Arnie walked in and out of it. Probably, if he had had his druthers, he would have hung out there endlessly with me. That's because it was a lot more fun and nuts and boltsy than the vagaries of developing the sales and marketing dimension of Earth's Best. But it was not all unfairness heaped on Arnie. He got to play with the growers more than I did, and had adventures in the field that I only could hear about.

There was no measuring and there were no resentments. Our worlds always overlapped because we shared everything, but he kept me out of his minutiae and I kept him out of mine, unless there was cause to do otherwise. The only aspect of Earth's Best that was time-tested and bulletproof was our relationship. We did not let each other down—ever.

Well into the installation, probably somewhere in late July or early August, the first big-time stressor hit. The Natural Food Expo in

October was looming large, our cash was burning, and Arnie and I could feel deep in our bones the threat of not being able to bring it all together in time. This was the order of magnitude of PRESSURE surrounding us that we had never experienced before. Arnie and I both have an innate sense of how fast you have to move to fulfill a time commitment. We were in the thick of it and we both knew, despite never being there before, that we needed to move faster.

Bovine Excrement!

But the obstinate stars wouldn't align for us. There was a death in Bob's wife's family, which required his absence. Here's where it got interesting. As I recall, Bob's wife would not fly. The funeral was in California, and Bob announced that he and his wife would be taking the train. Of course, all civility and good form demanded accommodation to such a family situation, but the "pressures" beneath my veneer of understanding had me on the edge of panic. I believe I performed admirably and was gracious, as I had been brought up to be, but there was little that would comfort me, including Bob's promise that he would stay in touch to keep the installation moving forward. Remember, this was before cell phones. There were no train phones either, so where would that comfort really come from? Nowhere is the answer. There was no comfort.

Bob left. The subcontractors swarmed all over me. I was completely overwhelmed. When you're suddenly thrown into the deep end of the pool, if you don't drown, you either learn how to swim or are rescued. I don't think my flailing about qualified me as a swimmer, but by summer-camp standards, I did get my "Tadpole" certificate.

Bob called once from California, as I recall, to shockingly tell me that he was taking the train back from California as well. This triple-flabbergasted me. There were other family members to support his wife, and we were in the most critical of times. It was unbearable, and I felt angry and resentful. The honeymoon was over.

It probably was just an impossible situation; impossible for him, because he felt an obligation, if not a need to be with his wife, and impossible for Arnie and me, because years of work and our futures were on the chopping block.

But that's the perspective, subject to twenty years of softening. At the time I felt betrayed, in part, because Bob created the expectation that he would be available and wasn't leaving us in the lurch. Bovine excrement! The train ride back pushed me over the edge. It felt like desertion.

When Bob returned, almost two weeks later, the survival mode did not allow me to regress into these negative feelings. Our ship was losing steam, somewhat adrift and taking on water. My instincts were to frantically coddle, amuse, serve up tea and crumpets, and inspire rather than to blow bigger holes in the fragile structure and sink us. There was only one direction to move and that was forward.

I Thought We Were So Clever

The production line took shape, conveyor belt by conveyor belt, motor by motor, pump by pump, pipe by pipe. It was a great relief to have Bob back on task, bless his heart. My inner self remained pretty much in nonstop survival mode, pressing hard to keep the pace that I knew we needed to succeed. I was constantly watching out for the balls that were about to drop and for people's vibrations that weren't so good that needed tending to. But when I looked around and saw people welding and wiring and setting pieces of equipment in place, it was satisfying, and I was filled with the realization of my life's potential. This was what I had longed to feel when I was spinning around in that green-plush south-Florida swivel chair with Arnie. Joy is a wonderful thing. And what a joy it was when the first tractor-trailer load of glass arrived—clear glass that is.

But we were still scrambling to get the labels made. If you've never designed a food label, you can't imagine how much goes into it. Besides crafting the Earth's Best logo, the feel of the label, the skin complexion of the illustrated babies, and imparting the deliciousness of the fruits and vegetables, there was a universe of government regulations requiring print types of a certain size for this and that, and specific placement areas for such declarations as the product weight and ingredients. A baby-food label is small. It all has to fit and hang together.

Again, we, the entrepreneurs, underestimated the process and the cost. But when those labels arrived at Pond Lane, they were beautiful, and Earth's Best had taken another giant step from big idea to reality.

The production room became a little quieter day by day, as the subcontractors finished up their work. That's not to say that the scrambling stopped. It didn't and never did. September 1987 was upon us, the expo was breathing hot and heavy down our necks, and either we were ready for showtime or we were screwed. The next big step in front of us was to hire the production employees.

We advertised locally in the Middlebury newspaper, and Arnie orchestrated the interview process. I just remember seeing people come and go when I happened to be in the area of our temporary administrative space. Interestingly, I can't remember Bob or me being particularly involved in this process. Ideally, he would have been, but the press to have the production room ready would not allow it. That's my recollection.

Arnie was positive and upbeat about whom he was meeting. A start date was set for orientation and training. It looked like we might be ready for the expo. Actually, we had no plan B for not being ready. Arnie and I were in the "all-or-nothing" mind-set. Failure was not an option. This was clearly irrational behavior, given the long odds of actually *being* ready, but I guess denial had crept in. Neither Arnie nor I wanted to face a world that did not have the plant running and the products ready. That's because we didn't think that was a world we could survive in.

Of course the pressure was created, in part, by our assumption that not being ready would be a killer to the project or at least a major setback. Since we had bought into that assumption, it was in the driver's seat, and the ride was the ride. We fought to stay on the road and not crash into that world that threatened us with failure—a world that didn't include Earth's Best.

One day in early September the production employees came into my life: strangers who would become the heart and soul of Earth's Best, people who stood shoulder to shoulder with Arnie and me through thick and thin to make a dream come true. And I'm not gushing here. Employers are supposed to know what they are doing so employees can fulfill their job descriptions. We did our best to know, but we often did not, especially in the beginning. When we fell short, disastrously short, we needed to be saved, and from day one, it was Barb, Pam, Belinda, Leo, Brian, Nancy, Lynne, Sue, Dick, Scott, and Jim (to name a few) who did the saving.

My challenge from the outset was to let Bob be "the man." He was the plant manager, and needed to be perceived as the production authority, leader, and decision maker. I needed to step back and let him do his job, and it wasn't easy for me. It should have been because I knew so little, but my natural tendency was to spontaneously intervene, respond, direct, and decide, when I should have simply deferred to Bob or disappeared.

I had never been in the executive position I was in. I had always been just hands-on, in the trenches, doing whatever it took. Early on, during the training and orientation, Bob brought to my attention his concern about me undermining his authority. I'm glad he did, because he was right. I was unpracticed and undisciplined in this regard, but I understood that Arnie and I really needed him to be the production executive so we could focus our efforts on leading the company and developing the Earth's Best business.

Before we knew it, equipment company representatives from Mateer Burt (labeler), ELF (filler), Stock Rotomat (pressure cookers), and Continental White Cap (capper) were on board, training the key production employees. Belinda was on the labeler; Big Bob on the Rotomats; Barb on the filler and capper; and Pam seemed to be on everything else: the washing equipment, scrubbers, slicer, cooker, finishing equipment, kettles, and batching. Dick, Scott, and Jim were on line to manage all of the inventories, transportation, and scheduling and to coordinate the interface with the production-room needs. Leo and Brian were getting set up to fix everything that would soon be either breaking or just requiring regular maintenance and TLC (like that six-hundred-horsepower boiler that could make or break an entire day's production by either reliably delivering steam or not).

Then, the first tractor-trailer load of apples arrived from Canada, the first of many more scheduled for October through February. The apricot, peach, and plum purees showed up courtesy of J.R. Wood and Joseph and Richard at Organic Farms. All of the pesticide-test results were clean so far on the California stone fruit. The Canadian apples had shown up before their test results were reported. This really irritated and worried me, but the apples looked great and the results were imminent.

Kevin, the thermal-processing authority from Louisiana, was in residence now, meticulously testing the Rotomats and determining the processing times and temperatures for each of our introductory products. I took a great interest in this work because here lay the bottom of the bottom line of my fear: the safety of the baby food. This had been the domain of my greatest anxiety way back when, standing in the Ronald McDonald House parking lot with Arnie in 1984. I knew it would be my domain then, and here it was for real, smack in the pit of my stomach.

In that RMH parking lot I was just in my head, but now in that gleaming white virgin production room, there were tires to kick and people with in-depth expertise and hands-on experience to add dimension and perspective to that primordial fear. I learned about all of the safety checks, monitoring gauges, and automated record-ing devices that would be checked by Big Bob, then by Nancy from quality control (QC), and then finally signed off on by Bob as the plant manager.

There was plenty of redundancy even for my neurosis. And the final blanket of comfort was that standard operating procedures would require that jars from each retort run be set aside and incubated for pathogens, and other quality parameters (such as pH, taste, and color) before being released for distribution into the marketplace. There was a formidable safety net in place.

When we added to that the various organic certification entities, such as CCOF (California Certified Organic Farmers) and FVO (Farm Verified Organic), our own Earth's Best certification and verification program that we were developing, and the pesticide-residue testing that we were instituting, Earth's Best would be just that—the Earth's Best baby food. Nothing less would do.

The day arrived. We were ready for our first production run. Bob was in charge. He had purchased a new $16,000 bladder press that was designed for grapes, but supposedly would also work well for juicing apples. Apple juice seemed to be a "can't miss," straightforward first product to make. I thought we were so clever.

Goose Eggs

Twenty or thirty production employees stood around the torpedo-shaped press, watching in expectant wonder. Soon the juice would be flowing to a five-hundred-gallon steam-jacketed kettle. Arnie and I just stood there holding our breath. We were standing on the edge of joy. The apples were beautiful. QC was hovering, waiting to measure the acidity and the sweetness to make sure that we were pressing the proper mix of apple varieties.

The juice jars were on the conveyor belt. Barb had tuned up the ELF filler for the fill volume. The coder was set with the date and product code. Big Bob was ready with the Rotomats. Belinda had the apple-juice labels locked and loaded in the Mateer Burt. And Dick, Scott, and Jim were on the mark to take the finished cases into the warehouse.

It had been a long pregnancy.

The apples were first washed and then ground up to enhance the efficiency of the juice extraction and fed into the press. Pam was all over that. It was a happening. The moment of truth arrived. Press the living daylights out of those apples! I had made any number of yield calculations to arrive at how many apples we would need and what the ingredient cost would be in arriving at a cost-of-goods number. My hope and expectation was that my assumptions were conservative and the yields would be improved and our costs actually lower. Bob thought this would be the case.

And I of course would then become a hero and bask in the warm glow of delivering realistic projections.

We all stood there waiting for the flow of juice. There was a trickle; the calm before the storm? The flow never came. Where the heck was the juice? There certainly was plenty of it in the apples. They weren't the problem.

First, Bob made adjustments in the loading and the amount of organic rice hulls used as a pressing aid. The air pressure was varied. A colossal uneasiness grew. The production employees started looking at each other. The morning was passing by. Nothing was working. Arnie and I threw some "bright" ideas into the ring, but we were basically clueless. It was Bob's show, and it was looking like a flop.

But in actuality it was my show and Arnie's—mostly mine. Arnie was counting on me to deliver the baby food. It was my job. Standing there with no tangible results was a nightmare. I could see the cash burning as everyone stood around. I could see my projection estimates going up in smoke. I held out hope because Bob was still trying. But there was a part of me that was already imagining the worst. What if everything we had set in place didn't work? What if it were true that we had no business being in the baby-food business? What if that prospective investor who provocatively asked us way back when, "Who the hell are you?" had his feet on the ground, and Arnie and I never did and never would?

There's nothing as painful and disorienting as being stripped bare to the core, where your identity disintegrates into dust, and nothing is left. Perhaps this sounds liberating, and perhaps if I had been on a vision quest, this shedding of self would have been hailed as a triumph on the path to enlightenment. The path to the Inferno was more like it.

Day one, cases produced: A big fat goose egg.

Day two arrived with new hope. I remember Bob packing the press with apples and rice hulls. He had a new plan for success. Everyone stood around watching expectantly. I just stared hard at the pipe where the juice was supposed to flow and simultaneously tried to push the image of cash burning out of my mind. Bob ratcheted up the air pressure and kept on ratcheting. There was an explosion.

The press cover blew open and apple pomace and rice hulls blasted off into the production-room atmosphere. You could say that the people standing in the line of fire were the first tasters of Earth's Best Baby Food made at Pond Lane—albeit unexpectedly. Apple mush was splattered thirty feet onto the ceiling and onto the walls everywhere. Now the production employees had something to do.

I'm still a little silly about it as a means to divert some of the overwhelming stress that I find in telling the story. Day two would be another goose egg. We were very fortunate that no one got hurt. The production employees were shocked. I even caught a few looks of disgust. Or perhaps it was cynicism. And it was a little early in the game for that to be creeping in. It definitely was demoralizing. Bob's credibility took a big up-front hit. And it never really recovered. And what about mine?

Imagine having to tell the investors that we failed at making apple juice, of all things. This was a sickening prospect. How could Arnie and I have ever projected that making apple juice with a guy with forty years of food-processing experience at the helm was not possible? We had spent $16,000. The equipment was new. Inconceivable—but it happened.

I knew we had to shift gears. Juice was not happening and I saw no prospect that it would. We had to give up on it. This was a huge concession and change in our plan. We still needed to have products for our introduction at the Natural Food Expo. Applesauce was next.

If Only We'd Had Google

You could argue that the making of applesauce is not a pioneering endeavor. I probably made that argument hundreds of times along the way to investors, bankers, and government officials. It is a plausible argument, isn't it? After the juice fiasco, was there anything about Earth's Best that was plausible?

Bob made all of the necessary equipment adjustments for the puree-jar size. The bottle washer, the capper, the filler, and the coder all needed to be changed over. Disappointingly, this took another day, another goose egg, which I had not anticipated or projected. The anticipation on day four was off the chart.

I remember the apples happily bobbing in the washer. The production-line inspectors removed any bruises, extraneous leaves, and of course, any bad apples. QC hovered. The apples shot through the brush washer because they didn't really need brushing. That piece of equipment was reserved for carrots and sweet potatoes. The Urschel slicer worked perfectamente. Every quarter-inch slice was fed into the twenty-foot-long direct-steam applesauce cooker. Did I say "direct steam?" I followed the path of those apples inch by inch as if I was their personal escort. When they dropped out of the cooker, nicely cooked, I was ecstatic. Next stop was the finishing equipment where the skins were removed and the puree form was achieved. We could make applesauce! There was a collective sigh of relief. I started breathing again.

The puree was pumped into the five-hundred-gallon steam-jacketed kettle, ready for quality control to make the required checks for taste, texture, color, sweetness, and pH. I remember someone from QC bringing me a sample.

Anticipation.

It was terrible . . . yuck.

How could this be? Delicious-tasting apples making terrible-tasting apple sauce? Somewhere along the way, a disgusting taste was imparted. The equipment was all clean and sanitized. There were no extraneous chemicals lurking about. But there was an undeniably "off" flavor.

And weirder yet, Bob barely perceived this taste. QC certainly did and I did. Now what?

Here's where there lies a potentially deep fault line in food production and probably in any manufacturing: quality either dies by the sword or prevails in the face of economic loss. Financial ruin was actually what I was thinking was on the line, but I knew as Arnie did that our greatest failure would not be a failed company, but the failure to deliver Earth's Best baby food. There was no fuzziness around this value and our determination to fulfill it.

Bob might have filled those jars with that applesauce. I remember the gist of a conversation with him that suggested the product was good enough to get started; pretty scary actually, and another blow unfortunately to Bob's credibility. The production employees grokked what Earth's Best was really about before he did.

There was a problem somewhere in that production line. The detective work and sleuthing began. What was the cause? The applesauce sitting in the kettle was dumped down the floor drain; painful, but really a nondecision. Day four was another goose egg, as were days five, six, seven, and on and on. You can probably see why the Inferno comes to mind.

We deduced that the steam in the cooker was imparting the flavor. So we blasted the steam for hours trying to purge the lines. Then we ran more apples through in hopes of achieving Earth's Best Baby Foods. There was some improvement, but not enough. The off flavor persisted. The pressure to say "good enough" was beyond excruciating. Bob thought we were trying for perfection and he became increasingly frustrated and perturbed. QC continued to insist on thumbs down. Arnie and I were dug in. It had to be right and it wasn't. And Barb, Pam, and Belinda watched us like hawks, wondering if we were all full of shit with our talk about Earth's Best or were for real.

We finally came up with a theory for our misery. When the pipefitters put the steam lines together they used a certain compound around the fittings. There was nothing unusual or extraordinary about this. It was business as usual for those guys. So we thought that the high temperatures might be causing that compound to become volatilized and hence incorporated into the steam fed into the cooker. Another complementary view was that there was a manufacturing film present in the pipes that was slowly degrading. Whatever it was, it was killing us.

Bob devised a plan to open all the steam lines throughout the building to once and for all purge them. We did this under the cover of a weekend night. The noise was deafening as the steam blasted through the pipes everywhere and filled the building. I could barely see Arnie standing next to me. I remember the hope I was holding and the sweat beads of desperation dripping off my face. We just let it rip through the night.

The obvious question, my obvious question, was why the hell was this disaster happening? How could Bob not have known about the necessity of purging the steam lines? I was the rookie. Bob was the veteran. This was a rookie mistake in my rookie estimation. I still don't get it.

Arnie and I tried so hard up front to defend against our own inexperience and ignorance. Maybe our Earth's Best dream was preposterous, but we weren't arrogant. But there we were, standing in that plant like idiots, hoping along with Bob that this cruel beginning to our adventure would finally end.

I guess we thought the problem was licked because a full-scale production was planned for the following Monday. The applesauce got to the kettle, no problem. QC batched it up, ready for filling, and passed some samples around to me, Bob, and Arnie. Bob liked it. QC was debating the acceptability. Arnie and I said unequivocally, "no." It just wasn't Earth's Best. It was okay, but we weren't starting the "OK Baby Food Company." We still detected that background off flavor.

If there ever was a time to bullshit myself, this was it. Any hope of getting products to the expo was about to disappear. Remember, we had no plan B for product samples, and as far as we knew, we had exhausted the options to fix the problem. Bob was exasperated, but pleasing him was not the priority.

Instead of collapsing into a death spiral, the decision to walk our talk and not cave in to the pressures to compromise were empowering and energizing. In our heart of hearts we knew we shouldn't. This was our trial by fire—or rather steam. Instead of becoming brittle and victims of circumstance, Arnie and I fought for the Earth's Best we wanted to bring into the world. We forged a plan B for the expo and no longer were we waiting for Bob to save us.

If only Google had been around. I could have instantly been connected to the universe of steam filters, direct-steam applications, and suppliers. How easy it might have been. How difficult it was.

Our Little Secret

Maybe this recounting sounds self-glorifying. If so, then I have failed to capture the moment for you. It was a small miracle that we didn't get squashed right then and there. Obviously, Arnie and I had messed up big time in either hiring the wrong plant manager or just completely underestimating the demands and complexity of the manufacturing start-up. And we would pay dearly for these miscalculations, as would all of the initial investors.

But we also resisted the descent into mediocrity. We resisted fulfilling the dire prediction made years ago by that cynical (or perhaps wise) businessman who warned us with certainty that we would not recognize ourselves after we had a turn in the PRESSURE cooker of the big business world. The essence being that we would desert our ideals for greener pastures when necessity dictated so.

Well, we didn't.

Kevin (a.k.a. Red) finally jumped into the ring to put us out of our misery. He introduced the idea of steam filters to me. I wish he had jumped in sooner, much sooner, but I guess the prevailing politics with Bob discouraged that, or maybe it was something else standing in the way. Maybe he was just out of town on another job. The net of it was that steam filters were required to assure the presence of clean, unadulterated steam. This was apparently common knowledge in the food-manufacturing world, when live steam directly contacts food, yet Bob didn't know it or perhaps thought he could cut a corner.

When you're an entrepreneur and you decide to go off into the wild blue yonder, don't underestimate how ignorant you really are and the impact of any imposing vulnerabilities on your decision making.

Maybe, in fact, it was impossible or unlikely to expect one person to deliver the complete package of knowledge we needed at start-up without tripping up. Perhaps this understanding is what Les eventually awoke to. But from the outset Bob led us to believe otherwise. Arnie and I didn't know better, and at the time we probably didn't want to know better. There was an imposing vulnerability bearing down on us: the prospect of never getting into business.

The hard fact of our collective lives was that we were unable to avoid this disastrous start. It wasn't the cause of the calamity to come, but it contributed to it. You can't buy a sophisticated steam-filtering system out of a vending machine or the local hardware store. When all was said and done, it would take around six weeks for the equipment to arrive and for Kevin to install it. The cost was an unbudgeted $20,000 bill.

Plan B for the expo kicked into gear. We would make baby food in the QC lab and limit the number of samples to an attractive display. Everything was canned or processed, but not in the Rotomats, and hence not according to any approved FDA thermal process. Sampling, unfortunately, was out of the question, and we couldn't give any baby food away. The real stressor was that we would have to watch the jars like hawks because they weren't commercially processed, and we couldn't assume or represent that they were safe for distribution.

Arnie and I left Pond Lane behind for three days to introduce Earth's Best at the Philadelphia Expo. I believed we were over the hump with the steam problem, so in truth it was a relief to get out of there and stop worrying and obsessing. I'm sure Bob was happy to see me go.

It was finally our turn to come out and meet the world, but it was really hard for me to not be all that we appeared to be. We hadn't made Earth's Best yet, but that would be our little secret.

Euphoria Mist

ARNIE:

I remember walking onto the expo showroom floor. I felt like a gladiator walking into the coliseum. Would we survive to fight again or be eaten? The showroom seemed cavernous and was filling fast with row upon row of exhibits. There were newcomers to the scene like Earth's Best and industry leaders like Little Bear, Arrowhead Mills, and Cascadian Farm. Hope was in the air as old friends reconnected at this annual pilgrimage of East Coast natural-foods devotees.

Even as we were setting up the booth, curiosity seekers swept by to check us out. There was nothing more compelling at the 1987 Philadelphia Expo than the introduction of the nation's first organic baby food. There was a buzz in the air. Baby's Garden was there, but this time Earth's Best would be the darling.

Ron and I greeted everyone with enthusiasm, but I have to admit to feeling a certain paranoia that I could not push away. Who were the potential competitors in the crowd? Who was resenting me for paying top dollar to the California organic growers? The insecurity I was feeling was probably exaggerated by the little secret Ron and I shared about the samples we had brought. My eyes could not stop checking and rechecking to make sure that our display jars were not missing. This was a huge worry and distraction. I hated it.

Our trade-show booth was soon swamped. Thankfully, Sue Gilbert and Bob Donnola were there with us. Sue was our consulting dietician/nutritionist and product expert and another great person to have on our team. Ron and I did make a few good decisions. Sue was one of them. I trusted her judgment, counted on her honesty, valued her expertise, and appreciated her flexibility, as we all coped with the tumultuousness of the earliest days.

Bob D. was our natural-foods industry sales manager. We were both wet behind the ears, but I knew he was the kind of guy I wanted in the trenches with me. Funny, smart, earnest, irreverent, and hard-working, Bob D. brought Earth's Best to life in that marketplace.

I was very encouraged by the pre-expo responses we had gotten from the trade, so I was primed to expect to close some very big distributor deals. Tree of Life in particular was a prominent player that loomed large. The plain fact was that Earth's Best desperately needed a home run in order to slow down the cash flow hemorrhaging at Pond Lane. Amidst the hoopla, I felt a lot of pressure.

Bob and I were busy writing up retail-store orders. I could see across the crowd that Ron and Sue were happily animated with booth visitors. Wow! I was ecstatic. We had arrived. "Mission Accomplished," if you know what I mean. That's what I was really thinking. It seemed like everyone was going gaga over what we had done. It was instant celebrity and instant success. I thought it was going to be hard because everything else had been and was, but finally something easy, the natural-foods marketplace, our home turf. Finally, an outcome that made sense.

There must be some kind of "euphoria mist" they put into the air-conditioning ducts at these trade shows. What else could possibly explain the stupendousness of my misperceptions and misjudgments—that soon would become evident?

The Tree of Life buyer strolled by the booth, ready to rumba. This was a make-it-or-break-it meeting for me and Bob. Tree ruled the Southeast, and without them on board it would take many more months to cobble together a network of small distributors to service the numerous independent stores found throughout the South and Mid-Atlantic states.

Bob had been working in concert with a Tree sales rep on an aggressive introductory special. I was concerned that we were sacrificing too much margin, but figured that this was the least-expensive way to secure shelf placement and a workable selling price at retail. The stage was set. All that was left was to meet the vice president of purchasing, shake hands, and write the order for eight tractor-trailer loads. If this had unfolded as expected, Ron and I probably wouldn't be writing this story, at least the redemption part that lies ahead.

Bob and I greeted the buyers as we all got seated around a small conference-room table. We were all smiles. The VP asked some questions about our products, delivery schedule, and pricing. He said, "Guys, I like what you're doing, but frankly, if Tree is going to get behind this and push it, we need you to give up more." I felt my body temperature rise, as if the sun had just lurched forward toward the earth. "How much more?" I asked. "Oh, I think 15 percent," said the VP.

Bob started to jump in to protest, as he stared at his sales contact looking for help. There was no one from Tree coming to his rescue. This was an ambush. I leaned forward in my chair and said, "Excuse me, do you mean 15 percent more than the 20 percent we are already giving you?" "That's exactly right," said the VP, looking as if he had just uttered the word "checkmate."

I tried to reason with the guy, telling him we didn't have any more to give, but would do all we could to support the intro with our 800-line, consumer brochure mailings, PR campaign, and advertising. I felt like a piece of bait fish trying to reason with a great white shark. The Tree VP said, "What's it going to be?" I calmly said, "We can do the 20 percent we offered and nothing more." He stood up, thanked me for my time, and exited. When all was said and done, Tree of Life took two trailer loads, not eight. This was a crushing blow that sealed the fate of our emerging cash-flow crisis.

Bob D. and I stumbled out of the meeting, shell-shocked. What else was there to do but run for the bar? Actually, we didn't do that. After fuming and blowing off (filtered) steam for a while, we started to strategize how to cope with this new crisis. There was no way we were rolling over and playing dead. I would have, if I thought we could have, but I already knew our margins were dangerously anemic. We had to find another way. Fortunately, Bob was a fighter. He was on the case, and I was thankful.

Ron wasn't at the Tree meeting. He was stationed at the trade-show booth, no doubt still feeling euphoric. He had a long way to fall when he heard the news.

The Glass Slippers Were Stripped from Our Feet

What we all didn't know was that around the bend there was worse news. Many of the distributors would not be passing on our intro-ductory discount deals to the retailers, and the retailers who did get the discounts would be pocketing them and taking higher margins than usual. This of course translated into disastrously high retail prices and consumer sticker shock.

I failed to appreciate the nature of pioneering a new product category in the natural-foods industry. Baby's Garden was out there trying to cut a trail through the distribution channel, and now so were we. There were well-established protocols in place that the channel players routinely assumed for product introductions. Kind of like a "one size fits all" approach. Baby food did not fit. Bob D. and I had to find a way to bring a new understanding to both the distribu-tors and retail accounts nationwide. At a $1.10 per jar, organic baby food would not fly, and that's what we were facing if the industry would not budge from its business-as-usual approach. We faced a huge unanticipated hurdle.

The showroom floor had been open for about an hour Sunday morning when I showed up to see how things were going at the booth. Bob D. and I had been in meetings with other potential distributors and were feeling hopeful about overcoming some of the damage Tree had done the day before. As we approached the booth with some good news, it was obvious something was very wrong. Ron and Sue looked very worried. "What is it?" I said to Ron. He whispered in my ear, "There are samples missing. Someone took samples, and some of them are low-acid." I immediately went over to our sample rack and took a quick inventory. There were seven missing jars, including one carrot and one sweet potato. A dreaded moment we feared was now real.

It's amazing we made it to Sunday before this happened.

Ron and I started walking the showroom floor with the hope of finding the samples. He was obsessed. This was his worst nightmare. Sue was confident the samples were safe, but still they had not undergone the official thermal processing in our plant. We had better things to do than to look for seven missing jars, but the priority was clear: find them. Ron and I rendezvoused throughout the day to check in. It seemed hopeless. Who were we kidding? They were gone.

Bob and I discussed the state of our sales effort and the number of orders we had in hand. Our review quickly revealed a developing dilemma. There were many retailers who wanted to pick up our line, but their preferred distributors were not yet on board. Translation: Unless we shipped to these retailers direct, they could not stock our products.

I was tempted to consider a direct sale to the retailers, but Bob was decisively opposed. First, the freight would kill us, and second, if the freight missed the mark, the industry distributors would find a way to skewer us for not being loyal to the established way of doing business. Bob and I agreed to press on to establish distributor accounts and to try to convince some of the retailers to go with secondary distributors who were already on board.

It was going to be a schlog. And a schlog was going to kill us. It was obvious right out of the chute that we were never going to meet our sales projections and our cash needs if we just looked to the natural-foods industry for business. We needed to cast a wider distribution net much sooner than planned. We had to somehow quickly find our way onto the big stage, the mass marketplace.

At the time, there were few if any products that crossed over from natural foods to grocery, unless they sat in a natural-foods set. The natural-foods industry considered it a betrayal to play both sides of the fence, and a move to do so was ill-advised. Earth's Best could not play by this rule. It was either perish being a well-behaved natural-foods player or die trying in a crossover effort to the mass-market stores. Sink or swim? We of course tried to swim.

I knew Bob was not going to be our mass-market guy. He was too much of a straight shooter. We needed a smooth talking pit bull disguised as a grocery-market sales veteran. In any case, Bob had his hands more than full with the natural-foods market and, not surprisingly, was strongly opposed to embracing a mass-market strategy. He knew once the word got out that Earth's Best had crossed over to the dark side, he was dead meat within the trade. Bob wanted a chance to succeed and a job.

The expo hall was growing strangely quiet as the exhibitors broke down their show booths. Ron and I were making a last-ditch effort to find our missing jars. As entrepreneurs, we had learned to persist against all odds, not knowing of course if what we were doing was what it took to succeed or just certifiably stupid. If the matter at hand was important enough, the odds were not the final arbiter for the degree of effort. Rather, it was hope and want.

Unexpectedly, our persistence paid off. As we cruised the show floor, I caught sight of one of our jars sitting behind a display rack. Ron and I stopped dead in our tracks. We knew the booth and the people. The company was a prominent organic-foods company, and the people were our friends. I felt relief and dismay in the same instant. Why would they take our samples? My paranoia sprouted wings. An awkward moment was about to go down.

Ignorance was professed. "Sorry, Arnie, I thought they were for the taking." Naturally, since the jars were all taped together and had been surrounded by signs that said NOT FOR SAMPLING, it was a lame excuse, but it didn't really mattter. We each knew the truth. Earth's Best was new and potentially big, very big. Even our friends had to figure out where they were going to stand in relationship to us. The unfolding of the organic-foods industry was a brave new world. Everyone was scrapping to find a place to survive and succeed. There were no crystal balls, so why not a little subterfuge? Fortunately, the relief dwarfed our dismay. I could clearly see that was true for Ron. The color started to reappear in his face for the first time all day. We had our samples and could stop worrying about worst-case scenarios. It was time to go home.

As we packed up the van early Sunday evening, exhaustion and crankiness were setting in. It was going to be a long ride back to Vermont. The van was even more crowded now, with the addition of show trinkets collected from other booths. Things were not fitting in. We foolishly forced our wooden display easel into the last remaining space and slammed the sliding door shut, hoping for a happy ending. The sound of exploding glass filled the van. "Perfecto," I thought as I surveyed the tiny pieces of window scattered on the parking-lot pavement. The wooden easel protruded through the new opening, now comfortably situated. We cleaned the mess up, taped some cardboard over the hole, and merrily went on our way—*not*.

As I drove north to the snores and wheezes of my Earth's Best team, Ron and I wasted no time assessing the depth and complexity of our predicament. This much we knew. We had to meet with our board sooner than later, a dreaded moment for sure. We hadn't run the numbers, but it was obvious we were going to need more money in the very near term. It was also obvious that we needed a mass-market sales manager pronto and a natural-foods strategy that would ensure a consumer-friendly retail price point. And we needed a plan to survive a cross-pollination plunge into the mass market, so we could sit next to Gerber, Beech-Nut, and Heinz.

There weren't any footpaths leading to where we needed to go. It was all bushwhacking. Now, in hindsight, I could have summarized all of the relevant information in our Louvre-destined business plan in five pages, followed by a hundred blank pages representing what we missed or didn't know and were now discovering.

Whatever we were going to do, we had to be ready for the Anaheim Natural Foods Expo, which was scheduled for early April of 1988. The question lurking behind everything that needed to be done was, "Would we even be in business by April?"

Here's a painful lesson. The Philadelphia Expo was in October 1987. All of that excitement was generated. All of those orders were placed. But as it turned out, we couldn't fulfill them until December. That delay hurt our credibility with the trade. Was Earth's Best for real? The initial excitement cooled, and we lost momentum. Orders were cancelled or drastically reduced. The glass slippers were stripped from our feet.

We overpromised. The steam fix took longer to resolve, and all Ron and I could do was wait and hurt. But we experienced the potential of Earth's Best at that Philadelphia Expo in a way that we never had before. It was real. The audience was live. Ron's initial organic baby-food whim back in 1976 was not crazy. We were not crazy. We just had to execute.

RON:

I came back from the expo intending to make good on all of the promises we had made in Philly. But, as you know, with the steam-filter fiasco still lingering, it was a waiting game for us—but not for calamity.

We were set to receive a lot more of those Canadian apples, but the belated pesticide-residue test showed positive for a fungicide. We couldn't take delivery. This was a nightmare for both us and the grower. And it would not be the last time. We sent Joe Smillie, our roving organic-foods production consultant, to check it out. Spray drift, from some neighboring commercial orchard, didn't appear to be the cause. You know what that means? The grower insisted he hadn't sprayed with the detected chemical. Joe wasn't so sure. At best, it was a muddle. At the end of the day, it didn't matter. We were apple-less. Arnie headed for the airport on an emergency mission to Sebastapol, California, the heart of organic apple country. And there was a silver lining: Our pesticide-testing program worked.

We also learned and never forgot that you have to have the analytical test results in hand before you buy and take delivery of a crop. I thought those Canadian apples would be clean as a whistle. This was an assumption. Assumptions and toilet paper offer the same utility. As it turned out, if we hadn't had the juice folly and steam problem, those Canadian apples would have been bottled and labeled and then we would have received the test results and had to throw it all away.

As Arnie zoomed off, there was only one thing to do: hold my breath and hope we weren't too late to buy California apples.

Nutcase?

ARNIE:

As I drove north from San Francisco to Sebastopol, I wondered if we were imperiled, if all the apples had been already contracted out. Jordan Smith was the big grower out there, and I knew companies like Organic Farms and Santa Cruz Natural were aggressively pursuing contracts. The stakes could not have been higher as I introduced myself to Jordan. He didn't say get in line and take a number, but he did confirm what I had suspected. I was very late to the scene, and being a newcomer with no track record and big plans he naturally viewed me skeptically. Jordan shared some of the horror stories of failed promises and relationships. Talk was cheap. Trust would have to be earned.

As Jordan and I walked through the mostly 'Gravenstein' and 'Yellow Delicious' orchard, I began to understand the dynamic that the organic apple growers were wrestling with. The picture was not pretty. The few big buyers out there like Organic Farms and Santa Cruz Naturals were offering to pay $80 to $120 per ton for processing-grade organic apples. Unless there was a short crop, there was an oversupply of apples. At depressed prices like this, there was no money in it for the growers. Jordan could not take care of the orchard, and his operation was not sustainable.

In that moment, I became inspired. I saw an opportunity for Earth's Best to separate itself from the entrenched adversarial paradigm between buyer and seller. What followed was a decision that rippled through the barely visible organic-foods industry. I asked, "Jordan, what do you need to get for your apples to make it work, to take care of the orchard and to be in business next year and the year after?" Jordan thought for a few moments and said "Arnie, I need a $170 a ton." I trusted him. Without hesitation, I said, "Then that's the price I'll pay you." But I went on to say, "Jordan, if there's a short crop next year or the year after, I don't expect to be gouged. My price will still be the $170 per ton." He was all for it.

Who knows what Jordan was thinking in that moment? Nutcase? Maybe I was. I just knew that business as usual was not the way I wanted to do business. I didn't want to be a winner and Jordan a loser and vice versa. And vice versa was what I was looking at big time, if some of those beautiful apples I was walking by didn't find their way to Vermont. In our projections, Ron and I had actually used about $170 a ton for a cost-of-goods assumption for the Canadian apples. So it seemed like a harmonic convergence. Jordan and I sealed the deal with a handshake.

Wow, did that feel good. I called Ron in Vermont and told him not to worry, the apples would be there. I had committed to purchase sixteen tractor-trailer loads, which in theory would meet our first year's projected-case requirements. You could say I averted disaster. You could also say I courted it.

My persistent dream was that Jordan, along with the Olsen Brothers and Paul Buxman, would be part of a great wave of growers who bonded with the intention of the way Earth's Best wanted to do business. We would be a community that took care of each other, in good times and bad.

RON:

I wasn't worrying. I was panicking. Arnie's harmonic-convergence moment did not comprehend the real costs to ship sixteen loads of apples from Sebastopol to Pond Lane in Middlebury, Vermont. He wasn't thinking $3,000 a load, because he didn't know it. Dick, our trusty transportation guru, could not find a way to reduce the pain. We hadn't budgeted for this. Add another $50,000 we didn't have. How can you know to put things like this into your projections? If you're an entrepreneur or intending to be one, take the time to reflect on that question.

The fact was, the transportation costs could have been $75,000 and we would have been stuck with paying the number. Earth's Best literally hung by a thread right here. No apples, no business. Arnie's successful mad-dash scramble made him the hero of the day. Our relief to be surviving was so great that we could not take in the financial consequences that were accruing for some future painful moment(s).

The apples showed up. The steam was now clean, and we were finally ready to rock and roll. And we did, sort of. The apple puree made it to the five-hundred-gallon batching kettle, thanks to Pam and all of the women running that line. QC approved. Bob was well beyond exasperated at this point. Arnie and I gave it the thumbs up, and finally we were ready to fill the first jars of Earth's Best. Hallelujah!

Ready to Be God

Barb wasn't the most patient person in the world, and she waited a hell of a long time to give that ELF filler a workout. It turned out to be finicky, very finicky. It worked great in practice runs with water, but hot puree proved to be a different story. The fill levels were inconsistent; some nozzles underfilled, some overfilled. Instead of it taking just Barb to run the machine, we needed two and sometimes three other people making hand adjustments to get the jars filled properly. This work was tedious, and of course it meant that the production speeds were much slower than we had projected. And this meant that our cost-of-goods per jar was inflated because the plant overhead was being spread out over fewer jars.

These first jars of Earth's Best didn't roll off the production line until November 25, 1987. We produced one hundred cases of apple-sauce, probably 10 percent of what we expected to produce on that first day. We were almost two months later than we had anticipated.

The good news, however, was that, although the line limped along, it did work. The jars were capped and coded. Big Bob ran the Rotomats flawlessly. Belinda sweet-talked that dinosaur of a labeler to apply those labels. And Dick, Scott, and Jim had pallets of baby food to move into the warehouse.

And there was no reason at the time to think that the line would continue to limp along. Bob was working with the ELF technicians. Changes on the machine were being made. It just seemed like a matter of fine-tuning. But it wasn't. The machine was essentially rebuilt with new parts in the first ninety days. In the meantime, filling the jars verged on drudgery. Barb just kept on doing whatever needed to be done. And so did every amazing woman on that line.

What we needed from the outset was a tried-and-true rotary piston filler. Bob knew this, but we didn't have the equipment budget. At one-fifth the cost, the electronic filler had a certain allure. It was a gee-whiz high-tech gizmo. Bob and I were both seduced by its mesmerizing potential. We bought it, knowing it had never been used to fill baby food.

We were the first. Sometimes you don't want to be first. Sometimes you should go with conventional wisdom. We should have found a way to start with a piston filler. It would have paid for itself in no time.

The ink coder would also soon prove to be another weak link in the line that would need to be replaced. It just wasn't reliable. And what was reliable cost an additional $16,000. Coding jars wasn't a luxury we could postpone. It was a necessity. Every time that original ink coder failed, either the line had to stop or the finished uncoded cases had to be reopened at a later date, each jar pulled out and run through the coder, and then each jar repacked and the case sealed. Re-work, as it's called, happens in all food-production lines, but in our beginning, it was the rule and not the exception. This was not okay.

And then there was Belinda's best friend, Mateer Burt. She coaxed all she could get out of that labeling machine, but there were days, too many days, when we had to pack jars into their finished cases, unlabeled.

And a lot of those days dragged on into overtime, major overtime. The filling was slow. The coding was hit-and-miss. The labeling was start and stop. This was the way it was. The production line worked, but it demanded ongoing heroics from all the production workers. Days that were supposed to end at 5:00 p.m. were sometimes stretching to 9:00 p.m. and later. This was bad. It was asking way too much of everyone. And overtime was not budgeted. And the number of cases produced was still far below what we had projected and what Bob thought was realistic to achieve.

We were not in a "perfect storm" scenario because we were making baby food, but it was perfect enough to make anyone who had a vested interest in Earth's Best feel seasick.

Needless to say, there was a lot of stress in that production room. Part of it was related to the ongoing equipment problems, but a growing undercurrent concerned both Bob and his son Dave, whom he hired as production manager. I want to fill this picture out, but need to explain a little bit more about the role I had fallen into.

In these earliest of days, I was worrying about everything but predictably was most obsessed about quality. Every baby that was going to consume a jar of Earth's Best was Gabe or Aaron. Every anxious and attentive father was me. Every exhausted, loving mom was Carley. The making of Earth's Best was very personal for me.

After the steam problem, I had my doubts if Arnie and I could count on Bob to deliver what we intended to sell as Earth's Best. Trust had been fractured. But Bob was the captain of the production-room ship, and I needed to let that be or risk an implosion with him (and his son) that we might not recover from. I held out hope that as the start-up wrinkles were ironed out, that fracture would heal. Until then I was compelled to watch from above, walking as lightly as I could, but ready to be God if I had to.

The Triumvirate

I first became the apple guy, recommending to QC which apple varieties should be blended in the course of the production. Inserting myself here did not trespass on Bob's turf or anyone else's toes. It brought me into the production room with a clear and focused role. I did the same for the peach blending and plum blending. In doing so, I started to come into relationship with the production flow, yields, and problems.

I watched the production struggle. I saw the looks from Pam and the eye rolls from Barb. They weren't subtle. I heard the complaints about Bob and Dave. "They don't listen." "Bob doesn't always wear his hairnet in the production room or take off his watch." "They're condescending." "They're sexist." "They don't know what they're doing."

I listened. I urged patience, but in truth I wanted to fix everything myself. And I couldn't. I couldn't because it would be irresponsible and counterproductive to undermine Bob. All I could do was pass on their feedback and try to help Bob adapt to and figure out a way to work with this collection of rural women and men from Vermont and across the lake in New York. And it was mostly the women that Bob polarized.

He really was a sweet guy, but he was from the "old school," and he had assumed a management style that just wasn't flying in that plant. The question that weighed heavily on me was, "Could Bob change to meet the situation?"

First thing each morning, I would check in with Dick, Scott, or Jim and make sure the apple varieties were lined up for the day. Once the production line got going, I always checked in with the apple inspectors who were standing there at the ready, gloved with their paring knives in hand. It was a very long day standing and staring at apples. Many times I would join them when there was more trimming than normal or just for the camaraderie. These women were the first step in the quality of Earth's Best, the q. Their work may have been described as menial or unskilled, but to me it was just the opposite. Their judgment and their grit to do a tedious job was the difference between success and failure. I always wanted them to know how important they were to me and to making Earth's Best the earth's best—every day.

I could do this fairly innocuously under the guise of checking out the apples. Besides, I was out of Bob's hair. I may have even been perceived as having nothing better to do. In fact, I was doing what was most important to me and what gave me the most joy. I was satisfying myself about the quality and infusing the production employees, as best as I could, with the understanding that I was accessible, that I genuinely cared about them and their working conditions, and that I would stand with them, side by side, doing whatever it took to succeed making Earth's Best.

And then I would casually check in with Pam, who quickly became the shepherdess of whatever was being made in the batching kettles. I saw that Pam was all about quality. She was all about hard work. And like Barb, she was quick to judge right from wrong, had little tolerance for double standards, attitude, and men or women who got in the way. But Pam was not just a hard edge. She was warm, sensitive, and good-natured. And she grokked Earth's Best from day one.

With all those fans and motors working that production room was a very noisy place for conversation, but if Pam had something to say, I always listened. She had the pulse of that room, the undercurrents, the impending disasters, and what was needed to set things straight or at least in the right direction. As such, Bob and Dave often took it on the chin. But everyone was fair game, including yours truly.

Typically, next stop on these early-morning jaunts was Barb and the filling line. Although Pam and Barb worked within fifty feet of each other, their worlds in that production room were quite separate; separated by noise, equipment, and disparate tasks. Again, I tried to make it a point to be only passing through, a neighborly, non-meddling visit from one of the founders. But you couldn't just pass through Barb's turf with a friendly hello. She would fill my ear with her take on the production-room politics, what her line needed, and the general state of affairs. Predictably, Bob and Dave again took it hard on the chin.

Like Pam, Barb also instantly understood what the spirit of Earth's Best was all about. She was a mom and a grandmother. She loved babies. I always knew she would put quality first. Nothing would slip by her on that filling line. It was a great comfort to a worrier like me.

Across the production floor, I could see Big Bob getting the retorts ready for the day's run. When Barb released me, I would make a beeline over to him to check in. "Big Bob, did you get a good night's sleep? You know you have the most important job in the building? Keep your eye on the ball? Right?" Big Bob was a friendly kid, probably in his late twenties. In his job as retort operator, there could be no automatic pilot or daydreaming. There could never be a moment of letting down his guard. His job required a constant state of beginner's mind: in a word, perfection. Big Bob never let me down. We established our own little ritual conversation each morning, plus a hand signal. I would raise my right hand to the third-eye position, fingers pointing straight, and move it back and forth. The meaning was understood and not so subtle: "Stay centered." He would signal back with a big smile, and I would move on to say hi to Belinda and the label line.

I might as well say up front that Belinda also grokked Earth's Best. She was the anchor at the end of our production line. Big Bob would wheel over the retort crates (filled with thousands of jars) after they were processed, and Belinda had to find a way to get those labels on. And it often wasn't easy. Many an afternoon, Leo and/or Brian, our two mechanics, stood there tinkering with that machine. These were two skilled, wonderful men who had mechanical abilities that I could only dream about. But that old, crotchety Mateer Burt would often confound them. When all was said and done, it was Belinda who became the labeler guru. I think she fell in love with that machine. I can't think of what else could have allowed her to transcend the challenges it presented.

Barb, Pam, and Belinda were a triumvirate of comfort for me on the production floor.

Although I haven't mentioned Bob or Dave, I of course was Ronnie-on-the-spot to also check in with them. I needed their sense of what was going on in the plant, to see how in tune they were with what was "really" going on. I wanted updates on their plans to fix the slew of problems causing our production output to be one-third of what we all thought it should be. It drove me crazy to see the line crawl along and the exhausting pace everyone had to sustain to compensate for the underperforming equipment. I always passed on the production-room concerns and issues I typically heard during my morning walk-through. And then I would leave the production room to let the chemistry unfold without me as a moderator or control rod, expecting Bob and Dave to respond and hoping that people such as Pam and Barb would see that things weren't as bad as they seemed.

I then entered the quiet space of our office, and Arnie would fill me in on Earth's Best's compounding financial woes. I would fill him in on the production woes. Our old two-dimensional life, when everything had been on paper and theoretical, was proving to be a lot easier than the three-dimensional reality we were facing now.

First Thoughts of the Sheriff

ARNIE:

Our conference room on Pond Lane had a viewing window that looked into the production room. It was a nice touch and a way to show visitors the plant without actually bringing them into the production room. The post-Philadelphia Expo board meeting was just after Thanksgiving, probably an early December afternoon. As I walked into the conference room, I saw all the board members glued to the window observing the production. It was great theater to see the jars on the conveyor bustling along toward the twist that turned them upside down for washing and then onward to the ELF filler. Everyone seemed to be in good spirits as we got seated to take care of business.

Ron and I circulated an update sheet on Earth's Best's status and waited in the silence as each member thumbed through the pages. Rick didn't waste any time. He was astounded by the cash-flow picture and the sizable incremental costs we were incurring to get the plant into production and now to truck the apples from California.

What followed was the equivalent of a busted football play where the quarterback, in this case quarterbacks, have the misfortune of being piled onto. Every board member expressed his alarm in his own unique style. I tried to present a plan of action to get us through and over the obstacles. They did their job of poking holes in the various assumptions and convincingly playing the devil's advocate. I wondered how Ron was holding up through the assault.

The overwhelming sentiment was that we didn't have the cash to execute a plan that included more hires (as in a mass-market sales manager), or supporting a more aggressive sales and marketing promotion for the natural-foods industry. Adding to the grim picture was the fact that we still had no cash flow and only about a $100,000 in actual orders.

After the venting subsided, we had a good meeting. I think it helped to see and hear the glass jars advancing. It was a visible sign of achievement and evidence that we could deliver something. If the jars had not been moving that day, they might have strung us up.

We had gotten into a dire predicament so quickly. No one expected it. This was a very positive group of people, but I'm sure it was hard to resist morbid thoughts, like a first-round knockout and money down the drain in an embarrassing fiasco.

Bridge financing was discussed, but there were no volunteers in the moment. The succinct message the board delivered to Ron and me was "stop spending and start selling product." What could I say? It was good advice we were already following.

The hard fact of life was that Earth's Best needed more money that instant. We had hemorrhaged. We now needed a transfusion. We had a plan to get into business with little room for error. No one hits every nail on the head. No one hits every green light. And no one expected us to. We just missed too many nails and got stopped at too many lights.

Was this because we were rookies or mutts as Ron likes to say? I can't dismiss the suggestion out of hand. But my answer is no. It was all of those bushwhacking moments compounding on top of each other. No one else had been where we were or where we needed to go. There were no directions or guidebook. Food-industry veterans would have probably seen more of the obstacles we were now facing, but then they would have also known better than to try. We were paying the price of being first. And despite the doom and gloom of our cash-flow position, we were miraculously well on our way.

The board had advised me to stop spending, but realistically, all I could do was stop paying. I had to travel west for more growers' meetings and discussions with retailers and potential West Coast distributors, and to hunt for a national mass-market sales manager.

I didn't know exactly how close we actually were to the fan that shit hits. I just knew we couldn't stop doing what needed to be done. Maybe when the sheriff came to take me away, I'd finally get the message, but not until.

What's That Twinkle?

As I looked for a place to park near Ken Winkler's Boulder, Colorado, office, I wondered if he would be the guy to help Earth's Best enter the grocery-market reality. Since these were pre-Internet days, it was the grapevine that told me Ken had a reputation as a high-performing, smooth sales guy. He had worked for General Mills and then as a regional sales manager with Mo Siegel of Celestial Seasonings' fame. In theory, Ken had the pedigree to impress potential investors and to help us break the ice in the mass market, so we could finally sit next to Gerber.

I walked into his office and immediately sensed Earth's Best could not afford the guy. That morning, I was probably predisposed to feel that way. I had spent the night before agonizing over the payable files, trying to decide whom not to pay. It was becoming an impossible situation, and soon I would be disappointing many people.

Ken greeted me with a twinkle in his eye, a firm handshake, and a round of chitchat about this and that. I noticed he had a slight drawl and also sensed he would be holding his best cards closest to his vest. As we eased into our introductions, it felt as if I was talking to a good old boy in training. This of course was not a positive association, but nonetheless, I knew it would be a positive for Earth's Best. We were both cloaked in pinstripes. But we were of very different stripes. On such occasions, I usually felt like I was dressed up for Halloween. Ken, however, seemed so at ease, like he was in his pajamas. He was passionate about selling and gamesmanship, as if it were a sport. I was passionate about organic agriculture and a smarter, better world, as if it were a matter of life and death. Fortunately, I was not looking for a clone of myself. I was looking for a sales gunslinger, someone who knew the grocery game, delighted in playing it, and had the cojones to slug it out and win.

It didn't take long for the gears to shift and for our discussion to turn to business. Ken could talk and I could listen, though I must admit, I didn't fully grasp all that he was saying. When it came to sales gibberish, Ken was king of the castle, flinging around words like scan data, SAMI numbers, cents off, and slots, and making up hybrid words, as it turned out, like only Ken could.

Ken made it clear that his expertise was not limited to the mass channel and that he could help us with our natural-foods rollout too. He was not shy about throwing around the names of his high-level contacts at the distributor and retail levels or reticent to hold back on his opinions. It was obvious Ken wanted in on the Earth's Best opportunity. He recognized the potential and had an interest in signing on with a company that could be the next trophy in his case.

As our meeting wound down and we both became talked out and punchy, Ken committed to sending me a consulting proposal within a two-week time frame. It was a good first meeting. I left feeling hopeful that Ken had the skill sets to dramatically move our grocery and natural-food sales program forward.

And he certainly did. We hired him soon after. What I did not know, at the time, was that those cards Ken kept closest to his vest would one day be thrown in my face and dramatically impact the future of Earth's Best and the fate of Ron's and my future with the company.

Woops!

My West Coast trip was a successful whirlwind. The grower meetings and follow-up sit-down with J.R. Wood were all encouraging. I was intent, as in hell-bent, on moving Earth's Best forward, yet offered financial flirtation and suggestion wherever I could avoid commitment. I was as fiscally conservative as a mobilized entrepreneur could be, but knew nonetheless that I was driving the company toward a brick wall. It was a game of chicken. Who would flinch first, the company or the brick wall? I guess I thought it would be the brick wall.

The next day I met with Ron to debrief him on my exploits and to get an earful about our production woes and some of the nonsense with Bob Fielder. I could only take in so much of his world and he of mine. We each had to apply a certain amount of anesthetic to our receptivity neurons to avoid being overwhelmed by discouragement or panic. Humor often worked.

I remember lightening things up with a "woops" moment that occurred when I was on a farm visit with our agronomist consultant,

Joe Smillie. Joe had asked me to keep this story quiet, but in that recap meeting with Ron and on select other occasions, often in Joe's presence, I gleefully reenacted the Van Dyke farm incident.

I depended on Joe to sniff out possible infractions of organic-certification standards while conducting farm visits. Joe was already a crafty veteran of the organic-farm scene and knew what to look for. We worked well together and traveled many miles in rental cars, talking story about the future of organic agriculture, certification issues, and industry politics.

Joe and I had arrived at the Van Dyke farm hoping to find a crop of California apricots that we could buy for next year. As soon as I met Betty and her teenage boys, I took a liking to them. They seemed genuine and matter-of-fact. We all walked through their beautiful orchard together, talking about the market, the tonnage we were looking for, and pricing. Joe casually wandered off to do some inspecting. He was like a bloodhound hunting for someone's mischief and misdeeds.

"Arnie," I heard Joe bellow, "Can you come over here?" I excused myself from my discussion with the Van Dykes and walked over to where Joe was poking around. In a quiet voice, Joe said, "I think we have a problem." He had in his hand a pile of some kind of white substance. He kept smelling it and tasting it. "I think this is a synthetic fertilizer. I don't know what else it could be." I had no patience when it came to these matters regarding the legitimacy of an organic claim, so I said "Joe, let's go find out."

We walked over to the Van Dykes, who did not have beads of sweat pouring from their brows. Joe fingered the white stuff in the palm of his hand, took another sniff, ate another pinch, and asked Betty if she knew what it was he had in his hand. The Van Dykes looked at each other and grimaced. Betty got right to it. "Joe, that's owl shit you're chewing on." Joe looked pained and paused his chewing. "Are you sure?" he said. She replied, "No doubt about it, Joe. We see lots of owls in the orchard and that's their business."

Woops. We all had a good laugh. Actually, I don't remember Joe laughing. He was embarrassed, but I was grateful he was so dedicated.

Ron loved these stories. He probably thought I was the lucky one, having all of these adventures.

Where the Hell Was the Sheriff?

I remember the very first eighteen-wheeler being loaded up with finished product. Talk about a labor of love. I took the greatest pride and pleasure watching that truck lumber out of the Earth's Best parking lot. It was a miracle that each jar had a paper trail certifying its organic authenticity. I also stood there hoping the driver would make haste, so I could finally hang a dollar bill on my office wall.

Now that the plant was running, I established a daily routine. When I was fortunate enough to be in Middlebury and not on an airplane going somewhere, I would enter the Pond Lane building, drop my briefcase in my office, put on a hairnet, and walk directly into the production room.

I envied Ron for being the one immersed in the day-to-day production reality. I loved being around the production. It was a sensory extravaganza. The food smells were different each day and comforting. The sound of the glass jars being conveyed to the filler was accompanied by intermittent bursts of hissing air and steam. It was loud, but to me, it was the sweet sound of success helping to quiet the surrounding worries everywhere else.

As I moved from station to station, I kidded with the employees and thanked them for their diligence. Sometimes, when I could not bear to be in my office studying the payables file, writing reports, or taking calls from irate creditors, I would join the apple-sorting line, put my head down, and escape. It was satisfying to actually touch the produce I had so intensely fought for. No one could possibly appreciate the complexity and effort it took to have certified California apples sitting in the Earth's Best plant in Middlebury, Vermont. The fifteen or so minutes I spent each morning in the production room was my fix. It energized and inspired me to be my very best.

My office was an organized mess. I had piles of papers on every surface and one impressive stack that I kept in the middle of my desk that was my current sedimentation pile. It was a layering of paper by date. I could find anything I needed despite the chaotic appearance. My worst nightmare would have been an open window and a gust of wind.

There were many days in late December 1987 when I would close my office door and just ponder. I traveled down numerous imagined roads and entertained scenarios and shortcuts that might deliver a sales breakthrough I could leverage or a cost savings that would free up some cash, so I could pay some bills and assuage my guilt.

Sometimes I just daydreamed. It was my escape valve when I couldn't make it to the apple-sorting table. I felt lonely and cloistered away in my office. The brick wall hadn't budged. No one was coming to the rescue. Where the hell was the sheriff?

Going Bananas

RON:

During my product-development days with Dr. Bartel way back in 1985, I knew after a few trials that Apple Banana would be a great Earth's Best flavor. I didn't want to do straight banana puree, like the other baby-food companies, because bananas needed to be acidified with citric acid to keep the thermal-processing temperature down and to avoid discoloration problems, such as browning or pinking. I always found that acidified banana puree burned the back of my throat a little, and my solution was using apples as the acidulant, rather than the citric acid. I wouldn't go so far as to say that it was a stroke of genius, but it was a practical solution, given that there was no organic citric acid at the time, and I didn't care for banana puree as a single baby food.

Flash forward three years. Apple Banana was penciled in on the production schedule. There was a source of organic peeled frozen whole bananas from MexAm, a Mexican company. They were in fact delicious, a little pricey (but not off the charts), and available year-round. You could say it was a no-brainer to buy them, because the alternative was crazy. That would be buying 4,000 pounds of bananas in 40-pound boxes, ripening them in the warehouse, and hand-peeling them one by one.

I wanted Earth's Best to be just like homemade. I held that ideal so tightly that at times inflexibility restricted the circulation to my brain. Objectively, there was no compromise in buying frozen whole bananas. Yet, I took a principled stand and decided we would ripen and peel them ourselves at the plant. My zealotry unfortunately completely inhibited the availability of my imagination to do the job it was supposed to do. Anticipate. Have you ever hand-peeled two tons of bananas?

The bananas showed up green and were stacked in the warehouse. I have no doubt that Dick, who managed all of the inventories and shipping logistics for us, thought we must have lost our marbles. In truth, we had gone bananas. Every morning I opened up a few boxes to give them their daily checkup. The ones closest to the boiler room were ripening more quickly than the ones closest to the warehouse door. That's because it was winter, the outside air was freezing, and the bananas closest to the door wanted to take their sweet time. So we had to do the banana-box shuffle. They all had to be ready at the same time.

The day came and the grim reality struck. We had an awful lot of bananas to peel. At first it was kind of fun, kind of like sitting around the camp fire, shooting the breeze, making breakfast. But it went on and on and on. There was no fire. It was messy. The warehouse was cold and damp, and the misery descended. There was always another banana to peel, which in my case, served me right. I peeled like crazy, hour after hour, as if I could make up for my misjudgment. But of course I could not. Sorry. Lesson learned.

Dick, the voice of reason, was right this time. But just for the record, sometimes, as an entrepreneur, you do have to be crazy or look like you're crazy, which means you're going to make mistakes. The general idea is to avoid the disastrous ones.

Next time the production schedule called for Apple Banana, we used MexAm's organic frozen peeled bananas. All of the production women wistfully reminisced about Ron's banana folly, three weeks prior. To me it was Houdini-esque to have escaped from this error so easily without a cataclysmic downside.

The Dark Clouds, Stormy Skies

The days and weeks passed into the heart of January 1988, and the production line continued to operate in fits and starts. The wrinkles were not getting ironed out as I had hoped. Our finished-case production per day was averaging about 1,200 (for apple products), compared to the conservative 3,600 cases per day we were expecting. The sixteen truckloads of apples Arnie heroically found were now showing up in Vermont en masse, because we were supposed to be burning through them. And obviously we were not. Apple bins started to accumulate in every nook and cranny of our small warehouse. We needed to rent storage space, which of course was unbudgeted. My garage at home was packed to the gills, stacked three-up in cardboard apple bins.

To get the line up to speed, we needed to keep investing in equipment with money we didn't have. With the ELF filler, it was like throwing good money after bad. But how do you know when to stop, especially when it seems like you have no choice? To get the meager production we were getting, the production crew had to constantly work overtime. And because of all of the inefficiencies, we needed thirty to thirty-five production employees, which substantially exceeded our initial projections of twenty to twenty-five. We were a train running off the tracks. With that picture in mind, you know the prognosis could not be good.

Bob and Dave persisted in being Martians and the production women in being Venusians. Every time I walked out onto the floor, I was assaulted by a growing frustration and tension that clearly was not resolving itself. But it was not just Pam, Barb, and Belinda who were at odds with Bob and his son, it was also Nancy and Sue from QC. The atmosphere began to feel explosive. The poison daggers were flying around the room. Personally, the disharmony was unbearable. I had no choice but to insert myself more directly in the dynamic.

Bob had an endearing expression when he was angry and upset. He would say to me, "Ron, that irks my gizzard." Although a Martian, Bob was not a man of expletives. He did not like these uppity women questioning his judgment or directives. And they did simply because he hadn't won their confidence or respect. The psychology of the situation was transparent.

They had seen apples blasted all over the walls and themselves. They had waited and watched for weeks while the steam problem tormented us. They had seen the equipment failing to perform and in turn compromising their own performance. They witnessed questionable QC judgments that had to be overruled by Nancy. And they saw or perceived that Bob held a double standard, one for him and Dave and another for everyone else. But these were observations Bob was not particularly receptive to.

I remember a January 1988 day of carrot production. I was in my office, at peace knowing that we were making the best carrot puree in the world thanks to Rick Ihler and his farm in Idaho. Nancy came to the door red-cheeked and upset. Bob had refused to put on a hairnet. "Ron, you'd better get out to the production room." Immediately the moment became surreal. This was the plant manager she was talking about. Wearing a hairnet was as basic an ABC as you could get in food production. There was always a box of hairnets outside the production-room door. Reaching for one was reflexive. Why would Bob do such a thing?

The hairnet issue and the removal of all jewelry, such as watches, had swirled about previously in some underbelly production-room mutterings. I actually talked to Bob about it once to see if he had a problem with the policy. I'm sure my question irked his gizzard.

What remains of that day lacks in detail. What sticks are words like sad, shocking, discombobulating, and disaster. Hairnets weren't negotiable. It didn't matter if you were the plant manager or God. It didn't matter if you were a million miles away from any food contact. Belinda and the entire case-packing line wore hairnets, although there was no chance of a hair getting inside a sealed jar. Dick, Scott, and Jim wore hairnets even though they were just riding a forklift in the production room.

There was no hardship in wearing a hairnet. They equally disqualified everyone from looking glamorous. I thought I looked particularly goofy in one with my big poofy hair. I know Arnie did. Every day I just swallowed my pride. I got used to it, part of the uniform. For Bob, it wasn't an ego thing like it might have been for me. I assume, for him, it became a power thing.

There is a certain inherent tension between production and quality-control functions in food plants. Production employees and QC employees work shoulder to shoulder, but they have different job descriptions. Sometimes they are antagonistic. And sometimes they're not antagonistic enough. Perhaps Bob had come from a world where QC looked the other way when the situation called for it; a world where the balance of power was tilted more toward production and not QC. There are tremendous pressures to produce. You better do it, and a lot of it, every day or you're kaput. And so, in manufacturing, there is often a dance between perfection and imperfection. The balance between the two is determined by the culture and ethos that lives among the people, especially the management, in any given production room.

With Earth's Best, the pressures to produce were enormous. We started two months late. We had to carry payroll. Then we struggled mightily almost every day. My instructions, as a cofounder of Earth's Best, to Nancy, Sue, Marty, and Lynne, the women charged with quality control, were unequivocal. "Your job is to protect the quality of Earth's Best. Do not allow, under any circumstances, Bob and Dave or Ron and Arnie to compromise your job performance on behalf of the quality of Earth's Best. When in doubt, throw it out. When in doubt, hold everything, stop everything. My problems are not yours, nor are Bob's or Arnie's."

It was critical to me that QC knew they were empowered to be the ultimate decision makers, especially when push came to shove, in those excruciating moments, when a day's production was on the line, for whatever quality-related reason. Nancy, Sue, Marty, and Lynne were too smart and principled to have it any other way. They shared a great responsibility. And they were put to the test more times than I would have liked.

Because this was my message to them over and over, Bob's liberty taking with the rules was intolerable. There were no nods and winks or looks the other way to accommodate his transgressions or anyone else's. The QC team was empowered to question his judgments, if necessary; to challenge his authority, if necessary; or even in a worst case, to assume authority.

It should have been just a dance, everyone learning the steps together. An all-for-one-and-one-for-all type of experience. Sadly, Bob made it a battle.

There was no recovering from this moment. I could not support Bob. I could not fix the situation. We were not on the same page. His authority in the production room, while never fully established, was now completely eroded.

At the March 7, 1988, Earth's Best board meeting, there was a motion to terminate Bob's employment. Although Bob's stock had not vested, I advocated that he be offered a portion of it, as a gesture of goodwill and appreciation for what he did contribute. The board suggested that Arnie talk to the company's attorney to draw up the appropriate documents, including a general release-and-cooperation agreement.

Bob refused the offer. He wanted it all. He sued. He ended up with nothing. Back to that story in a moment.

Pink Slips

Another decision was made at that board meeting that was even more momentous than the one to terminate Bob. The board also voted, upon Arnie's recommendation, to suspend production on March 10, 1988. Six production employees were kept on the payroll. Twenty-one people were laid off.

That didn't take long, did it?

There actually was a serious discussion to shut down the plant at the February board meeting. That's how bad our financial plight was. The manufacturing start-up had sucked too much oxygen out of the room, and the natural-foods industry rollout was more of a single than a home run. The retail price-point issue made the going a lot tougher and the turns much slower than we needed to stem the extraordinary cash-flow hemorrhaging that had been going on. We needed a miracle, and we didn't get it.

These were watershed events in the life of the company, but I don't want to leave the impression that all we did was fall on our faces. Earth's Best's sales in the first sixty days of our rollout scored in the top 5 percent of natural-foods companies. National distribution within the natural-foods industry was achieved in ninety days, but only 1,000 stores were carrying the introductory line—compared with the 2,640 projected in our sales assumptions. Where we goofed was in assuming that the distributors would take an active roll in enrolling the retailers. It seemed logical that they would, but then a lot of things weren't making sense at the time. Initial inventories that were shipped remained in warehouses. Promotional discounts were pocketed and freight charges padded, raising the unit price to retailers and, of course, the consumer.

Reality was a lot more rough-and-tumble than we had expected, especially in our theoretical backyard. Arnie and I assumed so many times that we would be the exception to the rule, that we would, by divine decree, receive a universal Advance Directly to Go card. Organic baby food was so compelling and necessary that the natural-foods playing field would level itself for us. As it turned out, we were not the force of nature we thought we were or should have been. I'm not sure why this lesson was so hard for us to learn.

And there were other related surprises and setbacks.

Arnie and I had planned to advertise in *Mothering* magazine. Certainly *Mothering* readers would be interested in an organic baby-food alternative. Shockingly, the powers there at the time rejected us as an advertiser. Their judgment was that mothers should be making baby food and not buying it. Accordingly, Earth's Best threatened to undermine *Mothering*'s commitment to mothering. Maybe they threw infant formula and baby food into the same ring. They were not. Maybe the idea of commercial baby food was too corporate and cheap sounding to them, as in "guilty by association." Needless to say, Arnie and I didn't see this rejection coming. If we weren't supported by the people we thought would be allied with us, how could we possibly succeed?

As a footnote into the future, years later, when Earth's Best was established and highly valued as an alternative for parents who could not make their own baby food or find a reliable supply of fresh organic ingredients, Arnie and I received a heartfelt apology from *Mothering* for their allergic reaction to us when we were starting. Times had changed.

Entrepreneuring is adventuring. It's the Wild West and the Mysterious East swirled unpredictably into infinite texture and tone. It's living on an edge where staying on or falling off will surely be a story one way or the other. Often, entrepreneurial impulses are ahead of their time or out of step with them. Too far ahead, and an idea may seem bad and prove very difficult (if not impossible) to incarnate. Not far ahead enough, and competition will be breathing down your neck much sooner than you want. That's assuming you can get into business at all and with an idea that has legs.

I remember well the anticipation of announcing the layoff to the employees—definitely a falling-off-the-edge moment. It was terrible. I had already fallen in love with these people. It was unbearable to reward their heroic efforts with pink slips. I felt like I was betraying them, but I was powerless to do otherwise. Arnie would do the talking. My nervous system could not handle it.

ARNIE:

Wait up, Ron. I'm not ready for the layoff!

The first bridge of $225,000 from the initial group of investors was so welcomed and appreciated when it finally showed up sometime in early January 1988. The brick wall flinched, but the movement was almost imperceptible. I could see more clearly than ever that if Ron and I had started a lemonade stand, we would have been set, but not a national baby-food company. Before that cash made it into our account, we needed more. Everyone on the board knew it. This second investment was much riskier than the first. And we would need more, fast, or it would all be for naught.

The Apple Debacle

As the weeks passed and our production numbers failed to meet projections, a new huge problem surfaced. We were not using our stored apples fast enough. Some of the apples that were coming into the plant from our rented cold-storage warehouse were beginning to look a little peaked.

I told Ron we had to drive down to the warehouse and evaluate the extent of the problem. Dick, with his affectionate, all-knowing, you-guys-are-nuts grin, had told us there were a lot of apples down there, but he could not determine the extent of the problem. Was it a few isolated bins, or were we up the creek?

I was happy to be in the car with Ron for the forty-five-minute ride south to Rutland. We seldom had uninterrupted time to catch up with the issues circulating within our respective work universes. Fortunately, this was well before cell phones. We could actually talk without being disturbed.

The Rutland warehouse was more like an old barn turned into a large refrigerator. It felt prehistoric, probably chilled with chunks of ice cut from some Vermont pond. As we entered through the dim entryway and tugged on the metal sliding doors, our eyes adjusted to an impressively deflating site. From one end of the warehouse to the other, stacked two high, were large corrugated totes of apples. Ron and I just stared, dumbstruck by this apple nightmare.

We gamely started counting bins and pulling the lids off as many totes as we could to determine the extent of the problem. I wish I could have taken a picture of Ron and me hopping from tote to tote, peering into the bins, praying the sight would be pretty. It was not.

Somehow I had to find a buyer for about 250,000 pounds of apples and fast. We would keep the hardiest apples for our production, but Ron was going to have to use them up pronto. There was no compromise to the baby food. It was just dishearteningly obvious there was going to be a lot of waste. The result was our cost of goods was growing out of sight, and our margins were well on their way to zero or below.

The ride back to Pond Lane was very quiet. Neither Ron nor I had the energy to think or speak. It was just amazing how many things were going wrong. I would have to report this bad news to the board. Then a week later I would report the good news. I found a buyer for the apples—who would only pay five cents a pound or about a third of what we already had into them. It was a debacle.

An Angel Descends

Interestingly, rather than descending into depression, I reacted defiantly like Lieutenant Dan in the *Forrest Gump* movie who screamed out to God, "Is that all you got?" while perched at the top of the Bubba Gump ship mast in the middle of Hurricane Camille.

The ongoing stressor for me was disappointing so many people, especially those I admired and who were so supportive and loyal to

Earth's Best. I was in a situation where circumstances provided me little opportunity to please. I was pissing people off by failing to pay them.

I remember selecting from the payables file the lucky few who would get paid or at least receive a partial payment. I noticed that Paul Buxman, the peach grower I had visited in Dinuba, was not on the list. I thought that was strange and worrisome. Paul should have billed us by now. I knew he was in a very vulnerable position, and I wanted to pay him before our well ran completely dry. To put my decision to pay Paul in perspective, I had already stopped paying our $6,000 rent and was past due on our electric bill, which was in excess of $6,000.

I dialed Paul's number, and to my surprise he picked up. "Paul, this is Arnie from Earth's Best. I haven't received your invoice." "Oh yeah, hi, Arnie, how's it going? I have been thinking about you," he said. Without spilling my guts and sharing the gory details of our travails, I answered, "We're hanging in there, Paul. The production is going and we're shipping some product." "That's great, Arnie, I know you guys are going to make it."

"Paul," I said, "I haven't received your invoice for the peaches. I am guessing I owe you about $18,000." Paul hesitated and said, "That's probably close, Arnie, I don't have the paperwork in front of me." "Could you send the invoice, Paul? I want to pay you." "No, I am afraid not, Arnie," he responded. Paul's response was obviously unexpected. I blurted out, "Why not, Paul? I want to pay you while I still can." And then he said it.

"Arnie, those peaches are a gift from me to Earth's Best. If Earth's Best succeeds, the world is going to be a better place, and organic farming is going take a giant leap forward. That needs to happen, Arnie." For a moment, I was stunned and speechless. "Paul," I said, "That is incredibly generous, but I know you need the money." Paul responded, "You're right, Arnie, I do, but not as much as the world needs Earth's Best."

I was in awe of and inspired by this amazing man.

"PRESSURE"

By February 1988, I had little choice but to delegate most everything related to sales and the supply side and just focus my efforts on raising additional capital. Several more bridges would follow, but they were, in effect, band-aids. It kept us limping along, but we never got far enough ahead of the crushing weight of the start-up cash-flow demands. I always felt imperiled. The only news was that the investor pool was expanding. Now there was old money and new money. And the old subordinated to the new.

An unexpected entry into the pool was Ken Winkler's (our new Boulder, Colorado, sales VP) father, Ed, and another guy named Stan Klack, whom Ken thought the world of. It was impossible to really be discerning. Everything was happening fast and needed to happen fast. I wanted faster. My inner experience was so compressed and my focus so task oriented that I had no bird's-eye view to get perspective or access to hindsight. I trusted strangers.

Stan was a well-connected big shot, a former CEO of the Mix Corporation and, apparently, a thoroughbred whose interest in EB went beyond writing a check. He wanted in as a board member and was prepared to take an active role in helping the company raise more money. This was great news for a while. My job was to find a transfusion for Earth's Best, and it appeared I was going to do so.

Ken jumped in to work with Bob Donnola on righting our sales and marketing programs. I didn't have time to babysit them, but was aware that Bob D. felt imposed upon by Ken's autocratic, arrogant, and condescending style. To hell with the personality pettiness was my sentiment at the time. We had to fix the price-point issue. Nothing else mattered. If it did, we were dust.

Our target was the Anaheim Natural Foods Expo in April, where we would launch the "My Baby's Worth It" sweepstakes," a strategic program aimed at seizing control of the upward-spiraling price points at which retailers were selling Earth's Best. It could have been argued that it was hardly the time to pioneer a new sales strategy, but we had already learned from the Philadelphia Expo that business as usual was going to sink us. We weren't brave. We were desperate.

The heart of the "My Baby's Worth It" plan was a "case-stack" program that required each store to purchase a fourteen- or twenty-eight-case display and agree to retail our products for a per-jar price between $0.79 and $0.89. At the time, it was unheard of, if not sacrilegious, to dictate to retailers the margin they could take.

To reel the retailers in, we had to make it juicy, and we did. In exchange for their cooperation, Earth's Best would supply case-stack posters and window signs announcing the sweepstakes, which offered a featured prize of a free college scholarship. We sent a professional mailing to childbirth educators, day-care centers, and health-care practitioners. We only had one chance, and so we piled on the goodies. A four-color postcard was mailed to parents with babies six months and older, offering one free jar with the purchase of one jar. Lastly, we did the unthinkable: we guaranteed the sale. If the retailer was not satisfied with the movement of EB after ninety days, we would pick the product up and refund them.

We couldn't afford to do all of this and we couldn't afford not to. A gamble offered the future a chance. Otherwise, it was a foregone conclusion that we were that fiasco everyone secretly dreaded. I was learning over and over the "PRESSURE" lesson that the sprout business and Village Renaissance did not teach me.

On the supply side, Joe was busy with follow-up farm visits and pursuing new leads. We had a year-two plan that included the sourcing of greater volumes and new ingredients like peas and green beans. As much as I wanted to ease my insecurities, I was not in a position to sign contracts. That would have been reckless. At the same time, there was no way I was going to avoid contact with the growers or fail to project what was positive and the possibility of moving forward.

Simultaneously, I was in a tense process with our board trying to complete another bridge to maintain our operation. I told them of the impending disasters playing out on the horizon. I slowly learned that these were my problems. Their problem was figuring out if they were throwing away good money after bad.

My Bags Were Packed

The payables situation was really bad that February of 1988.

There was one thing that I did each week, while closeted away in my office, that probably allowed Earth's Best to live on through this prolonged financial drought. No matter how distasteful, no matter how tempted I was to procrastinate, no matter how many other critically important priorities there were squeezing me tight, each week I called every EB creditor to update them on the company's progress. This good-faith effort on my part worked wonders and diffused much of the tension inherent in a very difficult situation. I made it clear that my intentions were the best. When I made a commitment, I honored it.

The door to my office was closed most of the time now. Beth, our office manager and bookkeeper, sat on the other side of the wall closest to me. She knew I needed privacy and space to make all of these calls. She protected me from interruptions. So I was surprised when Beth knocked one day to tell me I had a visitor. Unless it was someone from the Vermont Lottery with a big fat check, I wasn't interested. I had no appointments on my calendar and was about to dial a creditor to explain why I was only sending him $200, when I was past due on $10,000. On second thought, maybe it was a good time for an interruption.

Beth stood in the doorway with a strange expression on her face that I had not seen before and could not read. "What is it, Beth?" I asked with as much patience as I could muster. She stepped into my office and closed the door. "I am sorry, Arnie, but you have to see this person. I can't tell him to go away." "Okay," I said, curious about who it was I had to see so urgently. Beth gulped and said, "Arnie, it's the sheriff."

Finally, the sheriff had come to take me away and put me out of my misery. My bags were packed.

"Are you Arnold Koss?" he said in an officious tone. "Yes, I am," I answered. "Mr. Koss, I have here in my hand a legal document that formally serves you with a summons brought against you by several creditors. Please sign here acknowledging that you have received the document."

I signed, but much to my disappointment he left without me.

Over the next several months the sheriff and I became buddies. "I am sorry, Arnie," he would always say, as if it were his fault. I thanked him for being so nice and told him not to worry about it. Being served papers became an almost casual event in my life. It's amazing what a person can get used to.

Strangely, I saw something positive about the quagmire I was situated in. There was an incredible swell of support for Earth's Best. It was heartening. The sheriff was just doing his job, but he knew something important was happening at Pond Lane. He wasn't serving a bum or deadbeat, and he took an interest in our progress. The creditors I spoke to week after week were sympathetic. Obviously, not everyone warmed up to my earnest company reports or I wouldn't have come to know the kindly sheriff, but many did begin to relate to Earth's Best as more than another aged payable. A certain unexpected camaraderie formed, and it buoyed my determination to make good on every account.

Some of the local creditors would pay me a visit each week to collect. Our landlord, Paul Carrera, who was a saint of a guy, would send his first lieutenant each month to remind me in a friendly way that it was time for my John Hancock. I wish I had those conversations on tape, because despite the difficult subject matter, the discussions were rarely about money, but rather about life and values. I looked forward to these visits.

I Felt Loved

Amidst the thorns there were roses.

The decision to temporarily suspend production was made at our March 1988 board meeting. I supported the decision because we were at the point where I could not make payroll and also meet our payroll tax obligations. It doesn't get more basic than that. Long ago, I had been cautioned that the failure to pay payroll taxes was the beginning of the road to prison. I didn't want to become one of those guys who could say, "been there, done that."

Nonetheless, I beat myself up trying to find a way to avoid closing the plant and laying off our production staff. It was so hard to accept because the result was so contrary to my expectations. It felt like a death. It was failure, and I wanted to find a way not to face it. Ron was in shock.

I sat in my office, preparing myself to break the bad news to the employees gathering in the break room. Minutes before, I had finished up a call with Stan Klack, who was rattling off ideas on how to get the company bridge financing on track. It's intriguing how hopelessness and hope can in one moment be in such close proximity.

Ron and I walked into the break room. As usual there was a lot of good-natured banter going on. I tried to keep it light, as I made my way to the front of the room and positioned myself in the middle of the assembly. There was nothing light about it. I was about to pull the plug on the livelihood of more than twenty people.

Playing the role of president stunk. It also reminded me that Ron was smarter than me because he was not the president. I knew this was part of the deal. He wasn't copping out on me or trying to evade the difficult stuff. There was so much difficulty that he did meet, but there were places where he had to step back. I could see it was survival for him, but that didn't make it any easier for me.

I did not mince words with a rambling preamble. My eyes moved throughout the room greeting each person as I began to speak. "You all know that Ron and I are trying to find more investment. I had hoped by now we would be in a position to close an equity-financing deal, and while things look very promising, we are going to have to temporarily suspend production until we complete the financing. You have all been amazing and so dedicated. We hope you will come back. I am very sorry."

These people were not employees, they were family. I wanted to protect them as if they were my children. "When, Arnie?" Pam asked. "Immediately, Pam, everyone will receive one week of severance. It's less than we want to offer, but our hands are tied. There is no money," I responded. Everyone was quiet, staring at Ron and me as if trying to take our pulse from a distance. More questions followed that were of a practical nature. Did we have a tentative restart date? Were we still planning to go to the expo in California?

As these questions rolled in, I began to see something incredible living within the group dynamic. It should not have surprised me, but how could it not? I had just laid them all off and no one was expressing anger. No one was focused on their own needs. All of the attention went to making sure Ron and I were okay and what they could do to help Earth's Best. Through their eyes, Ron and I were the children and they the parents. I felt loved.

After the meeting I spoke privately with Pam, Barb, Belinda, Leo, Brian, and Dick. The board agreed to keep them on the payroll, so we would have a nucleus in place to start up again. There was plenty of re-work to be done like coding jars and putting on labels. There was lots of maintenance to catch up with. We were shipping baby food, and the warehouse would be busy. Retaining these key people gave me hope that maybe we weren't dead, maybe we hadn't failed.

In the days that followed, I would come to miss the reassuring sounds and smells of the plant in action. I would miss the daily contact with the apple-sorting line and the sense of accomplishment when seeing a case of Earth's Best make its way through the case packer. For inspiration, I would walk through the now empty plant and stare at each piece of equipment, the puzzle of stainless piping, and the retort baskets still full of unlabeled jars. Somehow I would find a way; all of this could not die.

The Damned Ducks Didn't Line Up

RON:

We all fought the good fight until the writing on the wall had its way with us at that March 1988 board meeting and subsequent layoff. The fact is, Arnie and I and everyone else riding the Earth's Best roller coaster had no idea what they had gotten into. In terms of equity needed, actual cash-in, getting over the hump was still a stomach-churning eternity away. Even farther. What people imagined were the funds needed to get over the proverbial hump and into a cash-flow-positive business were just toll charges along the way to that hump.

No one had a clue what it would take, although they thought they did. Earth's Best fooled everyone, from the earnest entrepreneurs, Harvard MBAs, and the seasoned CFOs, to the venture capitalists, the risk-averse banks, and the hotshot corporate types that would eventually make their way into this story, flaunting their pedigrees.

This is why there would be so much stock dilution to follow. Each new wave of investors thought they were going to the head of the class. And they did, but the visit was much shorter than they ever dreamed of. Earth's Best devoured their equity, thank you very much, and the next wave would show up all greedy and frothy, ready to make a killing and steal it from the last group of unfortunates. For Arnie and me it became a free fall down the food chain.

We knew from the outset that it would take every duck lining up at attention to make a go of it with only $500K in equity. But the damned ducks didn't line up. They wouldn't even get into the same room with each other. Even though we had to impose this layoff, we still had the good fortune to be planning for the future. July was not so far away.

Who Is Serving Whom?

While Arnold and Ronald Koss, the president and vice president of Earth's Best, were struggling to keep their company alive in early 1988, Beech-Nut's president and vice president were being sentenced in a Brooklyn, New York, district court for selling millions of bottles of "apple juice" that they knew contained little or no apple juice at all. This subterfuge had started in 1978 and persisted until the summer of 1982 when the sky began crashing down on these men. Even when the jig was up and a seizure of Beech-Nut's ersatz-apple-juice inventory seemed imminent, these executives colluded to liquidate as much of the inventory as possible by selling it into the Puerto Rican and Dominican Republic marketplaces.*

The point here is not to beat a dead horse. Earth's Best was on the ropes as a start-up in 1988, and Beech-Nut Baby Foods, started in 1931, was on the ropes as well, prior to the sentencing of their top executives. It was both sobering and energizing to learn about the fall from grace of these two men. Arnie and I believed we were needed more than ever and that together we could survive the perils of mortal compromise and truly deliver Earth's Best Baby Foods.

We had already survived a few difficult tests. The start-up direct-steam problem had been a nightmare. In standing our ground there and delaying production and sales, we had put our company at mortal risk. But then again, what kind of company would it have been if we had done otherwise? Earth's Best would have just been a figment of our imagination. Our proud label tag, "For the most important little customers in the world," would have been snuffed out by smoke-and-mirror disease. Who could live with that? Certainly not Arnie or me.

Our loyalty was to babies. We were fresh. The Earth's Best vision was ours. I'm sure that the founders of Beech-Nut, way back in 1931, never would have abandoned the sacred trust implicit in getting into

---

* Buder, Leonard, "2 Former Executives of Beech-Nut Guilty in Phony Juice Case," *New York Times* (February 18, 1988), Section A, page 1; Traub, James, "Into the Mouths of Babes," *New York Times* (July 24, 1988), Section 6, page 18

the baby-food business. But that impulse was sadly long gone at Beech-Nut. Serving the welfare of babies had succumbed to babies serving the welfare of the corporation.

The gravity of business wears on founding values and inspirational aspirations. The line between serving and being of service and being served and self-serving is constantly in danger of becoming blurred and then lost. We see this flip-flop in public school education today where children are often needed by teachers to be good test takers to prove that they are good teachers. Jobs are on the line. School funding is on the line. Who is serving whom?

Everyone in business, education, and public service is subject to these gravitational forces. It's clearly a battle. Otherwise, there wouldn't be so much failure.

The Scariness Would Not Quit

After the trauma of the layoff and the separation from Bob Fielder, the halting of production was actually a reprieve from the stress of fighting all the equipment inefficiencies and malfunctions. I don't mean to suggest that there was an experience of leisure. It's just that we had a moment to pull our fingers out of the dike and assess the situation and how we might respond. My never-ending wish list for the production room was born. I actually have a copy of it somewhere (totaling a conveniently round $100,000). And every wish of mine had a corresponding price tag and a subsequent impact on Arnie's world of higher and higher finance.

The planning for a production restart began immediately, because we had to start anticipating what ingredients we were going to need and at what cost. It was so much all about guessing that it was ridiculous. How could we possibly get it right? Our first pass was so far off the mark that it was hard to argue that there were any signs of intelligence underlying it. We had trucked hundreds of thousands of pounds of apples from California and then had to turn around and liquidate them at pennies on the dollar. We had thousands upon thousands of pounds of frozen fruit purees that we were paying storage on, and that we eventually would have to liquidate as well.

At the same time we needed to plan for buying more ingredients to meet new sales projections that were being pulled from the ether somewhere by Arnie, Bob D., and Ken. The scariness would just not quit. Everything had to stay in constant motion—or we thought it did. We had to keep growing and expanding in the marketplace at the same time that we were shut down and gasping for cash. We had to keep investing in the facility so that it would function economically and safely. The backdrop was always, "We have no money, but we can't stop spending it."

Slippery and Treacherous

ARNIE:

At the time, in March of 1988, despite all of the problems, Ron and I actually remained in a strong position with the company. Unfortunately, we didn't appreciate the significance of that position. We were still naïvely caught up in believing that *we were the company* and reciprocally that the company was us; hence the illusion that we were innately strong and with power. Our strength was akin to our youth. It was hard to imagine ever losing it. In fact, it was little more than a narrow window of opportunity, subject to a brief moment in time.

In the beginning, Ron and I were an indispensable, absolute necessity for Earth's Best to have any chance at all. All of the early investors knew this, whether they liked it or not. And I believe, perhaps naïvely again, that at the outset, they did like it.

The new tier of prospects beginning to consider Earth's Best as an investment were attracted to our integrity and the uncompromising values Ron and I were aligned with and insisted upon. We could be trusted. Earth's Best was not a mirage or just a "sizzle" product.

The brand promise made the company a great potential investment opportunity.

Paradoxically, these same people were polarized by the authority that created these bedrock values that guided the company forward. They loved what we stood for and created, but at the same time they didn't like being dependent on us. Something made them uneasy. The comfort wasn't there. Maybe it was the twin thing or our mutt nature.

Maybe it was our intensity or odd résumés. In any case, whatever it was, it galvanized their need for control. As such, Ron and I didn't understand that the new money coming in would have a cloaked agenda that included cutting our hair, removing our strength, and sending us on our way.

The relevant questions for an entrepreneur are, "How do you know when you are in a strong position?" and then "How do you respond?" There may not be an easy or correct answer. Maybe, in fact, Ron and I did exactly what we had to do, or Earth's Best would have been in that business graveyard with a tombstone etched, "Born, September 16, 1984—Died, March 31, 1988."

In hindsight, one thing is certain. I regret not having access to the power we held or I believe we held. Since I didn't exercise it, I'll never know whether it was real or imagined, and what its impact on our Earth's Best lives might have been.

Also in hindsight, the entry of Stan Klack and Ken Winkler into the life of Earth's Best was the beginning of the end for us and the catalyst that began transforming the investor pool into a shark pool. This is not to suggest that the company did not benefit from their entry, but personally Ron and I did not.

The "D" word ("dilution") became a regular part of every investor meeting now. The Klack card that Ken had held close to his vest (during our first meeting in Boulder) was now sitting plain as day on the table. It was early on in the relationship, but there was something slippery and treacherous about him. Stan's investment strategy was to keep his money in his pocket. He would get points by bringing other people into a deal, much the way Rick had done. In principle,

I didn't have a problem with this. The hitch with Stan was that he wasn't a champion like Rick. He was more the bully and manipulator. Stan fooled a lot of smart people for a long time. And he rode with the company a lot farther than the ride Ron and I got to have.

I was there. I was a player. The navigable river I was paddling down turned into a raging Class 4 rapids. That was my inner experience, and that wasn't in the business plan. I couldn't slow it down. I was consumed by dodging boulders and snags. I missed a lot of the road signs and the scenery. Now, as I write this story, I'm reliving everything in slow motion, going back and forth, stopping the action and staring at each high-definition frame. My biggest regret is that Ron got bounced out of the boat way before he should have. I haven't played that footage yet, but it's coming.

I Didn't See It Coming

As we prepared for the April 1988 Anaheim Expo, I was leaning very heavily on Bob D. and Ken to set the stage for success. Theoretically, Bob's earnestness and Ken's nerve could form a potent package of professional salesmanship. Actually Bob D. was pretty nervy too, which is why Ken and Bob were often like poles of a magnet, repelling each other.

I knew the Anaheim results would make us or break us. Our sweepstakes program had to be spot-on. We couldn't miss. Otherwise, our retail price point would discourage trial and regular use by moms and dads, and our jars would grow old and wither away in obscurity. If I didn't have a light at the end of the tunnel to offer investors already in the deal and those contemplating jumping in, I would soon be talking to just Ron and myself.

We needed an equity bridge immediately after the expo to have any chance of being back in production for July. If not, we would miss the entire 1989 season and be out of business for a year, or more likely, forever. I also knew Joseph and Richard at Organic Farms had gone way, way out on a limb for us, and they would be hurt, perhaps even ruined, if we failed. As it was, we were pathetically delinquent paying them, and it weighed heavily on me. How could I ask them to keep on going out on a limb for the growing season ahead? I wanted to write them a big fat check and restart with a clean slate.

The Anaheim show was vastly bigger than Expo East. The showroom floor was an endless sprawl both of big-company and mom-and-pop displays. The immensity took me by surprise. Wholesalers, retailers, and consumers crowded that floor with the crush of rush-hour traffic. It was exciting. I'm sure the euphoria mist was raining down.

In 1988, the natural-foods industry had not yet been swallowed up by corporate mergers and acquisitions. The boom times were ahead, and the industry was still a wide-open place for entrepreneurs to claw their way to the top.

The Earth's Best contingent should have been sleeping in our rental car to save cash, but we all checked in at the Hilton, right next to the convention center. Back then, the Hilton was the place to strut your stuff and show the trade you were a player and an industry insider. The decision to stay at the Hilton was my attempt to show that we belonged, to create the illusion that Earth's Best was on a roll (or conversely, to dispel the notion that we weren't).

This time we had product, cases of it, and this time everyone walking the show floor could sample Earth's Best. The highest of highs were those moments when there was actually a new mom feeding her baby Earth's Best. It was a joy that Ron and I got to share together. And of course, there was no better advertising.

Our booth was set up to feature the case-stack program and the "My Baby's Worth It" Sweepstakes. We dished out colorful handouts to every retailer who came near our booth. Some of them offered perturbed looks as they scanned the sell sheet. They did not take kindly to having the retail price dictated to them. Most of them got over that when they realized that everyone was getting the same deal, and the sale was guaranteed, but if and only if they played by the rules outlined on the sell sheet. The guaranteed sale was especially attractive to the smaller stores, who often complained they could not compete with the bigger "A" stores.

Bob D. and Ken were taking orders as fast as they could write. It was working. We were bucking conventional wisdom by putting the retailer in the driver's seat, creating the pull rather than letting the distributor call all the shots. When a distributor who did not carry EB came by the booth, we were able to show them how many stores in their area were signed on to the case-stack program. They left our booth with plenty of motivation to add EB to their catalogs.

This success seems so understated, fitting into the small paragraph above, but it represented a momentous change in the way a natural-foods company could do business with the retail trade. And it was the light at the end of the tunnel that I needed to show to the Earth's Best board.

In Anaheim, people of importance were now looking for me, interested in me. This was a wonderful, almost disorienting sensation after years of looking for, if not chasing, people of importance. In that moment where Arnie the pursuer met Arnie the pursued, I realized how exhausted I had become from pushing so hard and how much I needed this moment of grace.

Ron and I had a tiger by the tail. This was our dream. What we didn't yet comprehend was that the setting for the dream was shifting. I had been so busy dodging those boulders in my ride down the rapids, that I hadn't noticed the shark pool that was under construction or the danger that Stan Klack would pose to our dream. I didn't see the ambush coming.

Building the Organic Wave

The 1988 annual meeting of the Organic Foods Production Association of North America (OFPANA), today known as the Organic Trade Association, was planned to coincide with Expo West. This made sense because most of the players in the organic-foods industry were already in Anaheim. The early OFPANA meetings were both fractious and hilarious. There were many dedicated and energetic entrepreneur types who tediously worked to forge their independent streaks and personal agendas into what is now a multibillion-dollar industry with uniform standards and certifiable authenticity. In the early days, it was hard to imagine that there would ever be agreement on anything.

As a founding member of the OFPANA organization, I was convinced that if there was going to be an industry identity, it had to be defined by strict standards and protocols in order to be credible and stand up to scrutiny. Back in 1988, the food industry at large was not allied with the organic-agriculture movement; quite the contrary. Organic food claims represented a nuisance, if not a threat, to their business-as-usual domination. If there had been a way to snuff out the organic movement, it would have happened.

To me, the obvious way to cause that snuff was to advocate for standards without teeth. As such, those who wanted, for example, a one-year transitional standard to become organic were a threat to both the future industry and any association Earth's Best would have with the word "organic."

Ron and I even went through a period where we thought the term "organic" was doomed. We contemplated creating our own word to define what standards Earth's Best would adhere to. I remember tossing around the word "whole-ganic" with Ron. Ultimately we concluded that despite all of its flaws and baggage, "organic" was already a nationally recognized word whose definition we had to fight for, so it could support the weight of an emerging industry.

There was often scuttlebutt about food-industry spies and saboteurs lurking about at our trade meetings. Maybe it was paranoia, but maybe not. After all, the flip side of all that was positive about "organic" was the understood message about all that was negative about conventional agriculture. "Conventional" was the agriculture that relied upon toxic synthetic chemicals and fertilizers that were dangerous to the environment, farm laborers, and perhaps even the consumer. Organic agriculture and organic products were the good guys on the white horses. It's not hard to imagine how polarizing and unwelcome this positioning was to the other side.

But apparently the polarization was necessary in order to bring about the consciousness and change that eventually led convention to embrace the organic wave, rather than try to resist it.

What Was His Hand Doing on My Throat?

Anaheim did prove to be the springboard we needed to secure enough financing to start making new purchasing commitments for the July restart. But just barely enough spring. There really wasn't much relief on the financial end, and the money talk and the parsing of money to our creditors just kept on going on and on.

The discussions with Stan Klack and the board entered a new phase. Now we were talking about preferred A, B, and common-shareholder rights. The subject matter became dense as we weighed the merits of voting trusts, super majorities, board control, financial control, and credit-line options. The deeper the discussions went with the board and Stan on how to attract and bring in new money, the more I fantasized about winning the Megabucks lottery. And it wasn't just fantasy. I tried every week to rid myself of the dilemma that follows people who need other people's money—I bought tickets.

I wanted to call a special board meeting and then tell everyone to go home. I wanted them to leave me alone to run my company and stop wasting my time with all of their posturing and jockeying for position. Ron also bought tickets. The morning after a Megabucks drawing, we'd look at each other. I would wait expectantly for Ron to share the good news. He would then wait for me. What I loved about the Megabucks was that each ticket had the same chance of winning. It was fair. I liked fair.

The next bridge was under construction. Stan Klack was touting

Vanmarkle, an English company he was chummy with, as the new rescue hope on the horizon. I can't remember how many all-expense-paid trips Stan took to England on our nickel, but I can tell you that the results added up to a big nothing. The one thing that Stan did with great efficiency and regularity was to submit his expense reports.

I remember a particular board meeting where our financial plight was especially acute. We had just burned through some more bridge money, but the new bucks we were anticipating were still on the sidelines, waiting for the right deal terms and conditions. During a break in our meeting, Stan approached me and quietly asked if he could talk with me privately. We entered a vacant office and he closed the door.

"Arnie," he said, "You're doing a really good job under some very difficult circumstances." "Thanks," I said, wondering where this was going. "The cash flow is really tight," he went on to say. I lamented thinking he was being fatherly and supportive. Introspectively, I offered, "I know, I am going to barely be able to scrape together payroll for next week." There was a brief moment of silence as Stan and I stood motionless in the dimly lit room. Stan then said, "Arnie, you do have a copy of my most recent expense report, right?" Surprised, I said, "Yes, I do." Without warning, Stan stepped toward me and grabbed me by the throat. "Arnie," he quietly raged, "You will pay me in full and you will pay me immediately, do you understand?"

Stan was fifty-six and I was thirty-seven. Stan was a cancer survivor, ironically for that particular moment, a survivor of throat cancer. What was his hand doing on my throat? I was shocked by this. He wasn't a physical threat, but who the hell was he? I didn't know how to respond or what to do with such a moment.

I pushed his hand away and left the room feeling shaken. The anger would follow close behind.

Stan didn't give a damn about Organic Farms or anyone else. He obviously didn't care what I thought about him either. Stan was about Stan. And the expression of that became unimaginably ugly in that moment. I walked back into the boardroom and never said a word. Stan got paid, but he waited like everyone else, although probably not as long as he should have.

The Kindly Sheriff

The pressure to advance the ongoing bridge process was enormous, but as fast as Ron and I were willing to go, we were constrained by the pace of others: investors, potential investors, lawyers, and accountants. And then of course there were holidays. When you're trying to raise money under pressure, it always seems like there is a holiday to work around. If you've been there, you know exactly what I mean.

Venture capital became the new buzzword in our board meetings. The bridging strategy was keeping us afloat, but it wasn't working as a means to capitalize the company for stable and rapid growth. It just kept us in a steady state of agitation and stress, although it did allow me to continue socializing with the sheriff. Some of the investors thought it was premature to attract a venture company, because we were still too much of a start-up. I didn't really know much about it. I had heard cynical references to venture capital being called "vulture" capital, but didn't give it much thought. My strategy was simple, try every financing possibility and try it immediately.

In fact, I had heard some rumbles that Greg Leeds, the managing partner of North Atlantic Venture Capital, Vermont's only VC firm, was expressing some interest in us. Other money was circling Earth's Best, trying to size us up as an investment. I recall we were also talking to Touche Ross and Peat Marwick, both money managers and "Big Eight" accounting firms at the time.

The waiting game was disempowering for me. It made me feel stale and grumpy. I was a part of the process, but at this point, I was more of a spectator than a gladiator. I was mired in surviving. I wanted some action and a chance to make my own success, rather than wait for someone else to tell me who and what it was, and when. The opportunity graciously came with a knock on my office door.

I figured it was the kindly sheriff, who at this point didn't have to bother knocking. I didn't want to be harassed by anyone and hoped there would not be another knock, but there was. "Come in," I conceded. The door slowly opened and to my pleasant surprise Jon Corcoran stood in the entryway.

And There She Was

Jon was both a first-round investor and Earth's Best's public-relations manager. I admired him for having the courage to invest in our fledgling enterprise and felt his support and creativity throughout the start-up period. Before he spoke, he gave me that look I had previously seen many times. It meant something like, "Come on, Arnie, be adventuresome, keep an open mind, and be positive."

"Meryl Streep is going to be the keynote speaker at a Mothers and Others meeting in Montclair, New Jersey," he blurted. (Meryl was an outspoken member of this organization, who strongly opposed the proliferation of pesticides. Her celebrity status helped the group establish credibility and a high media profile.)

"That's great, Jon," I replied.

"Meryl is doing some really important work. I think you should go to the meeting," Jon advised.

"Now, why would I do that?" I questioned.

Jon did not pause. "Because maybe Meryl and some of her Hollywood friends would like to own a piece of Earth's Best."

"That's a very interesting idea, Jon."

I could already feel my energy returning. Even though I didn't know a thing about Meryl, except that she was a great actress, the thought of distancing myself from Stan Klack was a great motivator. Suddenly, I was feeling young and adventurous again. I never expected a 180-degree turnabout when Jon walked through the door.

"Arnie," Jon interrupted, "There are a couple of logistics to deal with."

"Like what?" I asked hesitantly.

Jon began, "If I had known . . ."

"Just say it, Jon, we'll deal with it." I was not prepared for what he meant by logistics.

"This Mothers and Others meeting is tomorrow evening and I don't know exactly where it's going to be."

"What do you mean you don't know where the meeting is? Make some calls, find out," I said, quickly feeling my temper get the best of my depleted patience.

Jon paused and said, "The meeting is being held at a secret location, at some church, and it is by invitation only."

I thought for a moment and said, "I'm going. I'll find it, and I don't care if I have an invitation."

I felt hope coursing through my veins. I started firing questions at Jon. "How big is Montclair? How many churches are there? How do I get there?"

Jon didn't waste a second. He abruptly turned and left my office to gather all the information he could find.

I jumped up from my chair to tell Ron about the plan to meet Meryl Streep. He took to the idea like it was the most natural and obvious thing to do, short of buying a Megabucks ticket. We started brainstorming on how best to approach her and what information on Earth's Best I should bring. The moment had a familiar frenzied feel to it, like the time we spiffed ourselves up to meet that Boston banker (who didn't know where Vermont was). We were pressing too hard and getting ahead of ourselves again.

It was decided that I would take nothing to distribute to Meryl and that I would steer clear of trying to sell her anything. The plan made sense. There would be no plan. If the moment was to be, it would just unfold.

Meryl was famous, I was not. I was in need, but was not going to play that card. I was the cofounder of the nation's first organic baby-food company, and that made me a player on any nontheatrical stage. Meryl and I would meet eye to eye, if at all.

I drove home that night wondering if I was losing it. I was planning a trip to meet one of the most famous actresses in the world, at an unknown location, and at a by-invitation-only event. I had no plan. I was just going.

When I told Anne of my plan to meet Meryl, she confirmed that I had lost it. She was nice about it, but advised me to sober up. "Arnie, go only if you can find out where the meeting is and only if you can get an invitation."

The advice was sound, but it wasn't going to get me in front of Meryl on short notice or out of the office on an adventure. I really wanted out. Sure it was a long shot, but so what? What was the downside? A wasted trip to Montclair, New Jersey? A snub by Meryl Streep, whom I never expected to meet in my life anyway? When contemplating risk, I always took the time to size up what might be the worst-case outcome. It was an important exercise and a part of my internal checks and balances. If I could live with my imagined worst-case scenario, then the mission was a go.

I spent the remainder of the evening shining my shoes, ironing my clothing, and figuring out how I would get to New Jersey.

The short notice made the air fare prohibitively expensive. The best choice was to drive to Albany and take the Amtrak into New York City. From there, I'd take the Port Authority bus to Montclair, and after that, I'd walk the streets until I found the undisclosed location of the Mothers and Others meeting. Is there a problem?

It was a strange feeling to step off the Port Authority bus in Montclair and be clueless about which direction to walk in. I was now out of my mind, living my choices, and reaping whatever consequences were to follow. The only clue I had was that the meeting was going to be at a church. I walked for some time without lucking out. It was getting close to what Jon thought was the start of the meeting. My pace quickened and my indecision to approach the strangers I passed ended. I asked almost every person I saw who looked approachable, until someone knew what I was talking about. They guessed about the location and provided me with directions. I started jogging and wondered if my trip to Montclair would be a complete bust. Time was just about up.

After a few lefts and rights, I was relieved to see in the distance a church with people streaming into it. As I neared the entrance, I realized this was the place and that there was an obstacle between me and the church interior. Standing behind a card table at the front-door entrance were several ushers, who were obviously assigned to turn away any uninvited guests.

I was feeling hot and sweaty as I approached the ushers. A middle-aged woman who was clearly in charge politely asked, "Excuse me, sir, do you have an invitation?" I hadn't concocted any crafty story. "I'm sorry I don't. I traveled all the way from Vermont to attend."

"That's a long way to travel to get turned away at the door," she mused.

"I apologize for just showing up at the door," I conceded. "I am the cofounder of Earth's Best Baby Foods, and I . . ."

A young woman who was standing nearby excitingly interrupted and asked, "Are you really the founder of Earth's Best? I feed my baby that."

I had said the magic word, Earth's Best. In less than a minute, I was being escorted into a small vestibule where VIPs were gathered to meet Meryl before she took the stage to speak.

The room was crowded, and it seemed like everybody knew everybody, except me. I was the mystery man, but not for long. The word was out that the founder of Earth's Best had come all the way from Vermont. For a few minutes, I felt like a star, and then there she was.

"Oh, So You're the Baby-Food Guy"

Meryl Streep and I were in the same room. She moved through the crowd greeting everyone. She looked just like she did on the big screen. Eventually Meryl made her way over to where I was standing. I did not hesitate. I extended my hand and introduced myself. "Hi, Meryl,

my name is Arnie Koss. I am the founder of Earth's Best Baby Food."
She smiled warmly and said, "Oh, so you're the baby-food guy."

The night was young and would turn out to have more twists and
turns than I ever could have imagined.

As I listened to Meryl speak, it was apparent her interest in the
pesticide issue was genuine. She was an excellent public speaker and
motivator. I probably didn't listen as closely to what she had to say
as I would have liked, because I was already busy trying to reconcile
that the moment with Meryl had come and gone.

A case could have been made that I had succeeded by finding the
church, getting into the event, and introducing myself to Meryl. I
wasn't going to make that case. I had traveled all the way down to New
Jersey, and I wanted more of an outcome. What more could I do?

At the end of the Mothers and Others program, I had another
brief opportunity to speak with Meryl. Everyone wanted her attention and was hanging around waiting for an opening. I was no exception. To my surprise, Meryl said "Arnie, would you like to join me
and some friends at so-and-so's house for a drink or coffee?" I wasn't
expecting that, to say the least, and my face probably showed it.
"That would be great," I said in the most matter-of-fact tone I could
deliver. "Is it nearby? Because I don't have a car."

"It's close," she responded. A few minutes later I was in the car of
one of her friends and on my way to an evening with Meryl Streep.

For an hour or two, I hung out with Meryl in the kitchen of this
well-appointed home. Our discussion covered a rainbow of subjects,
including the story behind Earth's Best and the financial challenges
I was facing to keep the company afloat. I didn't divulge the gory
details, and I didn't grovel. We did not dwell on EB, but did spend a
majority of the time talking about organic products and, in particular, the absence of organic wines in the market. I told Meryl there
was some organic wine in the New York Finger Lakes region and
about a few small organic vineyards, like Frey in California, that were
becoming established.

During our conversation, there were a few moments where

something she said or the expression on her face transported me back to scenes in *Out of Africa*. It was a special moment that had to end. The hour had gotten late and I was setting myself up to exceed my worst-case scenario calculation—missing my bus and train connections in Manhattan.

Fortunately, the party was winding down and someone who had heard I was trying to get into the city offered me a ride to a bus stop. As I said goodbye to Meryl, she gave me the name and number of a family member who might be of help. I thanked her and said goodnight.

A Portent

That night, I was riding high on the food chain. It felt good, but for this superhero, it wasn't going to last long. The rain was falling and the air was chilly as we sped along the back streets of suburban New Jersey. I was soon standing on a dark street corner, cold and drenched. I wondered if being the president of Earth's Best would ever have any perks, like an umbrella, for starters. Ironically, the answer to that question would be yes, only it would be someone else enjoying them.

It was after midnight by the time the bus pulled deep into the bowels of the Port Authority. I started making my way up some stairs and through some deserted corridors. Where the hell was everyone? This was New York. Seconds later, I noticed I was being followed by a few shady-looking characters. Then a few more guys were on my tail. My pace quickened, but my mind didn't. I had lost my sense of direction and could not find my way through the maze to the street level.

Without warning this young-looking guy walks up beside me and says, "Man, if you wanna make it out of here, I'll take ya, but it's going to cost ya. I am your only hope." The contradiction between having just been chitchatting with Meryl Streep and now deliberating how to survive in New York's Port Authority did not escape me.

"How do I know you aren't just setting me up?" I quickly asked. "You don't, man, you're just going to have to trust me." I felt surrounded by howling wolves. It was a portent. I agreed. My escort looked around, and with the wave of his hand, he barked, "This one is mine." "Follow me," he said.

By the way, this development was not in my worst-case scenario calculation when contemplating the trip to Montclair.

As we traversed the dim corridors and climbed the dank, vacant staircases, I wondered if I was being set up for an ambush. I was preparing for fight and flight or vice versa. When I finally opened a stairwell door and walked onto the main thoroughfare of the Port Authority, I felt a great sense of relief. I wasn't home free, but I could see the light at the end of the terminal.

As my escort and I strode side by side in silence, I marveled at how different each life can be. I was trying to start a baby-food company and this guy was hustling me for a safe-passage fee out of New York's Port Authority.

Unexpectedly, the silence was broken. "You know, man, I'm really not a bad guy. I'm just tryin' to make a buck and this is what I do." I didn't respond and just kept walking at a fast pace. "Really, man," he went on. "I could be out on the street committing crimes, doin' drugs, you know what I am saying?" "Yeah," I said, not knowing where to take the conversation. "Think about it, bro," he went on. "I'm helping you out, providing a service—I'm legit."

We walked a few more minutes in silence. I could see the exit and a few cops standing in the entry. My escort suddenly stopped and turned to me. "Time to pay for my services, bro," he said half smiling, half smirking. "How much?" I asked. "Tonight, for you, let's call it twenty dollars," he asserted. "Twenty bucks, huh?" "That's it," he said, looking right through me. I pulled a twenty from my wallet and said, "Thanks for being a man of your word." I turned and walked toward the exit, glancing back over my shoulder to see what the guy was doing. He was gone, vanished like a mirage.

"Cautiously Bullish"

I returned to Earth's Best a hero. Everyone gathered around me to hear the story of meeting Meryl and my escape from the Port Authority. Jon was so proud and amazed that I had pulled it off. As a follow-up, I asked him to track down some organic wines to send to Meryl, hoping that would help keep a dialogue going with her. It did not. After the commotion and excitement dissipated, I walked into my office to face the mountain of irate messages left for me, the hero who wasn't paying his bills.

Instead of focusing on my to-do list, I lapsed into a daydream. There was something about that guy in the Port Authority that I liked. He was a thinker in his own right, sharp and honor bound, streetwise and chivalrous. In his own way, he too was making a difference. And as it turned out, he proved to be more trustworthy than some of the white-collar guys coming my way who had the cash and the pedigrees.

Stan Klack finally acknowledged that Vanmarkle had vanished. This was old news, as far as I was concerned. Touche Ross went away for reasons unknown or forgotten. But Greg Leeds (of the Vermont-based North Atlantic Venture Partners) had become, as I specifically recall, "cautiously bullish." I found it very difficult to be patient with all of this calculated, nonsensical wordsmithing. Cautiously bullish? Phrases like that made me want to scream, because I knew they just meant more delay and more sorry phone calls to people like Joseph and Richard. But to a fault, I learned to exercise self-control and restraint. I had come to recognize one of my greatest fears. I didn't want my scream to be the spark to blow a prospective deal apart or sideways and perhaps kill the company. I knew I was in a combustible environment, and I think my sentiments were actually pretty transparent to everyone.

Unexpectedly, what I first liked about Greg is that he seemed to grasp the urgency of our timetable and was willing to roll up his sleeves to get the due diligence done. He also impressed me as being genuinely appreciative of the job Ron and I were doing to guide the company through the chaotic start-up period. Greg would say to me (on more than one occasion), "Arnie, you really have earned the right to lead the company going forward. If we invest, you will carry on as CEO and president." The position that Greg was immediately focused on filling was that of chief operating officer (COO). I was completely enthusiastic about this.

Finally, we were getting on a capitalization and executive-level management track that seemed to have a solid foundation under it. Contributing to the brightening picture were ongoing discussions with the bank to extend us a line of credit on our receivables and our inventory. Also, a guy by the name of Carl Reed was considering a $500,000 investment. We even had some first-round investors offering to loan us money that would be secured by finished-goods inventory. I began to feel hopeful that all was not lost.

Greg's plan was to stitch together a group of venture funds to both spread the risk and capitalize Earth's Best for aggressive growth. The idea of "venture capital" did not scare me outright. Why would it? You might say I was "cautiously scared." Ron and I could not move away fast enough from our hand-to-mouth, day-to-day existence on the edge of financial ruin. Surprisingly, Greg was also prepared to participate in a bridge loan to help us get the plant up and running again. This type of investment was well outside of his comfort zone, but he too saw there soon would be nothing left to invest in without another bridge.

The gears were grinding toward a closing that included Greg, Carl, Stan Klack, and some first-round investors. It's important to note that everyone understood that the bridge falling into place would lead to nowhere without a major round of venture financing coming in behind it. There were enormous pressures building everywhere to satisfy creditors, to ramp up to meet projected supply-side needs, to spend on sales and marketing campaigns, and to make needed improvements in the plant. It was crystal clear the new bridge cash would not last long. The good news was that more and more people were beginning to care about our predicament, because they were in it too. The great news was that we were getting traction in both the grocery-chain and natural-foods marketplaces. Ken and Bob D. were both movers and shakers.

We began to notify employees that the plant would reopen sometime in July. I was on the phone day and night talking with growers about our needs. I was also trying to smooth things over with Organic Farms, to whom we still owed about $100K. Complicating my discussion with Joseph and Richard was the discovery that they were considering the idea of getting into the organic baby-food business themselves. We had a noncompete agreement with them, but the term was not very long. What I didn't know at the time was that, in part, thanks to us, Organic Farms was on the ropes too and would never be in a position to enter the baby-food business.

Was the Screwing Necessary?

RON:

The turning of the tide, the changing of the guard, was now imminent at Earth's Best. The original group of investors was still sitting in the catbird seat, but the U-Haul moving truck was on its way. Their preeminence was receding, and they knew it. The challenge for them was how to best protect their investment going forward. The new people kicking the tires of a cash-starved company had different aspirations. To maximize their advantage, they wanted to leverage the vulnerability of the pre-start-up and first-round investors, and, of course, of Arnie and me as the founders.

It boiled down to the pain threshold of the early people. How much dilution and loss of control could they stand in exchange for the prospect of some return on their investment? For those contemplating a rescue, it probably was a cold return-on-investment calculation. The promise of Earth's Best must have been somewhat obvious, because we had no shortage of suitors. Or perhaps, more cynically, it was just the smell of blood in the water that was bringing out the sharks.

All I knew from my sheltered view in the now silent production room is that Arnie and I had started with 60 percent of the company, and we were on the elevator down. I could only hope that it wasn't the express.

I really had not given much thought to how I was being perceived by the investment crowd, but I should have. Everyone looking at Earth's Best as an investment knew very little about food processing and production. It was the brand position and market potential that I think was the lure. It was more familiar and easier to understand. Branding was where the money was made and the glory lay. The processing was just a necessary evil. It was foreign, the more invisible the better. No matter how hard I worked, there was probably nothing particularly comforting about my presence. I did not have the power to make the production challenges invisible; far from it, unfortunately.

As such, the writing was probably already on the wall during this first shutdown in the spring, and definitely by the summer of 1988, but I wasn't reading it. Earth's Best would begin the process of "de-muttifying" itself soon enough. Mutts like me would have to give way to the promise and comfort of pedigree. I'm not sure if this was an inviolate law of the jungle or not. It makes me feel better to think that it was.

I had nothing back then against pedigree and nothing by decree for it. It just depended on the person. An MBA from Harvard and/ or a big name like Nabisco or Coca Cola on a résumé was not an automatic gimme for entry into my sphere of respect or trust. But it sure was for the new wave of investors approaching the Earth's Best shores.

Day by day, I became an outsider looking in at the company I had started. Some people understood my outsider status long before I did. I plodded along innocently and determinedly. My task at hand was to overcome all of the production-related shortfalls that Bob

Fielder had either missed, misjudged, or just couldn't afford. The list was formidable.

The ventilation system was completely inadequate. The floors needed to be epoxied. We needed a spare-parts inventory. The "direct" steam cooker was too short to continuously cook carrots and sweet potatoes. Believe me, this is just the start of what lay in front of me.

I inhaled the essence of that production room. What I lacked in experience, I made up for with dedication and determination. I listened to everyone's input. Maybe someone with a lifetime of experience in the trenches would have cruised through and been ten times smarter, faster, more cost-effective, and more inspiring. I never met that person, but I did think I was on the way to becoming him.

Maybe there's good reason to think that dedication and determination can't compensate for lack of experience. I can hear voices scoffing at my arrogance. In my view, those are the voices of conventional wisdom. There's a lot of expertise in our world that doesn't necessarily translate well into intelligent, ethical decision making, effective action, or capable leadership. There was a lot of expertise around the table at Beech-Nut, but it did not prevent the sale of phony apple juice. Bob had decades of food-processing experience, but couldn't make real apple juice for us or figure out how to keep a hairnet on his head. Les was also steeped in expertise, but he wouldn't put it on the line.

In fact, it was my ability to morph myself into just about anything that probably allowed the company to survive the long days of wandering through the desert without a true plant manager. Yet I felt invisible and unappreciated by the money people at Earth's Best, and this would only worsen in the months ahead. This is the place of pain where the mutt and pedigree talk is born.

It wasn't my ambition to be a plant manager. I was headed in that direction only by necessity. It is what survival demanded. My ambition had always been to nurture and shepherd the spirit of Earth's Best and what it stood for and the myriad ways its potential could be expressed.

Arnie was no less essential to the survival of Earth's Best than me. I feel the same way about many people who somehow became part of the constellation that birthed this company. To name a few, Jeff Coolidge, Lavon Bartell, Rick Shays, Paul Carrera, and Joseph and Richard at Organic Farms were there in ways that made an incalculable difference. And some of these people got chewed up by the tidal wave of institutional funding, which in all fairness also made an incalculable difference in the life of the company's ability to extend beyond its infancy into its young adulthood today.

But was the screwing necessary?

The Express

Raising money was old hat by now. Put on the uniform or Halloween costume, as Arnie likes to say, apply your game face, and start selling. The scale of what we needed was orders of magnitude beyond where we had started with the original equity offering. In turn, the players contemplating providing new monies were different. There were hundreds of degrees of separation between them and the angel-investor universe that favored us at the outset. Arnie and I really didn't sufficiently understand the significance of these degrees of separation. Again, we were familiar with euphemisms like "vulture capital" and got the picture. But the people whom we were meeting didn't look like vultures, act like vultures, or talk in a predatory way. The "vulture capital" rap was probably more hype than not. That was our hope. Nonetheless, our guard was stuck on high alert.

What I learned along the way is that when you've been in a perpetual state of mobilization for an extended period of time, your predatory-bird identification skills become dull.

There was also a certain separation taking place between my world and Arnie's. I wasn't putting on the uniform as often as Arnie did. We had done everything together, but less so as the production room consumed me and the money chase consumed him. Our dog and pony show was en route to becoming historical. I would not be nostalgic for it.

Arnie and I, as dog and pony, had probably been perceived by many as being attached at the hip, perhaps the lip. I'm sure we had been a curiosity along the way to many, but perhaps a little threatening as well to some. Too much of a good thing, perhaps? Were we separable? Could we be divided? Were we of one mind, or did we actually have two? I think one Koss was plenty for those already in the deal and probably for those looking at it as well. The business couldn't afford to have us both suited up. I didn't have the nervous system for it anyway.

And yes, we were separable and we had two minds, but we could not be divided.

The money got pieced together, but not in a way that brought any kind of stabilizing financing solution. It was a patch job to get us back into production, but not off the capitalization treadmill. And although the plan for July held up, we were still deep in the dark woods.

When July finally came, it was wonderful to welcome everyone back (and surprisingly, literally everyone did return). The energy was incredible, as was the expectation and underlying anxiety. Although finding a plant manager was on the Koss to-do list, it hadn't yet happened. Maybe it was the money and an ingrained poverty mentality that postponed this action. Maybe the prospect of another manager so soon after the unpleasantness with Bob was just too unappetizing. I also was confident in my own ability to manage the production, knowing that there was so much expertise and support behind me ready to be tapped.

The most challenging part of managing is often the people part. I was surrounded by people I liked and who I believed liked me. The chemistry of community and cooperation was alive. There was a trust that freed up a lot of energy that is often tied up in resentments and divisions. It wasn't perfect, but I know the group dynamic was on the right side of the tipping point where good things happen and the extraordinary is possible.

ARNIE:

It was the summer of 1988. The return of the production employees had the energy of a tenth-year high-school reunion. Everyone was still recognizable, and the youthful enthusiasm and fond memories of days past were still intact.

The sounds of the plant were familiar and so sweet to me. The conveyors were moving, the glass jars clanked toward the filler, the compressors were hissing, the employees were gossiping, and the distinct and wonderful food smells were making their way to my office.

I knew Ron was at the helm, and it gave me great relief. For all that he lacked in experience, he made up for in diligence, vigilance, and worrying. And he was loved by the production employees. They had his back. Ron and I never anticipated the developments that landed him in this position running the production end. Fortunately for Earth's Best and me, he had the capacity and the willingness to meet such an imposing circumstance. As my dad once observed, Ron was "as happy as a pig in shit" in that production room.

If I could have, I would have placed a lounge chair in a corner of the plant and lay there all day enjoying the miracle of a jar of Earth's Best being created. Unfortunately that was not in the cards, and the daydream I was enjoying did not last long. Instead, a storm blew into my office in the form of Ken Winkler.

"Bob Donnola has got to go," Ken blasted. "Arnie, Bob doesn't get it, and he's in my way," Ken went on. Ken could be passionate and put on an impressive harangue, but usually I could pacify him by keeping things on the light side and letting him vent till he exhausted himself. "Ken," I said inquisitively, "I thought you and Bob were best buddies, soul mates, comrades in arms." Ken chuckled, "Since when? Bob thinks the natural-foods business is going to save the company. He's fighting my proposed mass-market price-point strategy." "Ken, listen closely," I suggested, my tone becoming more serious. "Bob is only trying to protect our natural-food customers from feeling ripped off and exploited." Ken implored, "Arnie, the natural-foods business is the size of a flea on an elephant's ass. I already have close to 400 grocery stores on board and I am working on another 100-plus." Of course, Ken had a point, but I was determined not to create a schism between the two very different markets and sacrifice one for the other. "Ken," I said, "You and Bob have got to figure out how to work through this pricing issue. Find a solution that works for both markets."

Ken sat there, eyes bloodshot, and stewed. Ken drew his line in the sand that day and it forever changed our personal and working relationship. "Arnie, you're dead wrong, and I am telling you now, this is not going to stand." Matter-of-factly I said, "Ken, what are you saying?" Ken went on, "I am saying that Stan Klack is listening to me, and if you don't do it my way, he's going to pull out of the deal." The cumulonimbus clouds that were forming in my office suddenly turned dark and foreboding. "That sounds like a threat, Ken," I responded while beginning to stand up. Ken tried to soften it. "No, Arnie, it's just a fact. Stan is a family friend, and I am not going to keep him in the dark." Now I was pissed. "Ken, tell Stan, tell anyone who will listen, but hear this: Do your job, play by my rules, or you're out." Ken left my office without another word.

The battle lines had been drawn. Ken's loyalty lay with Stan Klack and not with me and Earth's Best.

I wish that had not been the case because there was something about Ken that I liked and valued. For starters, his appetite for sales and salesmanship surpassed my own by a great distance. I did it because I had to; Ken played the sales game because he loved it.

Ken was charming in his own salesmanlike way, but he could be vulnerable as well. He had a soft side that was oddly juxtaposed to his bravado. Even though Ken and I did not see eye to eye on sales strategy, and at the shareholder level were in different camps, I think he respected me and admired the socially responsible values that made him feel proud to be selling Earth's Best Baby Foods. Parallel to that respect and admiration was an impulsive, judgmental, good-old-boy personality that could and would turn on me in a flash and condemn me for not being in the real world, his real world.

For the time being, however, Ken and I would continue to work closely together, sometimes collegially enjoying each other's company and sometimes on opposite sides of the divide. He would throw his tantrums. Bob D. would be indignant and fight back to build the natural-foods business. And I would referee and do my best to keep both marketplaces integral to the growth of the company.

My day-to-day work life had come to feel like a battle, and the fun and excitement of changing the world was being paved over by the reality of doing it. More and more of my time was being spent and would be spent meeting with investors and selling the company's potential. The two to three million in bridging was the beginning of the carving up of Earth's Best. The investor pecking order would now constantly be reshuffled by the introduction of revolving advantageous stock positions, shareholder rights, voting trusts, warrants, options, and first rights of refusal. I did all I could to protect Ron and me from dilution, but the elevator that our ownership interests were on was, as Ron had feared, the express. It was going down fast and far.

Are You So Sure Our Food Supply Is Safe?

We were back in production and that was good news. However, we were losing money on every case produced, because our margins were abysmal. Gross margins of 25 percent or less would not do. Yet it appeared there was little we could do in the short term.

We were still producing only 25 to 50 percent of the projected cases we needed each day to break even, and our food costs had ballooned owing to excessive transportation, storage, and waste.

I found myself pressuring Ron to pump out more cases each day. I didn't want to hear why he couldn't do it—the cooker this, the coder that. Stop! No matter how legitimate the reason, I didn't want to hear it. I was beyond reason because VC guys like Greg had no soft spots for tales of woe. We were either viable or we were not.

My visits into the production area were no longer pleasure trips. I think everyone could feel the tension I was carrying and knew my presence was intended to somehow push, even though the weak link was the equipment or lack thereof, not the work that was happening out on the floor. I felt heavy and had become heavy-handed with Ron, who I knew could take it and swing back at me if he wanted. I feared that, the way things were going, I would be inviting everyone back into the break room for another round of pink slips.

Fortunately for Ron, I was often away from Pond Lane. I remember preparing to meet a prestigious venture fund Greg thought could be the linchpin for the stabilizing capitalization we really needed. If Boston-based American Research and Development (ARD) invested, others including Greg would surely follow. ARD was one of the first venture-capital outfits in the country. Their investment track record was stellar, and the level of scrutiny behind their due diligence efforts was second to none.

I prepared for that meeting like it was the first manned mission to Mars—meticulously, with no room for error. With the support of Ron, Bob D., Ken, Beth, and Jon, I was ready for launch. I had learned by now that if someone was looking for a reason not to invest, they would have no trouble finding it. Conversely, someone who was intrigued and taken by an idea could overlook a full-course disaster buffet and enthusiastically move forward.

Before I knew it, I was on the plane with Greg, headed for Boston to meet Courtney Maxwell, Charlie Panterri, and the ARD management team.

Walking into the ARD office generated a combination of feelings that surprised me. While there was nothing ostentatious about their office, I felt as if I had just walked onto a very big stage. For the first time, I also had the feeling that Greg and I were on the same side of the fight, rather than feeling like there was a line between us. This was a good feeling, although you will soon see that it was fleeting, if not delusional.

Over the next few hours the ARD team dug into our plan, financial results, management team, operations, supply-side picture, and everything else that mattered. It was like being in a Petri dish looking up into the microscope at an ARD eyeball. Every time I stumbled to answer a pointed question, Greg would jump in and help to clarify my answer. He did his share of stumbling too, but sometimes offering uncertainty is better than being slick and full of it.

As our discussion wound down, one of the ARD partners asked me if I really believed in the future of organic farming. I sensed he was the most skeptical. I leaned back in my chair and said, "The organic-foods industry is going to revolutionize the food business. The big food companies are watching, and one way or the other they will be dragged into it—kicking and screaming perhaps, but they will be in." "How can you be so sure? The food supply is safe," he intently responded.

I didn't want to end our meeting on a contentious note, but I could not be timid here.

"Are you so sure our food is safe?" I asked. "Do you want your baby eating vegetables and fruits sprayed with known carcinogens, or are you going to buy Earth's Best for your kid?"

Every eye in the room was watching my debate partner's response. After a pause, he smiled and said, "Earth's Best, but only if it tastes good." The tension that had been building had broken, and to lighten things up further I volunteered to send him some samples. He was not enthusiastic, but we all got to laugh.

After the ARD meeting, I knew our best shot at moving forward with a capitalized company was with Greg and the other venture investors we could bring in. We had to end the bridging phase of financing the company. It was little more than life support. Unfortunately, we weren't done with it yet.

I was feeling pretty upbeat when I returned to Pond Lane in September 1988. There was the usual avalanche of pressing demands. Ho-hum. Joe was trying to convince me to get my butt on an airplane to see the growers who were more than disenchanted with our slow- or no-payment plan. Bob D. and Ken, when they weren't duking it out, were in a full-court press to get me to meet with brokers, key accounts, and marketing consultants. The board members wanted sales, marketing, and financial updates and were anxiously circling the wagons to prepare for a term sheet Greg would be proposing.

Milty

But what was first and foremost on my mind was that Anne and I were getting married, and my dad, Milty, was traveling from Florida for the wedding and to see firsthand what Ron and I had been doing all these years.

I was thirty-seven now and wanted to feel that my dad was finally proud of the man I had become. Up until this point in my life, I think I was a disappointment in his eyes. Along with the tag of being a college dropout, I had been a long-standing low-wage earner and a fringy, puzzling character.

But at that time he was equally puzzling to me. I desperately wanted to understand him and to know him, but as it turned out, my dad had an encrypted security system in place, before there *were* encrypted security systems. He was a tough nut to crack. My hope was that one day we'd have a breakthrough together. Maybe this visit to see Earth's Best would be that day.

I can still see him walking up the sidewalk to the front door of our Pond Lane building. I suspect he was already blown away by the time he had parked his rental car. There actually was a factory, a brand-new, concrete tilt-up building with loading docks. This was definitely a step up from the factories he had started.

After hugs and kisses and a quick tour of the office and lab, we donned our white hairnets and walked into the plant. It is a moment I will savor forever. The plant was in full operation, and it was Apples and Bananas that Ron was orchestrating.

My dad stared in awe throughout the entire tour. He seemed to enjoy everything. The ELF filler was even behaving for him, cranking out 150-plus jars a minute. How did his boys do this? The answer to that question circled directly back to him. Milty was the prototype for his boys. As a lifelong entrepreneur, he had made a habit of slamming into new ideas—like injection-blow molding and an early iteration of computerized accounting and financial management. He too was an idea guy. He also liked steep learning curves. Ron and I pleasantly surprised him.

At the end of the factory tour our dad gave Ron and me a hug and said he was very proud of us. He also had lots of questions and ideas to help us improve our operation. It was a delight to feel his approval. I basked in the moment, wondering if we truly had just had that breakthrough. Over the ensuing years, I came to believe my dad did let go of the hurt and disappointment he felt when Ron and I veered off the beaten path to try roads less traveled. I'm sure it helped for him to see Earth's Best jars everywhere he went. "My sons Arnold and Ronald did that."

Maybe more than anything, what allowed the positive potential of that visit with my dad to be realized was linked to a very difficult decision Ron and I had made years earlier. We never asked him for a dime. He was not an investor in Earth's Best. Steering clear of that complication made the accomplishment of Earth's Best that much more satisfying for me. The fact is, as an early investor, he would have been creamed.

No "Easy Street" in Earth's Bestville

RON:

Arnie loved to give tours of the plant, and I couldn't deny him. He had the spiel down. I loved watching his delight that beautiful September day as he walked through the plant with our dad.

The restart had gone pretty well. I guess knowing that there was no longer a plant manager in the room galvanized everyone's pride and intention to be successful. I quickly found out where all the weak links were residing and often stationed myself where I thought I was needed most. And it wasn't a very glamorous place. I lived right next to where the applesauce (or carrots or sweet potatoes) completed its journey in the infamous direct-steam cooker. From there, the food was gravity fed and pumped through two noisy screening machines known as the pulper and the finisher and then finally to a five-hundred-gallon batching kettle.

The intersection of this cooking and screening equipment with its many pumps and valves was a Bermuda Triangle of production-flow problems and the cause for many slowdowns, shutdowns, and big messes. It needed to be fixed, but it was a big fix because the equipment in the triangle was mismatched. The job of managing this problematic intersection required hypervigilance, because acute problems materialized suddenly and (to the casual observer) without warning. I became so attuned to every sound and vibration in that nexus that I could anticipate the next adjustment, whether it be cutting the flow of cooked apples, speeding up one pump, slowing down another, or shutting it all down before the pipes would all shake apart in hot calamity.

Of course, this meant I couldn't wear ear protection in this high-decibel zone. Muffled sounds would not do. I needed to hear every note of the production-room symphony. And it really was a symphony to me. I loved the sounds and what they meant to my sense of well being—or not.

Now, I only have to look at the scar on the top of my right foot to remember how crazy it was living in that delicious-smelling web of hot stainless steel. Apparently, in a split-second decision, I zigged when I should have zagged. Boiling-hot applesauce poured over the top of my boot. The pain was excruciating, but I stayed at the station trying to prevent a much greater disaster from occurring, like the pipes bursting apart. I succeeded, but so did the hot applesauce—in burning itself right through my boot to my foot. An ugly, scary infection followed, and days of sitting in a recliner with my foot elevated, hoping that all would be well.

Arnie was dwelling in his own hot, pressurized situation. I never wanted to let him down, but sometimes I did. "Murphy" got a law named after him. There was no law named after me.

I did pull the occasional rabbit out of the hat. I remember one afternoon the retorts suddenly shut down. We were doing carrots. All of the unventilated moisture pouring from the cooker overwhelmed the electronic circuitry. The bad news drifted into Arnie's office. In terms of the day's production, we were looking at a complete loss. Arnie watched from a distance as Leo and Brian frantically tried everything they could think of. Brian shook his head dejectedly and told me the control box just needed time to dry out. We didn't have time. In theory, I was the last person to solve the problem. I knew more about particle physics than that retort. When you're ignorant, you're free to think simply and practically. "Brian, how about trying a hair dryer?" Brian smiled. "Ron, it just might work."

One of the production women, who lived nearby, got her hair dryer, and minutes later we were back in business. Everyone likes to crow. I remember reveling in the moment. Arnie was very relieved to see that rabbit. He drifted back into his office. I remember reading his mind: "More rabbits."

Sometime during this time frame Bob Fielder's (our first plant manager) lawsuit came down the pike. Arnie recollects that he charged us with age discrimination and claimed he was entitled to all of the stock options represented in his employment agreement. Age had nothing to do with it. I mobilized myself to do battle. I took no pleasure in it.

Although in my view Bob had failed us as a plant manager, I still liked him and cared about him. He had never been malicious. But to do battle meant exposing his shortcomings in a court of law, under oath, in front of a judge and the community.

Our defense relied on using several key production-room witnesses. Person after person swore to Bob's failure to fulfill his job description, including myself. All volunteered to do so. I wish it had never happened. The judge ruled against the merits of all of

Bob's claims. He ended up receiving nothing. In a perfect world, my perfect world, Bob would have received the stock we had offered him just the same, and that would have been the end of it. It was not a perfect world.

Bob had not been successful in establishing a spare-parts inventory or a routine-maintenance regimen. The spare-parts problem was in part tied to the lack of available funding. I don't have a favorable explanation for the absence of a complete maintenance schedule. All I knew is that Arnie did not take kindly to my excuses, and Bob was not there to blame.

I remember some pretty intense exchanges with Arnie where I felt attacked, hurt, and angry. The outcomes were falling short. He felt embattled. I could not offer more than everything I had. And we were really isolated from each other. I drove up to the Pond Lane building each morning and was immediately sucked into the production room or the QC lab. Arnie was in his office with the door closed, no doubt talking to money people like Stan Klack or sparring with Ken Winkler about some sales promotion or tiff with Bob D.

I lost any meaningful track of the people Arnie was talking to. I was not at the ARD meeting in Boston. I heard names and snippets of stories and possibilities when he would venture into the production room to take a vacation break from his piece of the insanity. I loved standing there with him when all was right in that production world. And when it was all going to shit, he would be standing over the carcass of a broken machine or failed O-ring, watching me try to get the production up and running or to salvage what we had already made.

Arnie was not unsympathetic to my dilemmas out there, but he also was not there enough to fully appreciate why I occasionally failed. Extenuating circumstances rendered me ineffective or inefficient at times. Heroics and shoestring catches were a dime a dozen, usually unnoticed and sometimes just not enough.

But Arnie did make me better. I might have tried to snap his head off when he was expressing that frustration, the insensitive brute, but

I listened. He was seldom wrong. His obvious was also mine. But it was much easier seen and said than done.

Eventually the production did find something of a groove. Adding a second coder was huge. Establishing a maintenance schedule and spare-parts inventory was also huge. Leo and Brian finally had more of the tools they needed. The ELF filler was overhauled for the third time with their latest and greatest valving and controls, which still weren't that great for hot baby foods. There was relative harmony out there on the floor. Barb, Pam, and Belinda were able to run the show more and more each day, because they were empowered to do so. Dick, Jim, and Scott had the warehouse covered. I loved and appreciated their collective capability and independence, and I counted on their good judgment to call me in when necessary.

However, cash had to be conserved. There was a lot of making do out in that production room, holding out on the big improvements until Earth's Best had confidently gained enough altitude to escape the catastrophic force of gravity that caused start-ups to routinely crash. We were not there yet. Gravity is a pretty intense, far-reaching force.

It all boiled down to a persistent mismatch between cash-in and cash-out. The production problems you're already quite familiar with. Getting all the sales programs up and effectively running on two completely different fronts (natural-foods and mass-market grocery) took many months of selling. Then there was the time needed for the bureaucracies of the various distributors and retail outlets to lumber forward and establish the right price points, set up merchandising displays, and implement promotional programs such as ad placements in store circulars. There was just no "Easy Street" to be found in Earth's Bestville.

Layoff 2

When Arnie and I were in the business-planning phase, the nerve synapses necessary to appreciate this lumbering beast and the related time, expenses, and cash-flow repercussions were on order or out of stock. We didn't get them in time to properly anticipate the order of magnitude of our future cash requirements. Just as well; we probably would have ignored them because the truths they told were inconvenient and unfriendly to what we thought we needed to see.

The compounding impact of both the sales and production realities was that by October 1988 we were gasping for cash again. We were in grave danger of failing to make payroll. A layoff was unthinkable, but it happened just the same. Arnie and I held it off for as long as we could, but sometime in December the shoe dropped, and we were all back in the lunchroom, Arnie center stage. This was not a speech you wanted to make twice in six months.

Arnie and I had thought it was possible to keep bridging our way forward. This had been our secret hope to spare us from "Layoff 2." We could see the new money coalescing around the table, but it just wasn't ready to sit down with us and get a deal done without another shutdown. You might wonder why. In any case, the dark woods got us again.

It's hard to convey the pain of that moment in the lunchroom. Arnie was his usual articulate, positive self, but the presenting situation was really inexplicable, and the shtick had lost some of its luster. On the face of it, the baby food was selling. There was all sorts of encouraging publicity. The production was improved. All signs were green and go to the naked eye, but Arnie said "layoff," not "blastoff." It didn't make any sense. The production workers were doing their part. What was wrong with Arnie, me, and the board?

No one said that, but that's what I would have been thinking. People were losing their livelihoods—again. All we could do was hold out the promise that we were very close to the money, and the layoff would be short. The meeting broke up, and people fell away dejected. It was hard to imagine that anyone would ever return—or should for that matter.

The launch of a nationally distributed food start-up in both the natural-foods and mass markets had never been done before Earth's Best. There was no template.

The mass market was the unspoken Holy Grail for natural-foods companies. No one had really been successful in cracking the code to get in on the main-stage shelves next to the big boys. There were so called "natural-food sets," where natural-foods products were herded and penned in together. Health Valley, a natural-foods cookie, cracker, and soup company, pioneered by George Mateljan in the 1970s, was one of the few well-established companies inhabiting those healthy-food supermarket islands. Frank Ford's Arrowhead Mills was another. But to a company like Earth's Best, it was not coveted ground, it was death.

Mothers were not looking for baby food in a dust-collecting natural-foods section, and that's what they often were back then. Most mothers didn't even know these sections existed. Baby food was found in the baby-food aisle. Gerber was almost always there. Beech-Nut and Heinz slugged it out to sit next to Gerber. This is also where Earth's Best needed to live to be viable.

But space on supermarket shelves, known in the trade as "slots," is prohibitively expensive. At that time, natural-foods companies could look and dream, but they couldn't afford to touch mass-market shelf space. And if they dared, they faced the certain wrath and condemnation of their natural-foods brethren.

Arnie and I never considered paying for these slots. In our early Tru-Vision days, we had never heard of them. Later on, we discovered that they were completely out of reach financially. To move forward in the mass market, the Red Sea, in effect, had to part for us, and it did. Slots were often waived for our baby food. Supermarkets wanted us.

Earth's Best offered grocery buyers profit margins (for baby food) never seen before; the other guys, like Gerber, did not and could not.

We were fresh, upscale, and on the cutting edge of a movement that was about to explode; the other guys were stale and passé.

Arnie and I couldn't hide our mass-market efforts and successes from the natural-foods industry. In fact, because Earth's Best was the first natural-foods brand to land outside those dusty islands reserved for so called "health foods," we were glaringly visible and received both the scorn of some and the envy of many who closely followed our journey. But all these firsts were small consolation for Arnie and me in that December 1988 lunchroom.

A venture-capital deal with Greg Leeds and North Atlantic Venture at the lead had been looming large for some time (large being $6 million of new capital). If that amount didn't put us out of our fund-raising misery, what would? Of course, Arnie and I desperately wanted this deal to close because we wanted Earth's Best to live and to thrive. Earth's Best was our baby. And it seemed, from various conversations and signals along the way, that Arnie and I would be secure in our positions as parents. We had earned it. We still took people at their word.

In the meantime our payables were crushing us. We were doling out $100 here and $50 there. The squeakiest wheels got the grease. The sheriff became a regular office visitor again. I even got a knock on my door at home one night. Gabe and Aaron were pretty excited to see the uniform and the gun on the hip. At least there was a positive.

What were these prospective investors waiting for? It was like having firefighters standing at the ready, hoses in hand, just watching the fire burn. Arnie and I were in the blaze filling Dixie cups as fast as we could and running to where the flames were most threatening. It was exhausting.

Of course nothing happened over the holidays, except people calling for money; Happy New Year, 1989. February was the worst. Life at Earth's Best was reduced to fielding phone calls, expressing good faith, and promising as little as possible.

You still might be wondering why it was so bad for us. Here's an example of one unanticipated monumental setback to our cash flow.

A large groundbreaking sale had been made to a Mid-Atlantic grocery chain. We're talking something like ten trailer loads of baby food. This was cause for celebration at Pond Lane. There was the feeling that we had finally turned a substantial corner with this transaction. Success is a wonderful feeling, but it didn't last long. We got a call from one of the drivers, relaying that the chain had refused delivery. What should he do?

Predictably there was a frantic scramble. Ken was all over it. The first thought was, it must be a clerical error. Or maybe the trucks had arrived at the warehouse after deliveries were allowed. For some reason, an easy fix was not built into the script. The shelf space we were about to land on was apparently bought out from underneath our feet by Beech-Nut for $250,000, ten slots at $25,000 per slot. At least that's the explanation, from the sales trenches that made its way back to Pond Lane.

Here's the rest of the story. You would think with a purchase order in hand, the supermarket chain would have been bound to receive our shipment. But apparently Ken had received only a "verbal" purchase order from the buyer. He said ship, and we did. We also ate the transportation expenses. We had no recourse.

Big gambles, as in cutting corners, are great when you win. There's the glory and the story. But when you lose big, who pays? Ken was likably slick, and he was well connected to the money bridging the company forward, as in Stan Klack. The net result was that Ken was insulated from the effect of his gamble. He would not lose his job in a layoff. He would not be inundated by creditors or have the sheriff at his door. Ken got off easy. He ate some crow. The grocery buyer was the bad guy anyway.

There is only so much real estate allotted for baby food. Our jubilant ten-truckload (almost) sale must have caused some panic at Beech-Nut, when they got wind of it. They would not allow Earth's Best to secure their prized shelf space in a key market. And they had the wherewithal to make an offer the chain could not refuse. Beech-Nut wasn't playing hardball, they were playing beanball. Earth's Best didn't have the budget for a helmet or the hide to take a blow like that without major consequences. Pink slips!

Alar

I optimistically worked on a plan for another restart. Apples were done. Carrots were still a possibility, although as we headed for March the window was closing. Sweet potatoes were very iffy. There were, however, four new products that Sue, Marty, and I had been working on that were ready and not subject to fresh, seasonable produce: Peas and Brown Rice; Green Beans and Brown Rice; Plums, Bananas, and Rice; and Peaches, Oatmeal, and Bananas. This is where we would restart. All we needed was the green light.

New product introductions were crucial to keep the marketing buzz going and the buyers jazzed. Momentum is slow to build and fast to disappear in the grocery-trade world. Staying the course would never do. Even while we were flailing about gasping for cash, we had to have an eye on the future.

The plan was to hire back a small group of people to work with Pam, Barb, and Belinda, whom we once again had not let go. Unfortunately, virtually no production improvements had been made during the second shutdown and no equipment accommodations added for the new products. The built-in inefficiencies persisted. This was very worrisome to me. How could we be successful? How could I be successful if my hands were tied behind my back? Maybe Bob Fielder felt like this?

One of the unbearable tensions was the pressure to sacrifice natural-foods distribution for the mass-market rollout. If there were only five hundred cases of Apple Blueberry left and no new production in sight for months, who would get them? Ken and Bob D. were the stars in this soap opera. Ken was the Colorado thoroughbred. Bob was the scrappy Vermont underdog.

I did not want us to abandon the natural-foods business. Undermining that momentum and reneging on our commitments there was unthinkable. On the other hand, how could we short a two-hundred-store grocery chain and lose precious slots or even the entire account? Or forgo rolling out into a powerhouse grocery chain to service five hundred mom-and-pop natural-foods stores who would do a fraction of the business?

It turned out to be a not-so-delicate joust with a lot of finessing and spinning by both Ken and Bob to their respective trades. Arnie was always in the middle, playing referee.

All I could think about was getting back into production. I couldn't stand sitting on the sidelines watching these wrenching choices taking place. I hated it.

While we were standing still, the world, fortunately, was not. On February 25, 1989, *60 Minutes* aired a show featuring the Natural Resources Defense Council's (NRDC) condemning report on the use of the plant-growth regulator Alar on apple crops and its carcinogenic danger, particularly for children. Reports like this were presented as breaking news, but for Arnie and me, it was just another confirmation of the obvious. Children were vulnerable. Synthetic chemicals and foods should have nothing to do with each other. Many of the safety studies done on these chemicals were incomplete at best when they were approved and registered by the EPA.

But when an ugly truth rears its head in a forum where millions of people are tuned in simultaneously, there is a tsunami-like impact. Alar had the mainstream reality in a tizzy. The apple industry mobilized to do damage control. There were refutations defending the safety of the food supply and counterattacks on the NRDC's credibility.

Earth's Best was on the right side of this news report. Arnie and I started to look pretty smart, in theory at least. The interest in organic foods would now leap ahead. Gerber, Beech-Nut, and Heinz could only take a backseat to our now elevated market position. Even as our cash flow crushed us, it felt pretty darned good. We were doing the obvious: protecting babies, protecting the environment, and protecting agricultural workers from toxic-chemical exposure. Our struggle was worth it.

The *60 Minutes* report was a big boost for us. We were in the right place at the right time. And I think the investment community began to clearly see the business potential and the power of Earth's Best as a brand name. It didn't matter if some found the name hard to pronounce. What brand promise could be better than best?

The emergency board meeting that soon followed created anxiety for me, because it was convened so urgently. Drop everything and get up to Burlington. Was this the big one, the deal that would finally capitalize us for the long haul? The expectation of a breakthrough had Arnie and me on pins and needles.

— PART FOUR —
The Ambush

Apples and Blueberries

ARNIE:

I fought hard to avoid that second layoff. The prospect was embarrassing and humiliating, and it was wrong. I didn't want to stand in front of everyone in that lunchroom again. It seemed like we were so close with Greg. The follow-up meetings with ARD were positive.

In an act of desperation to stretch our cash-flow position to the promised venture round, the company entered into a short-term creative financing arrangement that became known as the infamous "Apple Blueberry" inventory deal. I was directly responsible for spearheading this initiative of last resort, and as president it was my responsibility to administer the terms of this agreement.

One of our first-round investors generously agreed to loan the company $50,000, secured by our Apple Blueberry finished-goods inventory. The agreement specified that all receipts collected from the sale of Apple Blueberry cases would go directly back to the lender without exception.

I did not know it, but I was fast approaching one of my worst lapses in judgment ever. At first, I diligently took the precious cash coming in from the Apple Blueberry sales and began to pay down the loan. Even though a deal was a deal, I labored over the decision to do the right thing and unconsciously entered a delusional state of rationalization.

Beth had alerted me that, based on our bank balance and projected receivables, we would not be able to make payroll or pay the stay-out-of-jail taxes. As the pressures mounted, I foolishly decided to borrow against the Apple Blueberry receipts with the belief that I could cover my tracks in time and make good on the money owed.

I should have disclosed this maneuver to the board and lender, but I did not. In the moment it seemed harmless, but as so often happens, plans go awry, and best intentions fall short. The money I was counting on to make good on the payments due the lender did not show up in time, and I found myself in the wretched position of having to disclose my lapse in judgment.

The reaction to my transgression was intense. The lender went ballistic. I didn't blame him, but nonetheless it still hurt to be so harshly ridiculed for trying to keep the company from coming unglued. But a deal's a deal, and I blew it. Eventually, my Apple Blueberry misstep got fixed, and the lender was made whole, but the episode was definitely a low and humbling moment. I think it also hurt my standing with the board.

What I did wrong carried so much more weight than what I did right.

This time, in front of the employees, it really felt like I was walking the plank. The news landed with a thud. There wasn't the same resiliency as the first time. I felt numb and deflated. I no doubt spun the bad news the best that I could, but no one was going to tell me "Good job today, Arnie."

The period that followed was now quite familiar to me. My right foot was on the gas, and my left was riding the brake. I was becoming quite an expert at this technique, except for desperate and foolish blunders like the Apple Blueberry deal. I had to push our sales and marketing agenda forward, or there would be nothing to invest in. I had to assume we would restart again soon. We were heading into March, and commitments for peas and green beans had to be made. The Anaheim Expo 1989 was just ahead in April, and I had to assume we'd be there and plan for it accordingly. The My Baby's Worth It scholarship had to be funded. This was my job.

Paradoxically, my job was also to stop spending money the company didn't have. I was repeatedly cautioned by our attorney, accountant, investors, and advisors to not dig the hole we were already in any deeper.

Time passed quickly, and time dragged on mercilessly during this period of paradoxes. The long drawn-out drumroll to a venture closing was coming to a close. With Greg as the champion venture capitalist for our deal, the promise of a $6-million closing was in sight. We were down to dotting i's and crossing t's, or so I thought, to get a term sheet finalized.

Checkmate!

The phone in my office rang and snapped me out of a Megabucks daydream. It was Rick Shays on the line. He asked me to drop what I was doing and drive up to Burlington with Ron for an emergency board meeting.

On the way up to Burlington, Ron and I speculated on the possible subject matter that would result in an unplanned board meeting. I reflected on my brief call with Rick and concluded there was nothing in his tone that revealed the slightest hint as to what might be going on. Rick was well practiced in not tipping his hand.

It was late afternoon by the time we parked the car. Ron and I entered Rick's office. I could hear voices coming from the direction of the cozy conference room I had been in many times. It was the same room in which Ron and I had presented to Ben Cohen and a host of other potential investors. We were greeted with smiles, handshakes, and the usual pleasantries. Ron and I shared some of the latest reconnaissance coming from the marketplace and an update on the D.C. shocker that had ripped what we thought was the sale of ten tractor-trailer loads of product from our cash flow.

Up until that point, there was only one surprise visible to me. Greg was sitting quietly at the end of the table looking somewhat stressed. He had never attended a board meeting before, and it seemed odd that he would be joining us to discuss company business prior to becoming a director.

Without further delay, Rick called the meeting to order. The room went momentarily silent before Rick began to speak. "Ron and Arnie," he said with a half grin on his weathered face, "You guys have done a great job getting the company this far. We all have been impressed with your dedication and stick-to-itiveness." As I scanned the room, I noticed that Greg had his head down, staring attentively at the conference-room table. Everyone else was looking at Rick, listening to him set the stage for what was to come. Rick's face tightened, and his half grin dissolved. The measured and positive tone he had begun with turned as quickly as Vermont's weather. Now Ron and I were suddenly hearing a stern rebuke capturing a laundry list of the company's failures and our lapses in performance and judgment.

Wow, this was surreal. I felt flushed. Ron and I exchanged flustered glances. We switched into mobilizing mode, reading each other's minds and plotting in a sixth-sense sort of way our response to Rick and the other board members.

On the count of ten, we would stand, calmly walk to the door and congratulate them for throwing the baby out with the bathwater and flushing their investment down the toilet.

"Arnie," I heard Rick forcefully say, catapulting me back to the unraveling situation. "As president of the company, you have had a chance to prove you've got the right stuff for the job." I heard Fred clear his throat. "Arnie," Fred said in a diplomatic tone, "What Rick is trying to say is that unless you are willing to step down as president, Greg is not going to go forward." Before I could open my mouth, Ron exhaled angrily, "What are you talking about? Greg has told Arnie all along that he earned the right to lead the company." All eyes darted over to Greg. Rick angrily responded to Ron, "Look guys, Arnie either resigns so Greg can bring in his own CEO, or the company folds. It's your decision."

It was my turn. "Greg, why are you doing this now? Were all your assurances that I was your guy BS? This is not fair, I trusted you, and now we're boxed in." Greg looked up and spoke in a solemn tone, "From my vantage point, the more clearly I see the road ahead, the less confident I am that Arnie has the experience. Arnie," he earnestly said, "I am doing what needs to be done to close the deal. I am not the only one who thinks that you are not credentialed to manage the company going forward."

I looked around the room at the traitors, the board itself. "Guys," I said, "you obviously don't support me either. Look what Ron and I have done with next to nothing. We've worked wonders. Now you're going to bring some stranger in."

Greg interrupted me. "Arnie, you and Ron are indispensable; the company needs your leadership and vision."

I felt so emotionally turned upside down by the way Ron and I were set up that the best I could do was say, "Ron and I need to discuss this privately."

We walked to my car in silence, each of us lost in our own dark and morose thoughts.

How did we get to this miserable intersection where all of a sudden the founders of Earth's Best were on the outside looking in? It was sudden for us, but of course it wasn't for Greg and the board. And then again, hadn't I seen and heard enough of Stan Klack's treachery to understand, if I had wanted to, that I was no longer in friendly territory? Didn't he put his hand around my throat? Then why wouldn't he stab me in the back? And, in turn, why would the others he was enmeshed with stand with me and Ron, rather than stick together as the unified "money" that was trying to stave off a huge loss?

I should have somehow anticipated the moment that just transpired. My Megabucks strategy was quixotic, it was fantasy. My foray to Montclair to see Meryl Streep was a step in the right direction, but I had plenty of experience along the Earth's Best journey to know that that one step would fall short, unless it was destiny to find the proverbial needle in a haystack on the first try. And it wasn't and it was predictable. I should have networked more on my home turf, the natural-foods industry. I should have mobilized myself to get the company out of Stan Klack's clutches the day after he grabbed me.

I had seen the many boulders and snags, but I had missed the obvious in my ride down the Class 4 rapids. The water had been disappearing. Now, the ride was over. It wasn't all of a sudden, but in that Belmont building parking lot, sometime in early March 1989, it felt like it was. I was hurt and bitterly angry.

In a matter of minutes, Ron and I were driving down East Avenue on our way to the India House restaurant. What else could we do but eat delicious food?

For hours that night, I lay in bed playing over and over again the content from the meeting in Rick's office. I beat myself up for sharing with Greg the gory details of Earth's Best's travails and giving him the inside track to use against Ron and me. I confided in him because I thought he was on my team and I was on his. But this was naïve. Greg's team was the investors in North Atlantic Venture Capital. His bread was buttered by what he returned to those investors, not by honoring and abiding by what he said to me. If Earth's Best had failed, would Greg want to stand in front of a jury of his peers defending his commitment to me, a no-name with no résumé? Or would he rather testify that he took all reasonable precautions by insisting that an "experienced" CEO take the helm before the big bucks came in? Greg was protecting his ass. His reputation was on the line. He played it safe and he played me.

I think there was another way. Greg could have just been honest with me, in a private meeting, and laid it on the line. He owed me that. He could have taken care of his business and taken care of me as well. It would have been a very difficult meeting, but I believe we would have survived it. What I can say with certainty is that a genuine relationship with Greg did not survive that so-called emergency board meeting. Why would I ever trust him again?

There really wasn't much for Ron and me to talk about. We were crystal clear that we didn't want to be the cause of Earth's Best demise. And we both agreed that the company would almost assuredly fail if I refused to resign. It was checkmate.

Use It or Lose It

There was some consoling clarity regarding the picture that surfaced. Ron and I had created the canvas that Greg, Stan Klack, Ken, and everyone else who was engaged with Earth's Best were painting on. It was our vision, values, and determination that were now creating their opportunity. We were the leaders. They were followers. It was our inspiration that they had latched on to. They knew what it was like to risk money, but Ron and I knew what it was like to risk everything. We knew we were the creative force behind Earth's Best, and that knowledge would always keep us at the top of the company, regardless of who called himself president.

No one could take away our accomplishments. There could be twenty presidents, but we were and would always be the only two founders of the company. I think Ron and I saw this now for the first time, and it helped to inflate us a little, after a very deflating moment.

The next day I resigned my position as the president of Earth's Best. After this difficult moment passed, Greg and the board tried to make some amends, or so it seemed, to take some of the edge off the bad feelings. I remember discussing the payment of our long-overdue retroactive salary increases and the job description for my new position as executive vice president of grower operations.

My resignation was a condition for the $6-million venture round, but it did not close it. Greg still had to seal the deal with the other venture companies. There was still, as it turned out, a lot of negotiating to do to finalize the multitude of terms and conditions. What would the net cash-in be after the closing costs and meeting the outstanding payable obligations that had been the bane of my existence? Our accrued back wages, for example, totaled around $38,000 by this point.

All of this old business made Greg and the venture investors uncomfortable, and understandably so. They wanted the fresh cash to pay for the way forward, but arguing that the past was the past (as did Leo in our failed Geneva, New York, effort) would not stick this time, because it wasn't true. Organic Farms was a creditor and a key supplier still hanging out there for more than $100K. They couldn't be blown off as the past.

The financial pressures began to shift from my shoulders to Greg's and the board's. I kind of liked the new dynamic. A series of meetings followed with Greg, Rick, Stan Klack, and on occasion some of the other board members. The dramatic content of two of these meetings still sticks with me. In one, Rick and I met to discuss a smorgasbord of issues concerning human-resource matters. The subject of accrued vacation and sick days was raised by Rick.

"Arnie," he said with that knowing look I had seen so many times, "the human-resources committee met and adopted a 'use it or lose it' policy regarding accrued vacation and sick leave." "When did this happen?" I asked, beginning to feel that Ron and I were the targets of this new policy. "Last week," Rick said matter-of-factly. "The company has to trim all soft excess obligations." "I assume Ron and I will be grandfathered in and that this new policy will be in force going forward," I said without flinching. "No," came Rick's response, "You made the choice not to use it." "That's crazy, Rick," I said, feeling that familiar heat enter my face. "You know Ron and I could not take time away from our job responsibilities, and for that matter, the board even asked us to defer taking vacation." "I am sorry, Arnie," Rick said, "a policy is a policy, and neither you nor Ron will be treated differently than any other employee."

Rick and I argued for some time, but in the end Ron and I lost about eight weeks of accrued vacation. I remember thinking that Rick's position on this matter didn't seem like Rick. I knew he could be a hard-nosed business guy, but I always thought of him as fair and reasonable. I respected him. This outcome was not fair and reasonable. I didn't know who he was anymore, and I certainly didn't respect him for imposing this position, rather than supporting Ron and me.

RON:

Now I knew what a coup felt like. I don't recommend it. I guess the lost vacation time should not have been a shock, but it was because it was so unfair.

All of our potential financing eggs were in that Greg Leeds–North Atlantic Venture basket. The recapitalization process had dragged on and on. Arnie and I allowed ourselves to be lulled into dullness. Or perhaps it was the five years of living on the edge that had dulled us. In any case, we jumped when we were asked to jump, bent over backwards, crawled on cue, and became entirely dependent on a one-deal scenario.

Dependency leads to vulnerability, and vulnerability leads to a loss of leverage and power. Arnie and I believed we were on the brink of success. The Alar broadcast was a nail in the coffin of the old, "just trust us," conventionally-grown-food paradigm. The sun was rising on organic foods, and we were the only baby-food company in the United States facing east.

Nonetheless, it was the brink of failure that Arnie and I had been running from, and we just wanted the running to stop. Greg Leeds had seemed like a good bet. He was a Vermont guy, or more accurately, a guy who lived in Vermont. He seemed earnest and appreciative of Arnie and me as founders.

Maybe he was, but asking Arnie to step down as president was a pretty grim sign of appreciation, at least as we read signs, especially since it was a condition for Greg getting into the deal. And colluding with our board to corner us with that kind of ultimatum felt underhanded.

I could barely sit in my seat during that meeting. My blood was boiling. My nerves were bare and synapses chaotically firing and failing me. I felt betrayed by the original board members who showed us no courtesy or respect, but rather complicit silence. It really hurt.

The argument could always be made for commending the board for doing the tough but right thing. In my view they were doing the easy and wrong thing. De-muttifying doesn't take a lot of courage because conventional wisdom supports the pedigree model. Arnie wasn't stuck on being president. He had worked his ass off to fulfill the vision we had for Earth's Best, not to call himself president and stick it in his résumé.

Greg and the board could have taken a collaborative and partnering approach instead of using the threat with which they offended and alienated us. But relatedness (as in genuinely relating to Arnie and me) would require some faith or trust that doing the right thing is worth a try.

Arnie and I could have walked out of the room and spurned the spurners. It's hard to say how that scenario would have unfolded. But we didn't have the nerve or the heart to take that kind of chance. The investors would be in for almost $3 million in bridges very soon. Would they have folded their hands when greeted with our outrage and just shrugged off the loss, or would they have rolled up their sleeves and tried to figure out a way to work with us?

These were "the" turning-point moments for our futures with Earth's Best. These are the moments I have relived over and over, wondering "What if?" And there were to be many more such moments lying ahead for us, where Arnie and I could have tried to steer a different course and chosen a different destiny.

But as it was, we would not be the agents of the company's failure. In turn, however, we would also be forced to recede from being the agents driving its success.

Make the Damned Baby Food

I never ever would have predicted the focus of such a meeting would be on Arnie. He was dead center in the investor-financing loop. Other than the Apple Blueberry–inventory deal mess, his success at managing an impossible cash-crisis situation ethically and with integrity had been irreproachable. His connection to the organic-food suppliers was tight and growing tighter. He had dedicated himself to building the marketplace, and the results were beginning to show. Why would anyone think an out-of-town gunslinger was going to move Earth's Best forward faster and with more integrity?

I was a much more likely target: isolated, low bullshit tolerance, and immersed in a dimension of the company that was absolutely necessary, yet unglamorous and definitely unfriendly to suits, ties, and coiffed hair. At that moment, however, I was "it" for the company's production future. And the board and Greg Leeds knew they would never get Arnie to bump me off the log. So, the first nudge went to Arnie. I'm sure it was a well-considered calculation. The board bet on our loyalty and commitment to the company. It really was a low-risk move on their part.

Arnie and I now placed our high hopes for Earth's Best on the new guy, Paul Mipperman. If this was what it was going to take to finance the company, then we were ready to get on with it. I remember how eager I was to make things work. I wanted Paul to be successful. Why not be a powerful three-legged stool instead of two? But it wasn't to be.

More bridge financing followed Paul's entry into the company. It set into motion my bare-bones restart plan, utilizing a minimum number of production employees focused on our new product introductions. The glaring problem was that our equipment was not well adapted to the new demands, and a day's production always fell short of what we needed. Not to mention it was such a grind for everyone.

Despite the imperative to produce, I, inexplicably, had no support. All I could do was write Paul memos pleading for his attention to the production issues and establish a paper trail reflecting my efforts. He obviously didn't know what to do, so, short of relating to me personally and professionally, he just stonewalled me like I wasn't there.

Paul and Arnie were also frequently away from Pond Lane through the spring and early summer of 1989, chasing the venture deal down, bobbing for plums, and God only knows what else. All that mattered to me was that the whole operating business fell on my shoulders in their chronic absence. I was *it* for executive leadership. I felt resentful and inadequate because I couldn't do my job and really couldn't do their jobs either. Paul seemed clueless about the needs and the lapses accumulating every day. Arnie knew I was drowning in an impossible situation. The stress for me was the worst it had ever been.

Ken and Bob D. were beating the bushes to expand sales, expecting me to do the easy part, make the damned baby food. The new products were critical. In March of 1989 the plant was producing only 250 to 350 cases per day. Tens of thousands of pounds of Rick Ihler's carrots were sitting in the coolers waiting for their chance to become Earth's Best. I couldn't get to them fast enough, and the losses started to mount.

I knew exactly what needed to be done. The equipment list and costs were laid out in detail with the rationale for each purchase or modification clearly outlined. The applesauce cooker had to be overhauled. Kevin, a.k.a. "Red," was waiting for the green light to make the cooker a double-decker with variable-speed screws to push the apples through quickly and the sweet potatoes and carrots more slowly, yet continuously. The ELF filler had to go. Enough! We needed a rotary-piston filler. Carrot production on March 22 and March 23, 1989, was 356 cases and 338 cases, respectively.

One word captures this scale of production output: "disaster."

Hot Under the Collar

ARNIE:

The second dramatic meeting that I distinctly remember occurred in Boston at the ARD office. Greg and I had flown down together to attend to some of the outstanding deal details. By this time, Greg was sweating these details and feeling the heat of our pressurized timeline. It was nice having him in the soup pot with us, although it didn't improve the flavor.

Since the ambush in Rick's office, I was naturally suspicious and untrusting. Greg had a halting, hemming-and-hawing style of speaking that tended to turn on itself until I had no idea what he was really saying. I didn't remember this difficulty in our earlier meetings. Was it there from the beginning and I missed it because of selective hearing? Or was it a post-ambush reflection of a lesson learned by him, not to confide in me? In any case, I listened very carefully to every word with that suspicion in tow. My guard was up and Greg knew it.

I never liked these trips. For starters, I was back in my Halloween costume. I was an outsider. My mission was not return on investment. It was return for babies and their planet, Earth. Don't misunderstand, I liked and wanted money. I had "bottom line" genes too, but they stayed subordinate to this greater longing for a world that made sense, beyond money. By necessity then, I had to consciously filter out this bias from emotionally leaking into the dynamics of discussion. The Earth's Best values may have been publicly lauded for their noble intentions, but privately I think they, and hence me as well, were threatening to that coveted bottom line.

I walked into the ARD office, post-ambush, and was greeted like a partner, but I felt more like the lone fish in a tank looking out at the strange air-breathers. There was now that divide that Ron wisely wrote about earlier, between me as an entrepreneur and them as institutional investors. We were and would always be different species.

I remember the ARD partners zeroing in on all of the soft closing costs. I was all for reducing these costs and enthusiastically contributed ideas on how to accomplish this. Eventually, we got to a line item that never occurred to me would be considered a "soft cost," the $38,000 of accrued back wages due the founders.

During this part of the discussion, I became a listener. I did not like what I was hearing; the gist being that it was bad form for the founders to deplete the company's resources with requests for accrued back wages. They were, in effect, calling into question our loyalty and commitment. I struggled to stifle the expletives cascading through my mind.

I restrained myself and insisted, "Ron and I were offered a salary increase to $60,000 by Greg, Stan, and the board more than five months ago, and this commitment to us was just reconfirmed after I signed off as president." After I disclosed the origin of the accrued-salary line item, I imagined hearing the pleasant sound of Greg's teeth grinding.

Courtney and company did not pursue the matter further, but clarified that if they became investors, their cash-management sensibilities would not support that type of consideration to us until the company was solvent. I kept my mouth shut, but had no intention of letting Greg off the hook.

The cab ride to Boston's Logan Airport started out quietly. Greg and I sat side by side, watching the city sights, and waiting to see who was going to break the ice and initiate the discussion about the accrued wages. As far as I was concerned, it was a done deal, and the onus was on Greg to break the silence. He did as we neared the airport, and it didn't take long for both of us to get hot under the collar.

As we exited the cab, he was giving me this lecture about adapting to the quickly changing investor environment and doing what founders do—make sacrifices to secure their company's future. I let him know that no one had to remind me about making sacrifices and that the back wages had been promised to us by him. There was no escape.

Being in a busy public place helped to keep the lid on the conversation, but by the time we were walking down the long corridor to the gate, our civil behavior had evaporated, and we were in a full-blown shouting argument.

"Arnie," Greg exhorted, "I never guaranteed you the accrued salary, it was a goal and regrettable." "Greg, stop!" I interrupted. "You cannot backtrack here. You agreed to pay Ron and me back wages, and you need to pony up." I loved using venture-capitalist jargon when speaking to one. By now we were both walking fast and pissed. Greg plowed ahead, "The money just isn't there, Arnie." Pleading poverty to me was dead on arrival. I fought the urge to lose my cool entirely. "Funny you should say that, Greg. Why is it that there is all kinds of money for Stan Klack to go on junkets?"

To Greg's credit, he did not answer. Instead, he corralled his frustrations and suggested we pick up the conversation when he had more time to think about the matter and we were both less tired. I agreed, but wondered if he was going to dump the issue on the board and try to escape through the back door.

The jury was still out on this one, but based on what had happened to our unused vacation time, I was not optimistic.

Ron and I Were Not Honeymoon Material

It was time to start confronting the fact that I was no longer the president of Earth's Best. The guy Greg apparently handpicked, Paul Mipperman, had not impressed me in our first meeting. It would have been a lot easier to accept my diminished status as executive vice president of grower operations if the new guy with his hand on the tiller was a dynamo. He was not.

Strangely, yet at this point predictably, Ron and I were excluded from the interview process that led to the decision to hire Paul. How stupid was that? It was beyond my comprehension that I would not be given the opportunity to weigh in on the various candidates vying to be my replacement. My role as president was in the past, but my role as a board member was ongoing. My opinion should have been sought after and my voice heard.

As you can see, I was very slow to grasp my low status on the totem pole. I persistently didn't get that I was on the outside looking in. Maybe it was some sort of spatial-orientation problem.

I have no idea why the investors picked Paul to lead Earth's Best. I suppose superficially he had the look—a tall, lanky guy with an angular face, a full head of graying hair, and a résumé that included several years of CEO experience. He must have sold himself as a take-charge hired gun, and Greg bought the package.

Ron and I expected there to be a honeymoon period, where Paul would lean on us and get to know the lay of the land inside the company, before he leapt into precipitous action. But I guess there either wasn't money for a honeymoon, or perhaps more likely, Ron and I were not honeymoon material. From the beginning Paul frowned at our suggestions and ignored our input. He was a "fire, ready, aim" sort of guy, who shot from the hip. That style of decision making can be spectacularly successful when you're intuitive, inspired, and inspiring, or just plain lucky. Paul was none of these.

The Mipperman era was underway, nonetheless. Ron and I did not want to undermine his authority by being spiteful or rebellious.

We encouraged everyone to give Paul a chance. He had a big adjustment to make and a culture to integrate into that was very much Ron- and Arnie-centric.

Unfortunately, Paul chose the heavy-handed and polarizing approach in his formative meetings and exchanges with key personnel. It seemed like an odd decision to me. Every relationship he touched turned rancid, especially with the old guard like Bob D. and Jon Corcoran. I recall Paul even alienated Ken Morris, the company's legal counsel, which took some doing. In relationship to the production room, it was as if Paul didn't exist. He never had any standing, even when he cut Ron out of the reporting loops and inserted himself instead.

The only traction Paul ever found was with Stan Klack and Ken. And this was a natural alliance that reflected the divide between Ron and me on one side and those who wanted to neutralize our influence, or wanted us out of the picture entirely, on the other side.

The Rah-Rahs Would Not Last for Long

The conflicts and unpleasantness with Ken escalated during this time. His Colorado location made it difficult to keep tabs on his daily efforts. I didn't think Paul was managing him well, and it was impossible for me to ignore the situation, just because I wasn't president. I was still a founder, and I would continue to be engaged in a hands-on way whenever I thought it was needed. But hands-on did not mean control.

I remember hearing that Ken had purchased $250 worth of booze for our sales brokers. This infuriated me. Hard liquor was completely inconsistent with the idea of Earth's Best. Organic wine would have worked, an organic fruit basket, absolutely. But hard liquor? I wanted to skewer Ken. Little things like this made the pain of losing control of the company more poignant.

The investors were all rah-rah, and Stan Klack was all lovey-dovey when the $6-million inaugural venture round finally closed. I knew it was coming, and it was discouragingly late. Many of the creditors, who in good faith worked so closely with me, had to wait far longer than anything I promised. The whole stretch of time was a misery. The production room was largely unimproved, and the rah-rahs would not last for long when the production numbers that Ron was generating were matched up to the high-octane growth plan coming down the pike. Grower relations had suffered because of long-drawn-out payments, and I was not proud of how far short we had fallen from what I had initially envisioned, and planned for.

Now that our cup runneth over with cash, Paul and Ken started to execute a very aggressive sales and marketing plan. The venture guys were not focused on the bottom line at first, but rather the top line—the gross-sales number. These *were* good instincts since making money would confound and disappoint them in ways beyond their imagination. If their thinking was that a big top-line number would prove both the potential of the marketplace and their brilliance for making such a risky investment, they were half right.

After the venture close, it was an all-out mad dash to expand sales and secure the organic-food supply. Both Ken and Paul knew how to spend money, and they did with gusto, until the company's cup started to runneth dry.

Lassies for Everyone!

Somewhere during this May to June 1989 time frame, the jury returned a favorable verdict on our accrued back wages. It was unexpected. I felt uplifted and guilty at the same time. I could see the company's decision making charging its way toward a massive hemorrhage of funds. Yet, I also understood or rationalized that $38,000 in total would not be the cause of the company's failure. Ron and I had each been making $30,000. Now we were at $60,000.

Though it may sound ridiculous in today's dollars, that check for back pay changed my life. For the first time, I had a cushion and wasn't living week to week, check to check. I actually opened a savings account. It was the little things that I noticed about not being near broke that I particularly enjoyed. Now I could go to the India House with Anne and Cora and not stress out about ordering three mango lassies. Lassies for everyone!

The Wrath of Ron!

RON:

Instead of rolling up his sleeves and engaging with the production people, Paul boxed himself in as just being another "suit." He probably thought the problem was me, and when he got his own guy in there to run the show, as plant manager, there would be a transformation of attitude and all would be right with the world. If so, that was a pipe dream. No one wanted Paul and the company to succeed more than me. I wanted harmony and a sane life. But inexplicably this intention was either invisible or just ignored. This was the dilemma I faced every day.

Thanks to the sheer willpower and determination of the production crew, average case production climbed to 563 cases per day in May. You cannot imagine the dedication of these people. They were constantly compensating for the nonaction of the company's new leadership. I urged everyone to have patience and put the best face possible on why improvements were stalled. But I wouldn't lie or cover Paul's behind. No one would have believed me anyway—especially Barb, Pam, and Belinda, the triumvirate, who could smell executive bullshit well before it walked into the production room.

One May day, from out of the blue, I learned that Paul had directed Nancy and Lynn from QC to report directly to him and not to me. No discussion with me or heads-up courtesy. No thought to how this change would be perceived within the production room. Wow! This action was just plain stupid. If there was ever a person to have as a focal point for quality control, it was me. In any case, at the end of the day, Nancy and Lynn would always report to me. I trusted them. They trusted me. In reality, other than being president, Paul's existence was inconsequential, as far as production went, except in his own mind.

I had never received a hint of a complaint about my performance as an employee. But somewhere deep down in the bowels of Earth's Best, a plan was under way to extricate me.

Paul soon announced in an open company meeting that I would no longer be able to sign checks greater than $100, except for freight. I was stunned by this.

No insult or clueless act should have surprised me at this point, but it did over and over again.

A new plant manager was, in fact, on the drawing board. I was all for this addition, if it was the right person. It would take a lot of pressure off me and finally allow me to focus on bigger-picture issues like the future product-development direction and West Coast production, which was clearly a necessity unless we were determined to kill ourselves with spiraling freight expenses.

Those six million big ones showed up at long last, and a crazy, greedy feeding frenzy soon followed. The venture mandate was to grow the company exponentially, instantly. Buy every apple out there. Corner all the raw materials and run like hell.

The new money must have been flaming hot because it burned big holes in the pockets of these new guys. They would show the founding mutts how to grow a company, for real. I thought they were completely out of control and reckless. Idiots! We would soon start to accumulate massive raw-material inventories that we had no way to use given our production capabilities. There were big plans to add a second shift and plenty of talk about new equipment, but sadly no leadership to execute much of anything. Earth's Best was like a party balloon let loose, streaking about here and there, expending itself like there was no tomorrow.

My hands were tied. I felt no resignation, just anger.

Paul introduced me to a prospective candidate for plant manager named Mike. Certainly a nice enough guy, but definitely not the right guy for Earth's Best. I was as diplomatic as I could be with Paul, urging him to keep looking for a stronger leader with baby-food experience. Paul promised me another meeting with Mike before a hiring decision. Paul lied and admitted as much. He hired the guy and completely cut me out of the reporting loop. Mike would report to Paul.

Mike knew a lot about infant formula, but not much about baby food. Paul was president, and as far as I could tell knew nothing about our production. He *did* know how to put on a hairnet, which was to his credit.

Everyone in the production room was baffled by these events. I stood by and bailed Mike out day after day. I wanted to give him a chance. And he was earnest and he tried, but Earth's Best was just not the right fit. It was too much of a start-up, too chaotic and unformed. Mike was in way over his head. It happens, but when you don't know that it's happening, it can be really dangerous.

I saw things falling apart, maintenance left undone, inputs from the production supervisors ignored, morale in a free fall. I kept trying to prop up Mike and fix things behind the scenes, but I could not stop the unraveling. I persisted in trying to warn Paul that we were getting into trouble in the production room, but he ignored me. I pressed Mike to get on top of the accelerating problems, but either he could not or would not.

A tragedy would soon be the result.

A Dark Horse Named Botran

ARNIE:
At Earth's Best on Pond Lane in July 1989 there was no warning rumble of thunder, just the phone ringing, and then the bright, blinding flash of light and ensuing shockwaves that ripped through our offices.

Beth leaned into my office and said, "Ken's on line one and he is fuming." "Perfect," I thought as I paused to gather my wits before picking up the phone. "Hi, Ken," I said cheerfully, "What's the good word?" "Botran, Arnie! Why the hell do we have Botran in our sweet potatoes? It's some kind of fungicide, and we are dead meat!" I had no idea what Botran was, but I did not feel panicked. I knew we tested every raw material we used for pesticides. There had been no positives with any sweet potatoes we had run, ever. "Ken," I said, "take it easy and tell me exactly what's going on."

As Ken began to explain to me the emerging nightmare that would immediately capture our undivided attention, Ron walked into my office to sign off for the day. I gave him the thumbs-down sign and motioned for him to take a seat. I scribbled "Botran in our sweet potatoes" on a piece of paper and watched the shock and disbelief sink in.

Ken's tone was accusatory, as he spewed out the details of our newest crisis. The Albany, New York, newspaper had published a story that Botran, a fungicide occasionally used when washing potatoes, was found in a jar of Earth's Best sweet potatoes. Apparently, the New York State Department of Agriculture and the local FDA office had conducted the test and were now investigating the matter. As I listened, I realized everything we had worked for was dangling by the thinnest of threads.

I asked Ken to fax me a copy of the newspaper article and if he had any idea how this news story became one, before we had even been notified by the FDA. He had no clue, but wondered aloud if someone with influence and a motive was behind the news release. I wondered also. There had to be a force with an "interest" behind the way this was instantly publicized.

I was livid by the time I finished the call. Ken blamed me, attacked me, and questioned my integrity. It was bad timing. We agreed to talk early the next morning and hash out a damage-control plan. It was going to be a very late night for Ron and me as we began to investigate Botran and how to best react to what would become a nationwide wave of negative publicity for Earth's Best.

The next day I notified Paul, the board, and the employees about the FDA problem. Everyone was stunned that a fungicide was allegedly found in our sweet potatoes and that the company was coming under attack. We all thought we were the good guys on the white horses, and now, out of the blue, there was a dark horse named Botran.

Ron found out that our lab did not test for Botran. Obviously, this was bad and unexpected news. We always knew and accepted that we couldn't test for every chemical out there. But this intellectual understanding offered no solace as we confronted the feelings of a real contamination situation.

I called our sweet-potato grower, Peter Ventro, a wonderful southern man with a drawl as slow as molasses in January. "Peter," I said, "This is Arnie Koss from Earth's Best." "Hello, Mr. Koss, you callin' about the potatoes? The crop's not lookin' that good, Mr. Koss, the weather been just awful." "No, Peter," I said in my best Yankee twang, "What can you tell me about Botran?"

"Mr. Koss," Peter answered a little defensively, "Botran isn't used much these days." I interrupted. "Peter, do they use it where you wash your potatoes, before shipping to us?" "Well, Mr. Koss, I don't think so. All the equipment is washed real well before my taters are run through." Peter paused and went on. "Mr. Koss, is there a problem?" "There may be, Peter," I replied. Peter cleared his throat and said, "Mr. Koss, we're real careful with our potatoes, we know they're for the babies." "I know you are, Peter, and I appreciate your efforts. Let me get back to you when I have some more information." "Okay, Mr. Koss, and thank you."

The next day, the mail delivery included an officious-looking letter from the Grim Reaper, a.k.a. the FDA. But the notice did not deliver the dread I was expecting. It explained that their analytical testing revealed a trace amount of the fungicide Botran in a particular date code of sweet potatoes. The trace found was in the parts per billion and well within the California organic standard. So we, in fact, were not in violation of our organic claim. Rather, the letter went on to explain that we were in violation of our label declaration that claimed Earth's Best was "pesticide free." There was good news in this bad news notice. The issue we were facing was a labeling problem and not a health and safety matter or a breach of our organic claim.

Of course, we also had to understand how Botran found its way into these potatoes and plug that hole forever.

I thought for a moment, "pesticide free." We don't have that on our label. I ran out into the plant to find Ron and a jar of sweet potatoes. Ron thought the same, that we didn't make that claim, but we did.

Ron and I stared at our Earth's Best label as if we were reading it for the first time. It was the same sensation I've had when driving a well-worn route and suddenly seeing a prominent topographical feature, like the presidential sculptures at Mount Rushmore, that were inexplicably invisible to me for years. How did we ever miss this?

It was never our intention to make a label claim of pesticide free, although it was clearly our internal standard to be pesticide free, to the extent that our analytical testing allowed.

Ron and I intended that the narrative on the label declare that the food in Earth's Best was grown without pesticides. And this was true, although the FDA would soon require that we specify that it was "grown without synthetic pesticides." However, there was no question about it, as Ron and I studied the label. We knew what we meant to say, but as it read, our label claiming "pesticide free" could be easily misconstrued.

By midday, I was fed up with knocking heads with Ken on how best to diffuse the crisis. The local media were calling to interview me, and some of the national media were already replaying the Albany newspaper story. Ken was screaming that our brokers were screaming for direction. The situation was spiraling out of control.

Ron, the production guy, jumped in, took the lead, and crafted a comprehensive response. It included a widely distributed press release that hammered home the point that there was no safety issue, but rather a labeling violation. Our organic claim was not compromised.

We were well within the California organic standards. A voluntary recall would be announced to address the label-claim problem and not for any other reason. Earth's Best was delicious as ever, safe as ever, and organic as ever.

We created a script for all our brokers, sales reps, 800-line operators, and executives to use when discussing the matter. A simple, clear, unified response was essential. The problem was a label violation, not a health or safety issue, and we would repeat that countless times during the next few weeks. My mantra to everyone at EB was, "follow the script."

We discovered that the Botran infiltration had resulted from our potatoes being rinsed in a washing plant that we had been told had not used any Botran for several years. Apparently, though, some residue persisted in the machinery and ultimately made contact with our potatoes. Improved analytical testing sensitivity, in the parts per billion, picked up this inadvertent contamination. The incident made us better.

Fortunately for Earth's Best and its new investors, Ron's response worked like a charm. He articulated the strength and integrity of our program to the trade and to people like Ken, who had a serious moment of doubt about whether Ron and I were for real or just two slippery sales guys. The crisis subsided. Sadly, Ron's contribution was lost on Paul, Ken, Stan, Greg, and the EB board. He was strangely invisible to them, yet so prominent, in my estimation.

RON:

When everyone else is going crazy and panicking, it is easier to be the calm, instead of joining the storm. At least that's how such dynamics play out for me. The Botran news focused me, while the hysterics of people like Ken played in the background. Not that hysterics were uncalled for. The crisis threatened to knock the Earth's Best planet out of orbit.

I instantly carried the burden of feeling guilty, as if the problem was my fault and reflected a lack of diligence on my part. I figured I would be blamed. In reality, I had been increasing the sophistication and the breadth of our synthetic-pesticide screens all along the way. Even when the well was dry, there was no compromise. Arnie and I were aiming for perfection. We were dedicated to minimizing the contact children had with these chemicals.

I knew perfection was impossible, but I never expected to be imperfect.

Although I needed a reprieve from Paul and Mike, even dealing with those guys was preferable to this Botran news, though not by a heck of a lot.

Arnie is very flattering above. I just did my part. Ken and Bob D., who were on the front line dealing with our customers, did a great job. Jon Corcoran handled the public relations with aplomb. It was a team effort. That's one of the beautiful things about a crisis: It can bring people together, who on any other given day, may be standing far across the divide. A crisis can melt ice, build a bridge, suspend distrust, and create community, where separation and dissonance prevailed otherwise . . . for at least a moment. Botran brought us all together for that moment. Grace shows up when it is least expected.

As the crisis waned, it was hard not to wonder how the FDA discovered this Botran with their very random pesticide-testing program. The fact that the news was broken in the *Albany Times-Union* eventually led us to a tip that it was Beech-Nut who had somehow instigated the matter. Our product introductions, in fact, had started to erode their shelf space and market share, especially in their home turf of New York State. It wasn't such a stretch to imagine that such an encroachment was cause for them to again take the gloves off and try to hurt us.

Instead of fighting us, Beech-Nut should have joined us. But in truth I would not have welcomed the association. The ersatz-apple-juice disgrace that landed their top executives in jail was still a fresh memory for me.

The Botran incident demonstrated just how pervasive and insidious synthetic pesticides are and what a mountain we would always be climbing in order to protect babies. I also realized that all of the distractions and energy I was expending with regard to Paul had caused me to take my eyes off that Earth's Best ball that I had been so devoted to. My worrying and focused neurosis served the company in ways that most people missed, because that was the point. Anticipate, prevent, protect, improve, and keep things as ripple free as possible. Botran reminded me how big my job was and how endangered my sense of doing it had become.

Ron Lived Across the Tracks in Production

ARNIE:

As Paul became more comfortable in his new role as CEO, there was a discernible difference in the way Ron and I were being treated. I was a board member, Ron was not. I was pulled into various investor meetings and strategic-planning sessions, and Ron was not. I was being offered more pay and option opportunities, and Ron was not.

Ron lived across the tracks in production, and he was clearly viewed by Paul and the new money as expendable. I tried to compensate for these inequities by entering into side agreements with him, sharing equally in any advantage offered me. Otherwise, there was no way to soften the blows for him. I was an A-team member. Ron was on the cut list from the squad. It was agonizing to witness.

This unfolded as it did for two reasons. Ron's position in the production room was perceived as more pedestrian than mine. As such, he was replaceable and less valuable. And since he wasn't even a credentialed production professional, what was he then to the outsiders like Paul, now positioned as insiders? My role was less tangible, but my elevated profile as the past president and conduit to the growers and marketplace insulated me momentarily from being the short-term celebrity write-off that Ron had become.

The other angle to this part of the story reveals that Ron was less tolerant than me in accepting the nonsense that was being dished out by Paul and others. He spoke his mind constructively and bluntly challenged any authority that deserved it. Ron left no doubt where he stood. I, on the other hand (and I think retrospectively to a fault), tried to finesse my way through the manure pit. By nature, I apparently was predisposed to assume a more diplomatic posture in the heat of a moment. It's not that I didn't have my line in the sand. I did. It was just that my line was more of an arc.

"Arnie," Beth said, "there's some guy on the phone who says he's from the *Enquirer* or *Esquire* or something like that magazine. Should I tell him you're in a meeting?" I've heard of that magazine, I thought. "I'll take it, Beth. Maybe they want to do a story on EB." As I clicked the line-1 button, it hit me that the *Enquirer* was a trashy, sensationalist tabloid. I could already see the headline, "Martian Babies Raid Earth's Best Baby Food Plant." "Hello, this is Arnie Koss, can I help you?"

"Mr. Koss, I am calling in regard to *Esquire* magazine's annual awards selection. Are you familiar with *Esquire*?" "Somewhat," I responded, "but I am not a subscriber." The caller was poised and professional. "That's okay; this is not a solicitation, Mr. Koss. Each year, *Esquire* recognizes six people in their respective professional categories who have contributed in a meaningful way to making the world a better place." "That's great," I said, "but what does this have to do with me and Ron?" "Mr. Koss, someone has nominated you and Ron to be a candidate in the *Esquire* business category."

Even though I didn't understand the significance of this, I was stunned into silence by the idea that somewhere in this world, an anonymous someone was recognizing the contribution Ron and I were making. "Mr. Koss, are you there?" "Yes," I quickly responded. "Mr. Koss, I am calling to verify you want to be considered for this award and that if you do, we will be sending you an info packet and questionnaire." "Yes," I said, "it will be an honor to be considered."

I shared the highlights of the call with Ron, but in the grand scheme of things, the news fell pancake flat for him. I understood. Ron was grappling with the production woes and was trying to convince Paul that we needed to immediately invest in plant improvements to have any prayer of delivering on Ken and Bob D.'s escalating sales projections. At the time, our annual production capacity was approximately 250,000 cases, and our planned production needs were at least twice that.

The reason for the logjam was simple. The equipment needed would cost at least $300,000, and Ron was some kind of nobody in Paul's eyes.

Concurrent with our need to improve the Middlebury plant was the piercing recognition that sourcing organic apples on the East Coast did not have a bright future, at least in the short term. True, there were plenty of apples growing from Canada all the way down to Virginia, but hardly an organic one to be found. The combination of apple scab and coddling moth quickly overwhelmed most organic apple-growing ventures. There were dedicated pioneers out there trying to improve root stocks and identify pest-resistant varieties, but at the time, the available quality and tonnage did not approach the 2.5 million pounds I was trying to source for the fall 1989 harvest.

The economics of transporting sixty trailer loads of processing-grade apples from California to Vermont was also a bankrupting proposition. It was absurd to ship our number-one raw material east and a growing percentage of our finished goods going west. I could feel the company drifting westward. The obvious solution was to find a West Coast apple processor. What was not so obvious was who out there would even consider jumping into the baby-food business with us?

The focal point immediately became Sebastapol, California. This was obviously the best organic apple-growing region in the United States. We already had Jordan Smith and Paul Kolling on board as growers in the region, and the potential acreage in transition to become certified organic would be able to meet Earth's Best needs for the foreseeable future.

The Barlow Company came into view. They were a prominent apple processor in the area, but they weren't running many, if any, organic apples at the time. I had already been down this road with J.R. Wood. Despite all of the inconveniences and extra demands to run organic, the profit margins for a processor like Barlow would prove to be pretty darned enticing. And with apples especially, since Earth's Best, even in the early days, had volumes that were viable enough to run in a commercial processing facility.

Organic made sense to everyone. Tom Barlow was a practical businessman. He saw the opportunity Earth's Best presented and agreed to work with us. "Rolaids" is not the only way to spell "relief." At the time "B-a-r-l-o-w" worked pretty well for me.

Once the relief passed, there was the daunting reality to face. Ron and I toured the Barlow facility, knowing that the only way it would work for EB would be if we invested in an entirely new processing line for juices and purees. Add the fact that our Middlebury plant was also in such desperate need of upgrades, and the sensation was dizzying. This was a very different kind of dizzy from the one induced by the swivel chair.

Multiply the above by the mountain of apples we had just bought (that would soon be sitting in bins), and you had a situation you wanted to be in, but wish you weren't. We were already well into July of 1989.

We would be getting started impossibly late on the new Barlow processing line. Would there be the kinds of delays that disabled our Pond Lane start-up? Would that mountain of apples I was envisioning have to be liquidated again, pennies on the dollar, or would it be juiced and pureed into Earth's Best? The good news was that we had the money now in hand to invest in Middlebury and develop Barlow. The bad news was that the company was running wild without any effective manufacturing management.

It delights me to recount that in this crunch-time moment, Paul and the board had to do the unthinkable. Who was going to figure out how to design, coordinate, and install everything needed at Barlow in no time flat? Oh yeah, the guy they needed was inexperienced, a self-described mutt of a man, an expendable guy who had been unceremoniously elevated to stand squarely on the chopping block. Yup, they needed Ron. Ron was their go-to guy. Unbelievable!

RON:

Unbelievable is right. As the Botran hubbub subsided, my situation with Paul took an unlikely twist. Although I no longer could sign checks greater than $100 or have QC officially report to me or have a direct hand in overseeing the production, I was suddenly now being asked to single-handedly establish a West Coast production line for our apple products, including juice.

On the one hand, I was being stripped of my responsibilities and standing, presumably because of my lack of experience and/or job performance. But on the other, I was being asked to take on a huge responsibility, requiring experience and expertise that I supposedly either didn't have or barely had.

I wasn't being asked to replicate Pond Lane in California. My task was to create an Earth's Best production line within an existing apple-juice-processor's line—without batching kettles or retorts of any kind. I had never done anything like this.

The management schizophrenia at Earth's Best was beginning to reveal itself. I'm in. I'm out. I'm in. Why?

    (a) Paul became desperate as he began to comprehend the enormity of the raw-material inventory that was being built juxtaposed to our anemic processing capability.

    (b) Paul was clueless in his understanding of the task he was asking me to steward.

    (c) Paul wanted me as far from Pond Lane as possible.

    (d) All of the above.

I have chosen (d). I was chomping at the bit to get a break from Paul's cluelessness and the stress of watching Mike fail in the production room. I couldn't drive from the backseat, and it was heartbreaking to watch the people I loved in that production room being forced into the regressed business-as-usual model of white-collar management versus blue-collar worker. What a silly charade that is.

My greatest angst at Pond Lane was around safety and complying with our wastewater-discharge permit. I didn't have to worry about quality. I knew that regardless of Paul or Mike, the women and men in that production room would protect the quality of Earth's Best. Everyone was a whistle-blower in waiting. I could imagine Barb, Pam, Belinda, Lynne, and Marty calmly telling Paul, "over our dead bodies," if they ever felt a compromise to quality was being imposed from the top down. I could venture off to California with at least that comfort, which was not exactly chopped liver to a guy like me.

But safety was another matter. People learn how to make do. They compensate for deficiencies in maintenance by taking chances. And if they are not embedded in a culture that expects safety procedures and precautions to be abided by, then guards are dropped, shortcuts are taken, and dangers abound.

I expressed my concerns to Mike and to Paul, because I saw a certain laxness beginning to take hold. A pump that dispersed a concentrated acid for cleaning was patched instead of being properly fixed. How can you be taken seriously as a manager if you don't jump all over a breakdown like that? Unfortunately, the ball was in their court, and their snail's-pace response showed that they obviously didn't get the significance of their responsibility for the safety of others.

I left for California sometime in early August 1989 knowing I had done everything possible to get those guys to wake up. They were both arrogant. They both knew better than me. They didn't.

Pride and Adrenaline

Since I loved "big" challenges, my journey to the Barlow Company in Sebastapol was incredibly exciting and intimidating. On one hand,

I didn't know what I was doing. On the other, I knew what had to be done. I believed I could be successful, because I was surrounded by information and know-how. I just had to engage it and skillfully direct the energy toward completing the task.

Here was my approach. Stay out of the way. Use my natural curiosity and neurotic tendencies to the advantage of the project. Work as if my third-grade teacher was standing behind me. Make no assumptions. And when I had Tom Barlow and his production-facility people, plus the Shaw Brothers (fabricators), and "Red" and his crew back in Middlebury, what couldn't be done?

It was fun. It was complex. There was money to spend to do it right the first time. If everything went perfectly (small p), the job could be done in ninety days for $260,000. The time frame was most critical since we were soon going to have an avalanche of apples knocking at our door. It felt like the whole company was hanging on me. That was not a new feeling. The difference now was that I felt like I had to heroically compensate for the choices of people like Paul who thought they were better than me and, worst of all, didn't grok Earth's Best.

But pride and adrenaline can accomplish amazing things.

Barlow was on line in ninety days for about $350,000. (p)erfect. I felt a great sense of accomplishment. Earth's Best now had, relatively speaking, an instant West Coast production facility for its apple products. Finally, we would have the long-awaited Earth's Best apple juice. The hemorrhaging of cash to ship apples and our finished goods across the country would finally begin to ratchet down. We had taken an important step toward financial viability.

Clearly, California production was inevitable for everything (e.g., carrots, sweet potatoes), but it never occurred to me that the necessity and permanence of our production in Middlebury, Vermont, would soon become otherwise.

We Were Not Just an Annoying Mosquito Anymore

ARNIE:

While Ron and I and Pond Lane were busy plummeting down this slippery slope toward what turned out to be oblivion, Earth's Best was making remarkable inroads in penetrating key mass-market areas. Ken and Bob D. are already fixtures in our story, but there was another force out there reshaping the baby-food world.

At first I thought Ken's decision to retain Michael Rice of the Sterling Rice Group to develop EB's marketing programs would leave me even further isolated and marginalized. How bad could it get? Michael and Ken were old Colorado cronies, and I naturally anticipated that what was coming my way was another stop on the same negative trajectory that Paul had so proficiently brought to the company.

But unlike Ken and Paul, Michael turned out to be a listener. This was so refreshing and unexpected. And he didn't play favorites. It was fun to have Michael in a meeting, because he could call Ken on his nonsense and bluff, and battle him as a marketer, with supporting data and prior experience.

When selling (Ken) and marketing strategies (Michael) are well coordinated, beautiful things can happen. In a remarkably short six-month time frame, Earth's Best captured 6 percent of the dollar share (for strained baby food) in the Denver market. But what really seals the deal for impressiveness is the fact that we did it with only eight flavors or SKUs. Believe me, the Big Three were taking note of these numbers. We were not just an annoying mosquito anymore; we were becoming a force. As we gained dollar share, one or all of them were losing it.

Michael turned out to be a difference maker for Earth's Best. He had his head screwed on right, when the board had its head in the clouds. He made Ken better, and he made my life easier, because I could trust him. Michael was a straight shooter. By now you know there weren't too many of those around me back in the late summer and early fall of 1989.

Blind Spots

RON:

I flew back and forth to California several times during this Barlow phase. Upon each return I was greeted by an incredibly intense and frustrated Middlebury production team whose members were at the end of their rope. It really was predictable, but it was also exasperating. There was no respite from my rescuing role. Instead of a harmonic symphony reflecting a well-financed company with new equipment in place or on the way, there was dissonance and grumbling in the production room, warehouse, and QC lab.

The problems really weren't complex at all, and in my mind the solutions even simpler:

(1) Help people do their jobs efficiently and safely. Help them be successful.
(2) Listen to these people.
(3) Facilitate the actions that are needed.
(4) Clearly communicate and frequently update.
(5) Check in frequently for feedback.
(6) Avoid avoidance.
(7) Assume nothing.
(8) Practice random acts of kindness, like the bumper sticker says.

Eight steps to glory. That's it. Problems subside. People smile. Trust is built. Divisions blur. That's all Mike and Paul had to do to both avoid the stink-eye that often greeted them when they entered the production room and to relieve me once and for all of the role of returning hero. And they couldn't or didn't do it.

Those steps might draw a big yawn, because they appear so obvious. But as Forest Gump might say, "Obvious is as obvious does." Paul and Mike were not dummies. The ability to truly be in relationship to others is a kind of intelligence that needs to be cultivated, if it is not found naturally in abundance. Knowing the obvious is as useful as knowing that you have to work to earn a living. It's a big step to actually get and keep a job, just as it is to actually effectively relate to others.

When I reflect upon areas where my intelligence is pretty dim, such as looking at and understanding the spatial complexities of a construction blueprint, I recognize that overcoming any deficit area is likely to require a tremendous and sustained effort. I have to spend hours trying to see what's represented in a drawing, where others see it instantly. It hurts. I can't deny it or blame someone else. I just feel stupid and inadequate. All I can do is to compensate by working extra hard and trying to be mindful to accept myself, pluses and minuses.

Relational intelligence or the lack thereof may be easier to dodge or avoid because there are obviously others to blame. In order to cultivate an intelligence, you have to somehow discover that it needs cultivating. A lifetime can therefore be lived in a blind spot, especially if there is a constant supply of people to blame. As I saw it, that's where I found Paul and Mike in October 1989: entrenched in their respective blind spots, failing to appreciate and value an intelligence they didn't know they didn't have enough of.

I find myself writing about blind spots and suddenly realize why I am.

That October Terri lost an eye. A salt-of-the-earth woman on the night cleaning crew, completely dedicated to Earth's Best, fell victim to that jury rigged acid-dispensing pump. Unfortunately, she wasn't wearing her safety goggles, which was indeed her mistake. But safety and adherence to safe-operating protocols must be vigilantly instituted and expected and re-expected by management. Mike failed. Paul failed. But I also felt that I had failed Terri. I blamed myself.

I lost control of the production room to two men who did not have the right stuff. They had risen, in my view, to a level of incompetence that was negligent and dangerous. There's nothing to finesse here. There is no kindness or rationale that I can extend in retelling this moment. Mike and Paul failed. They weren't bad people, just bad managers. They should have been booted out of the company on the express train. The nail in the coffin supporting this declaration is that weeks later, sanitation-shift employees were carrying around buckets of acid, because the correct acid treatment had run out and was not reordered. You would think that after an employee had lost an eye, management would be absolutely on top of this kind of situation.

I will never forget Paul insisting to me that everyone makes mistakes.

I'm Stuck on Ron for the Moment

ARNIE:

Unfortunately it was too early in Paul's tenure for the board to remove its blinders and get that he was the weak link and not Ron, but Paul still had his Teflon coating going for him. Terri's tragic accident should have scared them, and maybe it did, but short of criminality, like stealing, the newly configured board was not ready to backtrack on Paul as their man.

In the midst of all the good Ron was doing for EB, there was an expanding sentiment at the board level that he was a disgruntled and disruptive employee. No doubt this unwarranted perception was a result of Paul's poisonous barbs about Ron's supposed toxic attitude.

Wasn't it a wonder that such a toxic person could work so hard and accomplish so much for the company? Wasn't it a wonder that such a toxic person was approaching worship status by the production employees? Wasn't it a wonder that a disruptive guy like Ron was affectionately known as "the keeper of the flame" or the person who held and illuminated the spiritual essence of Earth's Best?

Paul ignored Ron. Mike ignored Ron. Terri lost an eye. I was so crushed to think that something I started, with the best of intentions, had led to another person suffering the horror of losing an eye. It was unbearable.

I'm stuck on Ron for the moment.

Years ago, I was watching the Big Apple Circus perform in Shelburne, Vermont. The circus would come to Shelburne each summer, and it became our family ritual to attend. I always looked forward with great anticipation to seeing the new acts.

On one occasion, there was a gymnastic troupe. This one guy with thighs the size of bridge pillars stood at the base of a human pyramid supporting the weight of at least ten other performers. While all the other members of this impressive pyramid of flesh maintained a smile as the pyramid grew, the guy on the bottom did not look as joyful. He was profusely perspiring with legs trembling. I was worried about him. The weight was too much.

In the circus that had become Earth's Best, Ron had become the guy on the bottom, and people like Paul, Mike, and Stan were waving to the crowd from their perches above. I remember Ron's franticness and was worried he was going to crash and burn from the stress.

For all intents and purposes, the weight of the Middlebury plant operation was on Ron's shoulders, and the Barlow start-up was piled there too. But that is not the whole picture.

Paul and the new investors were actively planning to expand the company's growth curve to near vertical. In order to accommodate this emerging and foolhardy strategy, the Pond Lane operation would have to add a second shift. We were barely keeping one shift going, and now Ron was looking at two. Who was going to pull that together? Paul? Mike? Although Ron probably had a choice, he felt and acted like he had no choice but to shoulder more weight.

I know Ron held on so tightly because Paul and Mike didn't grok Earth's Best. He wanted to protect the production employees, who were protecting the quality of our baby food. It wasn't magic that created the dedication in that production room. It was something Ron created, and it *was* magical and very special.

An incident comes to mind that perfectly illustrates the kind of impasse Ron had reached with Paul.

The QC staff—Sue, Nancy, Marty, and Lynne—had been on the warpath for some time protesting the ridiculously small area they were given to do the most important job in the company. With a second shift on the horizon and QC and product-development demands accelerating exponentially, it was obvious to everyone but Paul that they needed more space. The problem was there was only one option. Paul's office was it, and he said no way to surrendering or shrinking his space. I remember a demoralized staff turning to Ron.

Ron first pleaded with Paul and then argued that a change of heart to support the greater good would be uplifting to the entire production staff. Here was a home-run opportunity to be a mensch, not by conceding, but just by compromising. Like an impressionist painter, Ron used every imaginable color on his palette and every stroke in his repertoire to help Paul see the beauty of the picture that he could paint: "Paul the Leader," "Paul Who Sacrificed," "Paul the Staunch Defender of QC," "Paul the Wise." Paul did not see the beauty in Ron's picture, but did see that Ron was a pain in the ass who would challenge his decision making and authority to the bitter end.

And so the story to the board went that Ron was a guy filled with sour grapes. And they bought it.

The Kossmic Egg Cracked

RON:

The Kossmic egg cracked. I was so split down the middle emotionally that I couldn't keep the two halves together.

One half of me always loved seeing all of the women and men in the production room. There was the griping now, but I heard their grief and disappointment. They missed the warmth and camaraderie, when they knew it was all for one and one for all, when Arnie and I were the center of the Earth's Best universe. As the Paul and Mike era disappointedly unfolded, we all knew we had had a once-in-a-lifetime experience.

The other half knew it was over for me. I "went for it" and I had made it. I stuck with the manifestation of Earth's Best through thick and thin. My ideals were being expressed in the world, and my dreams for the organic-foods industry and babies were coming true. I had completely immersed myself, submerged myself, into the waters of life, and became initiated. I never gave up or lost my focus for long. I didn't knock myself out of the box with a mood, whim, or rationale. I never quit.

I was naïve about business and people. Perhaps I traveled more in my own world than the real one. The horizon for me had been the vision of sustainable food production on a grand scale, the love of babies, and care and stewarding of Gaia, our living Earth. I adapted as Earth's Best traveled down the road, and I became more grounded as I met the business I had envisioned. I never imagined either the high of family and community that I shared or the low of Terri's accident and the loss of control of the company's day-to-day operations.

I understood the definition of stock dilution, but not the reality of it and the feelings associated with the experience. Not since my third-grade head met that blackboard had I felt so unseen and violated.

However, there is no future living in anger. After Terri's accident, these two parts of me could no longer live side by side. There could be no peace. I could not win over the new money with my dedication and performance. They were not ready to see the mistake they made in hiring Paul, although they would. He had a golden parachute. I did not. I had a few Styrofoam peanuts attached to my butt, just in case of impact.

Any more compromise and I would have been lost. The painful truth is that I had already compromised too much.

Jousting with Walter Cronkite

ARNIE:

I was surprised *Esquire* would bother to send us a rejection letter, but there it sat in my pile of office mail. I opened it, as I did with all my junk mail, ready to peek and toss.

Shockingly, there was an invitation to attend the Sixth Annual *Esquire* Register 1989 at the 21 Club in New York City. This was a heady moment. Imagine being in the company of these names: Winfrey, as in Oprah; Jordan, as in Michael; Lee, as in Spike; Crystal, as in Billy; Lovett, as in Lyle; and Pfeiffer, as in Michelle. And then in addition to the celebrities being honored there was an amazing group of accomplished individuals: Faye Wattleton, president of Planned Parenthood; Peter Seligmann, founder of Conservation International; and Kurt Schmoke, mayor of Baltimore.

This was a surreal diversion in my day. It was a strange irony to imagine being in this kind of company, while Ron was getting shunned and shish-kebabbed and I was in daily mortal combat with Paul, Greg, Stan, and Ken. Someone up there in the heavens was having fun with us again.

Who was valuing our determined efforts to advance organic-foods production enough to nominate us for this *Esquire* award anyway? And why did they remain anonymous to us? Ron and I still don't know, to this day.

Esquire announced in their December 1989 issue thirty-nine people who are "making America a smarter, funnier, healthier, wealthier, safer, saner, livelier, prettier, all-around more interesting place to live." How strange it was to see a picture of Ron and me directly above Michelle Pfeiffer's.

It was exciting for me, but I was ecstatic for Ron. He needed to be recognized, and I gloated on his behalf, knowing that those who were so mean and condescending to him were seeing him nationally recognized for his contributions to changing the world. He was the all-star that they would never be.

The 21 Club? I pondered. What the heck was the 21 Club? And formal—did that mean tuxedo, bow tie, and scratchy shirt? This was a Halloween costume I was going to have to rent. I showed Ron the invitation. It was surreal for him too, but I knew it represented a moment of redemption. Predictably (to me), his first question was, "Do we have to wear one of those scratchy shirts?" Ron hated them more than I did.

Walking into the 21 Club all duded up with Anne, Ron, and Carley was a wonderful, unexpected moment I want to thank our anonymous sponsor for—finally, right here in these pages. I saw celebrities like Lyle Lovett, and I mingled with other unknowns like me, who were plucked from the trenches of difference making to share a magical life-affirming evening. I was surrounded by amazing stories and accomplishments, and I struggled to keep wrapping my head around the idea that I was one of them. The evening was a sensory extravaganza.

Ron and I made the rounds, bouncing from one conversation to the next as the twins and founders of Earth's Best. I remember meeting Faye Wattleton, the president of Planned Parenthood at the time, a striking woman with an obvious calm and admirable resolve. It was so energizing to be among so much talent and such a needed respite from the harshness and stresses of life within the company. I couldn't get enough of it.

At the end of the evening, Carley, Anne, Ron, and I meandered toward the exit of the 21 Club. Ron and I were striding side by side with Walter Cronkite and his wife. How odd was that? We were all chitchatting about something when Mr. Cronkite made a comment that Ron and I took exception to. I wish I could remember what the subject matter was, but that part of the memory has faded. Of course, it wasn't egregious, but our two fat heads were ripe to engage after a rare evening of adulation. Anyway, as we walked along, this debate took shape. Surprisingly, it became mildly contentious. Ron, who was capable of launching insightful zingers in a single bound, was verbally jousting with Walter. Fortunately, it ended well and at the curb.

It Was a Doozy

RON:

My dedication to Earth's Best didn't wane, but any interest in trying to build a relationship with Paul and Mike evaporated. I soon gave up on those guys. If they proved to be the "go-to" guys in this reality, I was on the wrong planet. Of course, deep down, I knew I was on the right planet, and this would soon enough bear itself out.

Paul and Mike, for all that they were not, were redirecting me back to my family and my life, separate from the company. I couldn't see this gift through my anger, but it was true. In order to move on and reconnect with the longer view of my life, I had to loosen my day-to-day grip. I wouldn't or couldn't do this of my own accord. I needed Paul and Mike. Of course, I'm not about to send them a belated thank you, but almost twenty years after this trauma and drama, I'm comfortable writing that life is mysterious and much that is, is unseen.

I discovered, as I began to come into relationship with my anger, that the unraveling of my Earth's Best life served as my opportunity to address once and for all that bitterness that I wrote about earlier, carried from one generation of Koss men to the next. The karmic thread of being screwed in business dealings was no longer a theory or a musing. It had just been reenacted. The encoded family trait was now in full play in *my* life. Now it was my turn to become angry and bitter and have righteousness take hold and calcification set in, as it did with my dad. That was the way it was playing out.

Once I saw the silver lining in the drama-trauma that was unfolding, I knew I was being given my chance to choose a different story from that of my dad and my grandfather. And perhaps, in turn, if I succeeded in at least being conscious of my anger I might not get stuck in it, and my two Koss boys, Gabe and Aaron, would be spared from reenacting the same old family story line.

Carley helped bring this awareness to me. My hurt and anger were so intense that I think it scared her. She saw the thread. I didn't want to see it or hear her, but I somehow did. If you pay close attention or actually any attention to resistance and defensiveness, you might learn, as I did, that it can be a gateway to important personal truths and subsequent opportunities.

Silver lining aside, I suffered during this time. That's as plain as I can say it. I had a constant lump in my throat, like I used to have as a child when I occasionally cried inconsolably. Not only did I have to contend with Paul's hostility and stand aside in Mike's production room, I had to watch Arnie become an insider with the new money guys. He was their favorite, now that he was safely taken down a notch.

While I was disappearing in importance, he was being offered perks and new stock incentives and greater financial opportunities. And he deserved it, but so did I. Arnie and I talked about all of this completely openly. He knew that what was happening to me was outrageous. He saw that they took a certain perverted delight in trying to divide and conquer us, but here the cold edge of their power was impotent. Arnie agreed to share every upside he was offered with me. All for one and one for all, but it was our secret.

With the lump in my throat persisting and the Barlow project on line, I immediately jumped into setting up the plan for an expanded shift at Pond Lane. The task was like a Chinese puzzle with overlapping job functions crisscrossing throughout a twenty-hour day. It was my cup of tea. And it was critical to the company, given all the produce bursting at the seams in the various warehouses storing our ingredients.

The expanded shift was planned out virtually overnight. The ELF filler was finally being retired, and the rotary Engler filler would take over. But it would be too little, too late. There was no way our manufacturing capacity, even with Barlow cranking out cases and an expanded shift in Middlebury, could approach digesting the mountain of ingredients that the first wave of venture pedigree was purchasing. Eventually, many ingredients would have to be fire-saled. Arnie and I had already made this rookie mistake. Now it was time for the sophisticated investors to make theirs, and it was a doozy, a cannonball that would just about drain the pool of money dry.

A Once-in-a-Lifetime Stroll

In early November 1989 I sent the board a memo that in effect said buy out the remaining part of my employment contract, which expired at the end of March 1990, or agree to change my position to three days a week at full pay with a focus on Barlow, the expanded shift, product development, and an analysis of an expansion plan for production. The buyout was rejected, and I can't recall if the three-day deal flew. What's most important is that I drove a stake in the ground. I expressed indignation and offense at my treatment and the resulting intolerable situation. I just couldn't take it any longer.

I didn't think I held any power with the board, but surprisingly I did. The idea of a disgruntled Ron apparently caused some concern among the investor group. I would discover this during January and February 1990 when my employment contract was theoretically up for renegotiation. Believe it or not, I was secretly hoping for a last-minute reprieve, another shoestring catch, and a new contract. Ever the eternal optimist, the child in me did not want to be rejected. He wanted to be valued and praised. He wanted to belong . . . and he didn't.

Arnie was so right about the feeling of redemption when I gazed at that *Esquire* invitation, in the midst of all of this angst and tumult. It was a jolt that reconnected me to a world apart from the rejection I was experiencing; a polar world that not only accepted me, but wanted to honor me. It seemed impossible.

The evening at the 21 Club is a blur to me. What stands out most is how happy I was to be there with Carley. I don't remember famous people. I remember fascinating ones with great stories, like Susan Spicer, a chef who was really impressing palates in New Orleans. I did feel important and did bask in the limelight. Was Oprah there? Billy Crystal, the bum, was a no-show. (I hope I'm right about that.)

I do remember sparring with Walter Cronkite. It was a surreal, out-of-context moment. I was out of context, dropped somehow into a city of eight million, walking side by side with a man I had watched on TV throughout my entire childhood. He was larger than life to me, which is why I was so surprised that he didn't tower over me, during our brief, once-in-a-lifetime stroll together. It was truly an honor to share the walk to his cab.

Paul Was Going to Win This Battle

ARNIE:

As a member of the Earth's Best human-resources committee, I naturally assumed I was in the loop regarding vanguard issues like new hires, compensation and benefits, grievances, and the development of company policies and procedures.

The committee had four members, Paul, Greg, Tony Daniels (who had joined us representing Orien Ventures), and me. Of the lot, Tony was the most approachable and outwardly sympathetic to my viewpoint. I did all I could to bond with him, hoping that he would recognize that Ron and I were not suffering from sour grapes, but rather from the frustration and anxiety of seeing the company put at risk. I had no chance of swaying the outcome of a Human Resource Committee decision without Tony's support.

At some point I realized the committee was secretly meeting without me to discuss sensitive issues—the most notable of which was what to do with Ron. I challenged this exclusion and even raised the issue with the other board members. The politics of it all was unwieldy. All these guys were amalgamated by their shared financial stake in EB. My investment was largely a sweat-equity one, and Ron was the only one that shared that variety of stake with me.

Paul, Greg, and Tony were in a predicament, because it was my twin brother and partner they had their sights set on. There never would be consensus on the matter of Ron with me in the mix, although I might have seen the logic of recusing myself, if they had tried talking to me about their dilemma. I knew Ron was persona non grata. His departure was not a question of if, but when and how.

I didn't know this for a fact, but I had no reason to think otherwise. Paul was going to win this battle.

I remember Ron's November 1989 ultimatum letter. He painted a bleak picture of Paul's performance. If his fate wasn't sealed before, it was after this communication. Ron made it difficult for the venture investors to write him off in a wholesale way. He persisted in being articulate and credible throughout. He didn't make up the story of Terri's eye. He pulled off Barlow, and it was hard not to see, through any prism, that everyone at Earth's Best loved him.

I've always wondered what it would have been like if Ron hadn't had to cope with his panic problem. It always seemed like he was on a tightrope, trying not to fall off. I had the capacity to just bull my way forward in any situation. Ron could not. He had to very carefully size up every situation and then micromanage it to stay on the wire. This is why it was so amazing that he held together as much as he did on the company's behalf—and so painful that he was not valued.

As Ron and the board hashed out the first steps of a separation agreement, a bucking Earth's Best was slowly winding up to give Paul his long overdue kick in the ass.

The Old Twin Switcheroo?

RON:

The board's verdict was, "Hasta la vista, baby Ron." No big surprise, but nonetheless, the finality was a huge, shocking disappointment and letdown. But they also played nice with an offer of a bonus, severance, and stock options. Why? Because they were nice guys? Nope. Because they wanted me to agree to extend my noncompete agreement for two years, as well as agree to not make any statements that might be viewed as damaging to Earth's Best (their) interests. Bingo!

These were easy decisions for me. I never would have done anything to hurt Earth's Best, including compete with it. But I was flattered to know that this was a concern to Paul and the board. They were afraid of me. Was I going to be the loose cannon from hell? They wanted me quiet, and they didn't want me on anyone else's team. Who developed the recipes? Who had become a baby-food-production expert? Who embodied the heart of Earth's Best and embraced its essence? Who had become a presence in the organic-foods industry? But they didn't want me.

What consoled me somewhat is that Arnie was still in the thick of it, representing the heart of Earth's Best and our interests. And of course the employees at Earth's Best, who were the greatest group of people ever assembled to manifest a noble cause, would be there everyday. They always had access to Arnie, who happened to wear the same genes as me, day in and day out. This, as you might imagine looking ahead, did not bode well for him.

As I began to feel the tide of relief creeping in at the prospect of being removed from the daily grind, I saw Arnie becoming more burdened. His contract was renewed. I would not be there. And the weight of it all would be on his shoulders. He would have traded places with me in a heartbeat. I guess we could have tried the old twin switcheroo, but my nervous system would have failed us—or my tongue. Arnie was destined to carry the burdens of an older brother, even if it was only by eight minutes.

Some entrepreneurs stay with their business for decades. They become it. It becomes them. Catch a wave and ride it to the distant shore. Others, like me, ride the wave while it's most intense and challenging and then turn and paddle out, looking for the next one. I didn't choose to turn out, but the outcome did suit my temperament, especially when confronted and confined by convention, the suffocating convention that Paul, Stan, Greg, and the institutional investors imposed.

I have often dreamt of what a longer ride would have been like. There was so much of my vision for Earth's Best that remained unexpressed as we moved into January 1990. I had a strong desire to keep going. I saw myself graduating from the production room and my intense preoccupation with it and reengaging with product development. I imagined the Earth's Best brand extending beyond baby food, even beyond food. I knew there were other vistas and steep learning curves for me at EB, with their shiny, tantalizing, slippery slopes, which could have captured my attention for years. In any case, I expected the ride to last much longer than the end of March 1990, the date of my planned exodus.

It Was Dusty in That Shark Pool

The days that followed were tumultuous. Arnie and I fantasized about a last-minute coup, demanding the board choose between us or Paul. There was a pervading sense of desperation and the need for desperate measures, but it was impossible to discern how that desperation might play out. What would happen if we actually pulled the trigger?

I watched, from an increasingly distant perch, as the $6-million venture-cash infusion virtually evaporated. How much would be enough if they just kept throwing money at wild-eyed, frenzied growth plans? Or at expense accounts that included liquor and dress shoes for work? It was as if they wanted their Earth's Best investment to behave like a high-tech one. Get in, get out, get rich—fast. They were more delusional than Arnie and me. Even pedigree cannot push a square peg through a round hole, but they would certainly try.

The life-or-death struggle persisted for the company, despite all the suits and ties and polish walking into Pond Lane. That surprised me. I thought that the days of life on the edge were history, like I was now. I didn't fully comprehend, until I saw that $6 million vanish, that money can go out faster than it comes in, even a lot of money. And despite my pedigree-snubbing rants, I believed on some level that those guys now sitting at the top of the heap would be so much smarter than we mutts who started the company.

Arnie was always exhausted and out of breath, running from fire to fire, playing the peacemaker and protector. I'm not playing him up.

He had an impossible role to play in a milieu that he had never known, the shark pool. He was always immersed in some big powwow. He would tell me stories about the conniving and agonize over how to maintain his integrity and survive the chaos that was gaining strength as the financial stakes in the company escalated. There were promises and side deals and perpetual horse trading, because the cash kept burning. New knights in shining armor would keep appearing on the horizon. And as they did and the cash kept pouring in, our financial ownership and the financial interests of people like Peter, Fred, Jeff, Jon, and David, who had all pioneered on behalf of Earth's Best in the earliest days, went the way of the dodo.

When you're in the kind of whirlwind Arnie had descended into, you really can't tell what's happening for sure until the dust settles. And it was dusty in that shark pool. Also, the front-row seat gave Arnie a great view of the stage and the actors, but a lousy view of backstage and dark deeds. I just tried to keep up with the cast of characters, listened, strategized, worried, and held out hope that we would all somehow land in place just right, the proverbial shoestring catch.

I was determined to finish strong. I mobilized to help make the extended shift work and to problem-solve at Barlow. There was naturally a buzz about me leaving the company. I had to be discreet with everyone, especially in the production room. And it was hard to do so because I felt alone with the truth of why I was leaving. I had to portray it as a mutual decision and pretend to be positive. I had to keep my hurt and anger to myself. I could do it or appear to do it because the quality of the energy in the production room was my highest priority.

Yet, I think it's also fair to say that I was also not a very good actor. I read my lines correctly, but my eyes told the real truth for anyone who really cared to look. I couldn't hide anything from Barb, Pam, Belinda, Brian, Lynne, Marty, or Jim. So much of what we said to each other all along had been written on our faces. Fortunately, they also knew what was most important at Earth's Best. They all carried on, and soon it would be easier than we ever imagined.

One piece of good news that was developing as the hourglass emptied on my tenure was the exit of Mike from the company. I can't recollect the timing of the event, but I know he's not in my going-away-party picture. Fortunately, Rick Keller is.

Based on everything you've read up till now, you probably wouldn't bet much money on the likelihood of me paying a compliment to either Paul or anything associated with Beech-Nut. I had an aversion to all things Beech-Nut back then. Of course, condemning an entire company for the actions of a few was unfair, but I'm not perfect, and this was my predilection.

Either way, Rick Keller moved from Beech-Nut to Earth's Best at this time and assumed the position of plant manager. Paul made the hire, and it was a good one, a great one. I knew he was the right guy the first time I met him. He had an open countenance. He was a listener. He carried authority, but was not authoritarian. He was respectful and appreciative of what Arnie and I had created. He was secure within himself, and I felt confident that the production management of Earth's Best was finally in good hands.

Of course, the true test would be the thumbs-up or down by you know who. Barb, Pam, and Belinda pointed their thumbs skyward with smiles.

There was a little bit of sweetness in those last days, because I could relax. I learned from Rick and he learned about the idiosyncrasies of our products and our equipment from me and the smiley three. Rick would quickly be plugging the holes left from the Mike era. A cloud had lifted, at least in the warehouse and the production room.

Here's What I Said

I could now indulge myself by connecting to my sadness and the change that was going to culminate with my going-away party. To Paul's credit, he supported the party idea. It was important to recognize the moment and send me off in style. There were a lot of feelings about my departure. It's hard for me to convey the place that I had grown to hold in the company.

I remember anticipating that I would be expected to make some sort of speech. It wasn't that I didn't know what I wanted to say. I didn't know if I *could* say it. I worried that my nervous system would not be able to hold up under the stress. I feared I would literally pass out, or in some way fail to keep my vulnerability cloaked (as I had always been able to do). So many different levels of my experience and life issues were converging at the same time.

Because time marched on, all I could do was go along for the ride and hang on and hope that I would survive, literally. Again, if you haven't suffered from panic attacks, this description might seem over the top, but it's not. This was my inner experience in early March 1990.

The party was held March 30, 1990, in the warehouse, and everyone was there. I was thirty-nine years old plus one day. Lots of children, including Gabe and Aaron, were there. It was festive, but a heaviness also hung in the air. I was going through the motions because the moment was like a bad dream. How could I be the one who was leaving and Paul the one who was staying? I felt humiliated by the way I was exiting. I had lost the battle. It was a victory party for Paul and a wake for me.

Fortunately, the warmth and good spirits of the employees would win the day. The outpouring of love and appreciation overwhelmed me. Their recognition was life affirming, affirming of *my* life and the bond that had been forged as we had traveled the path through a wilderness that we miraculously survived. The humiliation I had been feeling began to shift, crumble, and fall way during that party.

I felt grateful, proud, even triumphant. No one could ever take away my successes. Or diminish the best part of Earth's Best, the men and women who worked there. I received a plaque that was signed by all of the employees and that stated, "To the Best Friend and Boss Anyone Could Have Had." My heart melted.

Here's what I said.

The best part of Earth's Best has been working with all of you. The experience of knowing you and really loving you has presented me with one of the major lessons of my life. You know, people would always say to me, "Ron, you cheer us up, Ron, you're always smiling." But the nicest thing about it was that, without expecting it, you cared about me and we sustained each other.

It's not a small thing—maybe you've felt it in your family. But to have this experience in the workplace is very special to me, and I'm grateful because I leave Earth's Best knowing that it really does pay to love.

The other thing I've learned is that dreams can come true. I pursued Earth's Best to the extreme. I started out thinking, come hell or high water, I'm not going to give up on Earth's Best. And then, the high waters of hell came, and I thought, I have every good reason to give up. I mean, my father can't call me a schmuck, Carley won't say I'm a quitter. I really could justify giving up.

But I didn't. I have a lot people to thank for that. Now I have had the satisfaction of seeing that dreams can come true. And even though I'm leaving the company, I don't feel like any less of my dream has come true, because, after all those years, Earth's Best is in the world.

The last thing I want to say relates to something I read last night about Richard Nixon in *Time* magazine. Looking back on Watergate, Nixon said: "In retrospect, I should have set a higher standard for the conduct of the people in my administration. I did not. I played by the rules as I found them. Not taking a higher road than my predecessors and adversaries was my central mistake."

I think that Richard Nixon's lesson is our lesson. We

can no longer just play by the rules. Our world is in trouble. The challenge of our time is for each one of us to find "the higher road." As I used to say to you in some of the worst moments, "keep your eye on the ball." For me, "keeping your eye on the ball," is to always stay in touch with what you feel in your heart.

Thank you very much. I'm very touched by all this. I hope that you all work together to make Earth's Best everything that it can be.

— PART FIVE —
Ron Is Gone

Store Your Nuts, Guys!

ARNIE:

Things are quite murky as I reflect back on the first half of 1990. I think, as you will see, this is because chaos and turmoil ruled.

Ron was gone. I felt so alone and so angry at the board and Paul for orchestrating this unfathomable demonstration of shortsightedness. Ron was Earth's Best's operational glue and the employees' favorite. To mess with Ron was like messing with family—in the close-knit company sense.

In the same moment Ron was being pushed out, the board was doing its best to pull me in. My salary was raised to $88,000 with a 20 percent bonus upside. I was offered more stock options and extra options for each attended board meeting. It felt like they were trying to make me their floozy by liquoring me up with cash to keep me stupid and compliant. It wasn't a bad strategy. Anne and I were ecstatic about building our savings account by the thousands each month.

Yet at the same time, my entrepreneurial self was adamantly opposed to being offered this level of salary and bonus. Paul and Ken were making even more. The company was burning cash like it was a mad dash to get the last dollar conflagrated. There was the hope of improved gross margins, but you can't deposit hope and pay bills with it. It was the time in the company's life to conserve cash, perform, and prove itself. This sounds pretty basic, but that conservative, commonsense level of thinking and relating was not yet engrained within the company's venture-board culture. I had a very uneasy feeling about the spending, but I took the money.

Why wasn't conservative cash management engrained? I had been obsessed with it. I had lived with anticipating the sheriff at my door. I had strained and stretched to make payments to our creditors and lived with the angst of always falling short. I assumed "the money" was loose with their money because they had so much of it. It's hard to imagine desert life, if you're surrounded by freshwater. Controlling hundreds of million of dollars in investment capital gave them a certain swagger and immunity from vulnerability. But it also left them without the much-needed street smarts of an average squirrel. Store your nuts, guys!

The Mist No Longer Did the Trick

A certain "groupthink" infected the board, and the result was a possessed, almost giddy mood and exaggerated sense of power and control. Ron and I had already experienced our own version of this, sans the millions; the lesson being that power and control are elusive, with or without brute cash in your pocket.

With Stan Klack now as board chairman and chief persuader, the venture investors were locked in on the blue sky. The $6-million sales plan for fiscal year (FY) 1990 sales was on track, although the cash-out to keep it on target was hard to ignore, as in scary. FY '91 called for almost doubling sales to $11.9 million, and FY '92 sales were being projected at $21 million. The old euphoria mist must have been imported into Pond Lane from Anaheim.

Any vestige of invincibility had been well beaten out of me, and the mist no longer did the trick, owing to years of excessive inhalation. The board mania made me very nervous. I knew that behind the collective chest beating was a deep-seated fear and that the stampede could drop dead as fast as it was set in motion.

The board mandate to buy everything organic in sight reflected their frenzied attempt to preempt the greatest perceived threat to the company's future: competition, especially from the Big Three—Gerber, Beech-Nut, and Heinz. In effect, buy everything in sight and stifle anyone else looking to get in for as long as possible.

I must admit it was freeing to sign contracts without obsessing about every penny. But the purchase numbers were so big and so out of line with what we had done that this felt like a strange limb to be climbing out on. Strange, because I had never been on a limb that I knew couldn't break. Fresh venture money was supporting it. Even so, the limb was far too high and I'm not even sure it was attached to the tree.

Who Were These Masked Venture Men?

Moods have a short half-life. The consequences of my spending showed up in a board-meeting agenda item. Paul reported the inventory buildup was draining the company's cash reserves. Air was leaving the balloon faster than it was coming in. I knew all too well what it was like to plan to be the exception to some inviolable rule. Even so, I wasn't sympathetic. I didn't pretend to be all-knowing. The venture money did, and I expected them to be.

The translation was quite simple. Earth's Best would need more cash again —soon. In our Tru-Vision days, the suggestion that $10 million of working capital would still be far short of what was needed to break even would have been preposterous. But it was fact. And we weren't even halfway there to what the company eventually needed.

The explosive growth strategy caused the company to start raising an additional $2 to $3 million in the form of convertible subordinated notes. This was far in advance of what had been projected. It wasn't that the need for more capital wasn't anticipated by Greg and his compatriots; it's just that the expectation was that EB would be further along. As I saw it, this development played to the advantage of the venture players. They had the resources. They knew they would be going deeper. The fact that it was sooner rather than later was of little concern, at least as I read the tea leaves, because sales and market shares were impressively growing by region. All of the top-line business trends were favorable. And yet because the company was still a relative fledgling, they could leverage that vulnerability to effectively beat down the financial position of those already on the sideline.

They needed me from time to time to help convince the old guard that half a loaf or a hundredth a loaf was better than none. And I went along fulfilling that role because I thought it was true. But it was ugly, because it was wrong. Those who took the greatest up-front risks should not have been diluted mercilessly. And they were. The unknown was always how many new rounds of investment would be needed. And my assumption and the premise of all my earnest lobbying was that it couldn't go on forever. But it did.

The VC are the bad guys in this story. It seems cliché to demonize them and paint them darkly. I have no trouble doing this. But curiously, the Earth's Best venture board members and key players were very likeable people.

Courtney and Charlie over at ARD were professionals who had seemed fair-minded and genuine about relating to Ron and me. Tony at Orien Ventures always impressed me as an excellent listener and an engaging communicator. Gerry Smithe was the lead guy for Vista Ventures, and he too impressed me as a smart, low-key guy, oriented to a working relationship with me rather than an adversarial one. So how did that portfolio of venture investors coupled with Greg at North Atlantic Venture Capital (whom I did not like) and Stan Klack (whom I did not like) lead to the undoing of the heroes (and many others) of this tale?

I don't know. It's a mystery to me. Even with their loyalties committed to their respective firms, I never imagined what followed.

Ron's share in the company was on its way down the toilet. That was a given. But mine was not; at least that's what I wanted to believe. To an objective observer, I was in the swirl of the bowl too; maybe a little higher up in the vortex, but definitely going around and around and down.

True, I was being promised the freshest of stock incentives to keep me energized, but, as you will soon see, fresh stock during this time period had a shorter shelf life than a loaf of bread. I knew our financial ownership was a shadow of its former self, but I took comfort in seeing how much worse it could be (if I was also on the sidelines with Ron). I thought the situation was bad, but salvageable. I was still a player, albeit a minor-league one.

One consequence of my frantic splurging to round up all of those grower commitments was that other organic-foods companies perceived my efforts as greedy and threatening. Earth's Best was suddenly acting like a big, clumsy oaf, and although I was very concerned about the impact, it did not appear that way, because I was snapping up everything in sight. If there had to be someone in this crappy role, I'm glad it was me. I couldn't control the volumes and poundage that were being demanded by the board, but I could control the tone of the transactions and the interactions. Once again, the situation was bad, but not as bad as it could have been.

There was also good news. EB's expanded appetite for certified organic produce spelled opportunity for those who were still in the conventional arena, but were closely watching the organic value-added trend. Was organic a fad or the future? My purchasing in early 1990 was craziness for the company, but perhaps an indicator for many growers who were still trying to answer that question. Maybe early on, the organic premium we were paying seemed too good to be true. There was skepticism and doubt. But the demand for organic ingredients was exceeding the supply, and Earth's Best was doing its fair share to make sure that was the case.

By all appearances, in the spring of 1990, Earth's Best was a company fueled by fresh venture capital, stalking the blue sky by executing a precipitous growth plan, and burning cash like no tomorrow to do so. Now consider this.

Even before Ron was gone, sometime in February 1990, discussions were initiated to sell the company to Ralston Purina, the owners of Beech-Nut. I can't speak to the genesis of this development because, although a board member, I was plainly outside the inner circle that first considered it. The negotiation was under way when I found out. A Beech-Nut sale made no sense to me.

"Pedal to the metal" and "Get out of Dodge" were simultaneously in play. How was this possible? Here's what I imagined: In a more reflective, less manic moment, the way forward looked perilous, perhaps even overwhelming, to the venture players. Maybe writing more checks and going deeper would be a not-so-fantastic voyage down a bottomless hole. Maybe baby food wasn't as tasty as it looked, even Ron's recipes. Maybe an early and not-so-graceful exit would trump a later and possibly embarrassing one. Selling to Ralston Purina wouldn't look so bad, even if the return on investment (ROI) was less than expected.

In mid-February, I had sent Greg a letter challenging the wisdom of selling to Beech-Nut as well as the troubling idea of having Beech-Nut pack up to 250,000 cases of EB on a contract basis. Nightmare of nightmares!

We had just invested almost $400K at Barlow and were on track to improve the Middlebury plant with Rick Keller's assistance. Now the investors were contemplating spreading our production out further with a company that appeared to have been openly hostile to Earth's Best; a company that had a less than distinguished reputation (ersatz-apple-juice scandal), and its own issues with financial instability. Where was the Candid Camera? Who were these masked venture men?

A Pair of Shoes Pushed Me Over the Edge

The nonsense would not quit. The board, behind my back, began discussing a product-line extension with Beech-Nut that included meat products. This matter should have been directly in my purview as VP of grower operations. And not to be petty, I *was* a board member. This was a double whammy. I was incensed when I found out. Certified organic meat didn't even exist back then. I was surrounded by misguided subterfuge. Beech-Nut also did not have Rotomats, a quality advantage we proudly touted in our sales and marketing literature. Earth's Best was headed in the direction of becoming "Earth's Good Enough." I doubt the name had been trademarked.

The board's discussions with Beech-Nut's VP and director of

consumer-products business development may have reflected some well-calculated business strategy. I was oblivious to it. I saw "not-entrepreneurs" who weren't grokking what they were "not." I heard confusion and felt the stifling of panic. It was way too early for a May Day distress sale of Earth's Best. Fortunately, sometime in March of 1990 (about when Ron was leaving) as I recall, the Beech-Nut buzz fell mysteriously silent.

I appreciated the panicky feeling and the urge for an exit strategy and liquidity. But Earth's Best did not need its board to run from it. The company needed management and a steady hand. The moods and flip-flopping back then reflected the chaos of trying to figure out how to move the company forward before competition set in and concurrently how to maximize or at least salvage the investment.

Just to give you the full flavor of the time, the board was also talking about expanding Earth's Best into Europe and Japan. Like I said, it was turmoil.

Too bad Paul remained or appeared to remain in the venture comfort zone. My disgust with him was complete and uncontainable. The board seemed determined to ignore his awkward stumbling and the obvious mismatch with the company's ethos. They had completely misjudged the value of Ron, choosing to believe Paul's condemning characterizations. And now, despite Paul having uncannily shown no signs of life as an effective manager of money or people, the smiles and pretense persisted between him and the board. The stench of the superficiality made me sick.

Interestingly, a pair of shoes helped push me over the edge.

Ken's expense report was sitting on my desk one morning. I still wonder who put it there. A line item on the report included a pair of expensive dress shoes. I felt a wave of rage. Shoes don't usually have that effect on me. The early investors' sacrifices juxtaposed with Paul's purchase of expensive shoes for Ken was just too much. I confronted Paul. He feigned surprise and then defaulted to indignation and dismissiveness. I was very familiar with this passive-aggressive tactic. But these shoes got stuck in my craw. Paul and Ken made for a toxic stew in my cookbook. Add a pair of shoes and it was a threat to national security. I was obviously very ripe for the decision that followed.

Virtually no time had passed since Ron had said his good-byes, and now I was ready to join him out in the pasture. I could no longer endure the broken process I was in with Paul and the board. I was fed up with being excluded and treated like an afterthought. And maybe more than anything, I was exhausted from feeling powerless. The Beech-Nut prospect had alienated me. Ken's shoes followed my hard feelings about the gifts of hard liquor to the sales brokers. What was it going to be next, discount coupons for ChemLawn? I notified the board that I was resigning. What I did not know is that the board had secretly met in February sometime, again before Ron left, to set a plan in motion to call for Paul's resignation. They were a bunch of busy little beavers, weren't they?

"Arnie, I Want You to Co-manage"

Obviously, a heck of a lot was going on behind doors closed to me. You can see even more clearly now why the Beech-Nut interest was so tantalizing to the venture capitalists. In the midst of all the aggrandizement and fantasizing, the company was a mess, although the top line was still on the rise.

The board's response to my resignation letter was swift and brilliant in a diabolical sort of way.

Which board member do you think made the first contact with me after my letter was passed around? If you guessed Rick, you guessed right. It was no accident that they pushed Rick into the point position to bring me back into the fold. Rick and I had been through a lot, and it was understood that while we were not buddy-buddy, the relationship was not as dysfunctional as it was with Stan and Greg.

Rick urged me to meet with him and Stan at the Sheraton in Burlington. He teased me with a reference to some big changes on the horizon that included a change in my role with the company. Of course, I was intrigued. But I could not imagine what they could possibly say to sway me to reconsider my decision to resign.

A few days later I was in the moment at the Sheraton. I had no positive expectations. I'm sure my body language presented an unmistakable predisposition. Fed up and cynical captures it pretty well. I was done.

Rick was the warm-up act, and Stan patiently waited until he thought there was enough social lubricant squeezed into the conversation to take over.

"Arnie," he said, "I know we haven't seen eye to eye on a lot of things, but more than ever the company needs you to succeed." I could barely listen to Stan, and I'm sure he knew it. He leaned toward me, his raspy, hoarse voice muted to almost a whisper. "Arnie, the board has voted to ask Paul for his resignation."

My eyes widened, and for the first time since I had arrived at the Sheraton I gave a damn. In a monotone I responded, "When?" Stan wasted no time with, "Immediately." "When?" I demanded, detecting a slipperiness to Stan's answer. As Stan began to respond, I could feel an edge creeping into his demeanor. "Look, Arnie," Rick interrupted, sensing the tension developing between Stan and me. "At the next board meeting, Paul will be asked to resign or be fired."

I wanted to let loose and express my delight at the news, but I remained stone-faced. I knew that showing any sign of emotion might be used or leveraged later on to exploit me. Stan and Rick had both taught me how hard the "hard" could be in hardball. And although I didn't know it at the time, the ball was going to get harder.

"That's right, Arnie," Stan said. "At the board meeting, and we'll make the announcement of your return at the board dinner." "Stan," I said, playing the moment as best I could, "Why would you presume I'm withdrawing my resignation?" There was a sudden silence that enveloped the space we were sitting in. It was becoming obvious to Rick and Stan that this wasn't the Arnie they were used to railroading and manipulating.

Stan's face broke into a smile. He was ready to lay down the wildest of cards he had been holding in his hand. "Arnie, I want you to co-manage the company with me until a new CEO is identified." Rick was smiling too, as if he knew such an offer would be irresistible to me.

These guys were shrewd and they were right.

It's not that they really wanted me back. It was more like they were stuck with me. They still needed a founder on board to commiserate with the old money and to look good to the trade. I stood for something. They still needed me to tell them what was and what wasn't Earth's Best. I served as a security blanket of sorts. No one else could, now that Ron was gone.

Ron was stunned by the double-barreled news that Paul was headed for the exit and that Stan had offered me the opportunity to co-manage EB. He smelled a rat. I was more of the mind to smell roses and take Stan's offer at face value.

Arnie, You're in a Snake Pit

RON:

I didn't realize how out of shape I was. I guess those endless days of no exercise took their toll. I found myself mourning and celebrating at the same time. I had found a life and lost one. I felt guilty not being there in the production room and for my absence in the pressure cooker with Arnie. Emotionally, I couldn't cut loose, but physically I did.

I had missed my children so much, and somehow through this amazing web of circumstances and choices I was finally at home with them on The Land planting a garden and thanking my lucky stars.

I didn't realize how much I had been locked into a life of mobilized coping and how much living I had set aside. A phone call from Arnie would shoot Earth's Best back into the foreground. My reflexes and mobilizing energies were instantly at the ready, but there was no trench available for me to jump into, and all I could do are the things that can be done when you're sitting on the sidelines. I tried to offer Arnie advice and perspective. I tried to pep him up. I fumed and I worried.

The ongoing stock dilution was very threatening and depressing. The tendency to avoid the prospects of my financial future was strong in me, but fatherhood challenged that tendency. I could see the future being lost, and I seethed at the willingness of the money people to set no limits on how much they would take away from others whose shoulders they now stood on.

I no longer saw it as degrees of hardball because there's a certain misplaced prestige associated with hardness. It was weakness. They were playing the game the way they were expected to play, but they had the free will and the capacity to choose differently.

Arnie kept telling me about rewards and stock options for this and that, and I kept asking him if they had put their promises in writing. The short answer was usually no. The long answer was an excuse. Things were too chaotic to formalize the upsides, but Arnie had their word.

This is why I smelled a rat and Arnie smelled roses when the co-managing offer was made to him. From the view out in the pasture, Rick's and Stan's word meant nothing to me. I couldn't figure Rick out, but he definitely hadn't been an ally of late. Stan had never been an ally. He was a foe. But Arnie stubbornly just wanted to believe that they would do right by him.

I understood his longing. It's like the longing of a child for his or her world to be fair and painless and filled with unconditional love. Was this just Arnie's naïveté?

Arguably, yes, but it was also Arnie being Arnie. He didn't wear two hats, one as the loving husband, father, and man of values and integrity and one as the kick-ass, ruthless business person. Arnie was the same everywhere in his life. Morality and relatedness were not compartmentalized such that they fit at home, but not in the workplace and his professional life.

Arnie kept bending over for the board beyond the bounds of ordinary compromise. He kept assuming that if he pretended to be on the team, kept pleasing and acting like an exemplary team player, that he'd be assimilated into the roster as a walk-on. Wishful thinking ignores contrary results. The board met without him at will and excluded him from key decisions as if he didn't exist. Arnie had witnessed plenty of their treachery, including the meeting at the Sheraton, where the stabbing of Paul in the back was announced in a raspy whisper.

"Arnie, you're in a snake pit. Protect yourself, protect us." He knew it, but he didn't believe it. He did push to get the various promises made to him in writing, but he didn't wield his power, such that it was imposing and effective.

I was not immune from the same hope Arnie held. I wanted the same wonderful world he wanted. I also was prone to thinking that just maybe our Earth's Best story would have a fairy-tale ending that included us riding in the victory parade.

What I knew for certain was that Arnie was doing his best. I wasn't there to do mine, and even if I was, he would have been stuck figuring out how to dance with these two-hatted creatures wielding the money.

I did miss my old life at Pond Lane, but I loved my reclaimed life at home. The two crab apple trees the employees gave me at my party were newly planted. Somehow it helped to care for them. They brought me instantly back to the best part of my Earth's Best experience, the people. (And now, twenty-plus years later, those two trees still do.)

Say No More, You Conniving, Low-Life Scum

ARNIE:

I did not have to wait long to find out if my shaky optimism in Stan and Rick had legs or not. The board dinner at the Café Shelburne was only hours away. In theory, Stan would announce Paul's departure and my expanded role to co-manage the company.

I parked my car in front of the café, took a deep breath of the cool, crisp Vermont night air and centered myself in anticipation of my first slow dance with Stan, the other company co-manager.

Fortunately, I had arrived late and missed the foreplay—schmoozing and downing a drink or two. One by one, each board member greeted me enthusiastically. Everyone seemed to be in a good mood, and I did my best to join in and go with that flow.

But I didn't trust the flow because it wasn't mine. If it had been, I wouldn't have been cut out of all those secret meetings.

As we all migrated away from the bar and toward our tucked-away table in a more private area of the restaurant, I was comforted by a confirming observation. Paul was nowhere to be seen, and therefore I could inch a step closer to believing he was history and I was not. This surprised me. I was waiting for the shoe to drop. Maybe Ken had FedExed his new pair for the occasion.

After ordering, Stan began to speak to the congregation of assembled directors. "Thank you all for coming," he began. I listened attentively as the side conversations subsided and everyone directed their attention to Stan.

"First, I want to announce that Arnie has withdrawn his resignation." Everyone at the table nodded and looked at me with adoring eyes. I watched Stan shape-shift into a strutting rooster. He had just rounded up and penned in a guy he had grabbed by the throat. "As you all know, Paul will be leaving the company in two or three weeks." Say no more, you conniving, low-life scum. Paul was supposed to be already in the past tense as president of EB. That was the deal Stan and Rick presented to me at the Sheraton.

I remained silent as Stan continued his sermon. "Arnie and I are going to work in partnership to manage the company until a new CEO is identified. Once that is accomplished, Arnie will continue on as the executive vice president of grower operations."

As I munched on my salad, I began to think that the news was not all bad. At least Stan acknowledged I would be co-managing the company with him. That was a big step. The fact that Paul would linger on for another couple of weeks was disappointing, but I could roll with it. What lifted me up was knowing that a much-needed change had finally arrived. Paul was gone . . . or almost.

I had my doubts about the partnership with Stan. For one, he had some pretty big shoes to fill, as in Ron's. And two, I was plain stupid to think otherwise. If Stan had a hint of an intention to build a working relationship with me, he never would have blindsided me at the café by announcing the change in the time frame for Paul's exit. I guess I wanted in more than I wanted out, because I let it go.

Ron Was Right

Almost three weeks after the café dinner, I could no longer ignore the obvious. Stan had not contacted me once to discuss how we would co-manage EB or when Paul's last day on the job was. This was incomprehensible. I was at the office every day now, feeling entrapped by my own sense of duty and responsibility. Who else was there to run the company? It wasn't Paul, who was on his way out, but for reasons unknown to me, wasn't out. Stan had strangely disappeared. It was like the twilight zone. Arnie Koss was alone, stranded in an organic baby-food company.

Of course, I did try to find out what was going on, but whatever it was, I was kept in the dark. I just soldiered on, but make no mistake, I was at my wit's end.

Finally an explanation showed up. Stan and the rest of the board were still in discussions to sell the company to Beech-Nut!

Ron was right about the snake pit. I knew those rattling sounds I had been hearing for some time were not baby rattles, but I didn't know what to do about it. I needed the sage advice of a wise elder or mentor, but I was isolated. In theory, my dad should have been the go-to guy, but I just couldn't go to him.

Ron was right about smelling a rat. I was wrong about the roses. In a Beech-Nut deal, Paul was not needed, but as a founder, I might have been. Maybe my employment was an essential part of the deal discussions. Clearly, the co-managing offer was a ploy to keep me on ice until the Beech-Nut deal sugared out. Otherwise, I believe my resignation would have happily been accepted.

I called Ron. He was watering his crab apple trees. I wondered if I would get trees at my party.

In May 1990 I wrote my second and final resignation letter, giving thirty days' notice. I had waited five weeks since the board dinner at the Café Shelburne without a word from Stan. I think it's fair to say he proved to be the anti-partner. Paul was still apparently the CEO, and I had no reason to believe . . . anything. My letter included a request to continue on as a board member and an offer to provide consulting services to the company. The board responded favorably to both of these proposals.

It must sound odd at best (or more likely stupid) that I wanted to remain as a director, given all the preceding exclusions and my obvious status as a second-class citizen, because it does to me—almost. I should have extricated myself and ended the misery, but I wasn't ready for the separation. I couldn't walk away from Earth's Best. Despite my diminished stature, I believed that when it was crunch time on the supply side, the quality-standard side, and the early-investor side, all eyes would look in my direction for answers or inspiration. I still believed I was essential or at least important to the company's future success.

But there's also the flip side. The board said yes to me. I'm not sure if that seems as odd or stupid, but it either validates my sense of importance to the company or confirms the presence of a pretty confused group of people, probably both.

There would be no bon-voyage party for me, and sadly no crab apple trees. I think, in part, that was the downside of not making a clean break like Ron did. I was like a founder ghost, not there, but there. Nonetheless, the truth be told, I was hurt by the lack of acknowledgment and recognition when I left as an employee. I wanted a plaque, and I wanted some crab apples. I needed that nurturing, but it wasn't there for me.

A Vegetarian Alternative to Crow

Concurrent now with the board's pursuit of being acquired by Beech-Nut was an ongoing discussion with a powerful West Coast venture firm led by David Russell, of Transpac Capital Management. I didn't know how advanced the discussions were with David, but again, I would have if I had been in the same loop as the other directors. Trust me, I wasn't content to stay in the dark, but illumination was not a founder perk.

What would Earth's Best's future be? A break-even fire sale to Beech-Nut that would have guaranteed a drubbing for the early series-A stockholders; left Ron and me with little more to fight over than who would get the q-less typewriter; and end the employ of everyone at Pond Lane? Or a longer ramble down the venture path?

It may seem like everything else was standing still at the company, waiting for all of this drama to sort itself out, but it was far from it. The ingredient buying was still an ongoing fury. Sales and market share were climbing. Cash was evaporating into the opening of new markets and the propping up of the company's anemic gross margins. And I was still in the middle of it all, slowly making my way to the exit fringe . . . very slowly.

Suddenly it was necessary to compress even more chaos into the time frame, courtesy of a dramatic turnabout board decision. The euphoria bubble burst, and now there were frantic screams from the board to "Stop the raw ingredient buying."

The complexity of raising a baby-food company exceeded the collective wisdom of everyone involved. Earth's Best was like a precocious toddler whose first impression charmed the cash out of almost everyone, and whose second impression involved the dirty diapers. Success wasn't going to be as simple as knocking me out of the president's chair and driving Ron out of the company.

The brakes were slammed on, but that didn't stop what was already set in motion. Momentum translates into consequences. Eventually, tons of pureed frozen fruit would have to be sold for pennies on the dollar. As Ron noted, our first-year apple debacle would be dwarfed. The scale of that mess didn't even register compared to what I had just accomplished, courtesy of the venture group's impulsiveness.

Why did the venture bubble burst? I think it was as simple as fantasy meeting reality. The promise of the mass market was so tantalizing, but no one gets there via magic carpet. It's a grind, even with lots of money, good haircuts, and stylish suits. I imagine that Greg and the others had that terrible "holy shit" moment in which suddenly their next $2 to $3 million seemed inconsequential. It was now money chasing a mood that had fizzled. When moods replace moods, you're lost.

The lunge from pedal to the metal to an emergency stop made me a flake out on the West Coast. I couldn't explain the drastic reversal to the growers we were in serious discussions with. It was mortifying. I had to find a vegetarian alternative to crow.

Ron and I had never been in a position to have a mood swing like this one. We had turtled along, although we had to run like hares to do so. We never had the resources to cast caution to the wind and make things instantly happen through that brute cash. I'm grateful for this. The stress of having such a degree of choice would have overwhelmed us, maybe even divided us.

The board persona turned inside out. Statements like, "We are investing to further demonstrate the viability of the concept," became the jargon of choice. And there were now references to capitalizing the business on a "cash conservative" basis utilizing three-month time horizons, until a major new equity financing was completed or the company was sold. The square peg would not fit through the round hole. It looks like it should, if you hit it hard enough with cash or your head. But it doesn't for anyone.

The operative word became "retreat," but there was resistance.

Paul (believe it or not), Ken, and Stan made the case for precipitous growth. Ken was passionate. They all insisted that the company
was on track to achieve the $6-million FY '90 plan, and that $21
million for FY '92 was even realistic. The problem with those guys
was they were top-line thinkers and could not easily see beyond the
superficiality of reaching sales milestones.

Growing the top line did little to lighten the suffocating prospect of needing an additional $1 million of capital to grow the top
line an additional million. Do the math, and the company needed
another $10 million or so to have any chance of achieving the FY '92
expansion-plan objective. This was too much weight to bear without
the prospect of profitability.

Needless to say, entropy rained down during this time. Damage
control was a steady state. It was a wild ride with little amusement.

To my great relief, the Beech-Nut deal fell out of favor. I was gone.
Paul lingered longer. I lost track of when he officially left.

— PART 6 —

*The Tunnel with
No Light at the End*

Business as Usual Will Doom Us

RON:

It's June 1990. This is when I actually started to write the Earth's Best story. The stress of watching and listening to Arnie navigate his way through that chaos was unbearable. I needed an outlet and a means to start chronicling, reflecting, and processing what had already happened and what was continuing to unfold. I also thought it was an important story that needed to be told, that I needed to tell.

Arnie may have left the company as an employee, but he was far from gone. From my perspective, nothing had changed for him. He was as immersed and overwhelmed as ever. I could tell he couldn't get his bearings. How do you possibly reconcile the way he was excluded? Wasn't it illegal? Wasn't there some recourse? Maybe, probably, but there was no pause for spaciousness. Arnie was trapped inside a run-on sentence with no space between the words. I wasn't much help because I didn't see a way for him to break out.

He couldn't pull the plug on himself when the company seemed so adrift and schizoid. Our financial future was in his hands, and it seemed that there wasn't a moment when the peril ever abated. The situation was chronically acute.

Arnie genuinely liked many of the venture players, and they seemed to like him. But beyond that, what followed and what follows is just a head-scratching disconnect. Nix that earned vacation time, Arnie. Meet behind your back, Arnie. Exclude you left and right, Arnie. When there was something of real value on the line for the VC, like money and control, the relationship was "off." But when they needed him or nothing of substance was on the table, then the relationship was conveniently "on."

Arnie was not a victim, so this recounting is not about "look at what they did to me." It's a cautionary tale of look at what happened, look at what can happen, and ultimately what needs to happen if leadership is to emerge to meet the challenges, if not the crisis, of the twenty-first century.

The story now is about what happened to Arnie and the company, but the point is to wonder and question how individuals who know better choose to collectively act as if they don't. The same wonder and question applies not just to a group of venture capitalists, but to the political arena, top-level corporate management, and any other situation where the question of "might makes right" or "right makes might" hangs in the balance.

I well understand the notion that when you get into a shark pool, you shouldn't expect Flipper and his pals to show up for fun and games. At the same time, I also well understand that people aren't sharks. Business as usual will doom us. If you can walk all over someone who is working his or her heart out for you right in front of your nose, how likely is it that you can also rationalize choices that hurt people and places thousands of miles away?

The rest of the story that follows is the part I've always wanted to read.

The "Pièce de Résistance"

ARNIE:

Soon after Beech-Nut evaporated, Transpac signed on, and David Russell became the new guy at the board table. This was good news, but it wasn't all good, at least for Ron and me.

All of EB's management received additional stock options when the Transpac deal closed. I received nothing, for the obvious reason I was no longer on the management team. My employment contract had stipulated that I was entitled to 2.75 percent of the stock, post-financing. My upside was completely lost. Why wasn't I on the management team?

I expressed my disgruntlement in a memo to Charlie at ARD. I argued that my resignation was the direct result of Stan and the board reneging on their Café Shelburne promise to relieve Paul of his CEO duties and engage with me in good faith to co-manage the company during an interim period. I was severely compromised. I never would have resigned otherwise. I never would have lost those options.

My appeal fell on deaf ears. Maybe you're speculating why I didn't threaten to sue at this point or in some way rock the boat. I know that I look weak. Ron and I talked about legal action, actually frequently, as if suing were a primitive brain reflex. Our higher brains always said no. When we played it out in our imaginations, a suit always ended up a disaster flick.

The questions to reflect upon now are: What assumptions were operating for us? And were they valid? Was I in the dead center of a blind spot? Was I wise beyond my years or far too controlled and passive? Was there another path and another outcome for Arnie and Ron Koss? I still think not, but I still wonder.

With Paul finally gone and with me on the sidelines as a consultant and board member, Stan's role as chairman became even more prominent. This was hard to stomach, but now at least there were more penetrating eyes tracking his actions. He had to tighten up his act and follow the board's direction. One obvious priority during this time frame became the company's search for a new CEO.

There was one ideal candidate for the CEO position who was uniquely qualified, really the only one who had the credentials and experience to tackle the job. In September 1990 I sent a letter to Chairman Klack announcing that I wanted to be considered for the position. I made this decision to apply after interviewing two candidates the board was considering. Nice guys, but not the right guys.

I reasoned to Stan and the board that, as a cofounder, I understood the Earth's Best concept and was deeply committed to it. I made the case that six years in the trenches, senior management experience, plus being a leader in the organic-foods industry with strong ties to both the marketplace and grower universe added up to something substantial. I was thrifty by nature and a tenacious problem solver. I was their man.

I was not.

Not long after my request to be considered for the CEO position, the company hired Roger Stone. This was sometime, as I recall, in December 1990. I hardly remember Roger because his tenure with the company was inconsequential and short-lived. Of course, he came with his pedigree papers. Roger was an ex-Nabisco executive. What stands out for me is that my application was rejected. I was bitter.

Roger's appointment crushed me. Losing the opportunity to lead the company hurt a lot more than losing the financial opportunity. I felt that my capability and my potential were invisible to the board. The prejudice was palpable. My jaded read on their disposition was that mutt entrepreneurs like me, by definition, were not qualified to be serious business leaders. Entrepreneurs plowed the virgin earth and planted seeds so that those who were properly educated and a part of the elite establishment could do the harvesting and reap the benefits.

The "pièce de résistance" on this subject followed a short time later, after a board meeting at the Pond Lane, Middlebury, plant.

"Arnie," said Greg in an almost endearing tone, "I know you are disappointed about the company not supporting you for the CEO position."

"Very disappointed," I said bitterly.

"I understand," said Greg searching for a way to penetrate the dark cloud hovering directly above my head.

"You know, Arnie, you have a lot of fine qualities and you have grown immensely in the time we have worked together." Greg paused, his brow wrinkling as he thought twice before continuing on. "Arnie, have you ever thought about going back to school and getting your MBA?"

Defiantly I said, "Actually, Greg, I have not. I would have to work three more years to get my undergraduate degree before I could become a candidate for an MBA program." Greg listened attentively, and I could tell he really meant well.

"Arnie, Harvard is my alma mater, and I think you would be an

excellent candidate for the Harvard Business School. If you would
be interested, I would be willing to be a sponsor and support your
application."

Looking back on that moment, I should have been appreciative,
and I should have seriously considered the opportunity, but I could
not.

Why wasn't I good enough as is? Hadn't I proved in overwhelming fashion that I had the character, ability, drive, and leadership
qualities to be the champion and CEO of Earth's Best? The world
was full of Ivy League grads, was run by Ivy League grads and others
from the hallowed halls of prestigious educational institutions. So
what? If they were all so smart and capable, why after centuries of
being in charge was the world in such a mess?

"Greg," I said, in a much softer tone, "I appreciate your offer and
I will give it some thought." I never did.

EB needed me right then. What was I supposed to do, drop out
for five or so years to become truly educated and then apply for the
job? The truth is, at that point in my life, I thought I was qualified
to *teach* at Harvard. Besides, I was almost well credentialed. I would
soon have a prestigious MID (master's in dilution) from the School
of Hard Knocks.

I am sure if I had attended Harvard, I would have received a fabu-
lous education and maybe would have learned how to avoid the snake
pit I ended up in. Who knows? But one thing for sure would have
been different: I wouldn't have been a mutt anymore, and that would
have positioned me very differently within the start-up paradigm I
had unwittingly wandered into.

Maybe it sounds like Ron and I have whined incessantly about
this mutt thing, seeking a rationale for what some will judge as our
stupidity and incompetence for losing control of EB so quickly. After
all, there are famous contemporary mutts out there (I'm assuming
they are all mutts) like Ben Cohen & Jerry Greenfield of Ben &
Jerry's ice cream fame, Gary Hirshberg of Stonyfield Farm yogurt,
and Gene Kahn of Cascadian Farm (produce), who successfully built

national companies while retaining considerable influence and a meaningful financial stake in their respective enterprises.

Now, not to take anything away from their accomplishments, but rather to put in perspective our circumstance, all of them had pursued businesses that could be started on the smallest of scales and with minimal capital investment. To their credit, they chose to entrepreneur in areas that could grow "organically" and sanely, providing them the chance to have success and leverage that success in ways that supported their continuing role as company leaders and primary stakeholders.

All over the country, in the 1980s, you could find small regional ice cream, yogurt, and produce companies. Is there anyone out there in the peanut gallery who ever took note of a regional baby-food company? Those are actually springing up today in some fashion as gourmet and Internet-driven start-ups, but not back in 1984 when we began our Earth's Best journey.

There was a good reason, up until Earth's Best, that there were only three baby-food companies in the United States dominating the landscape and no organic ones. The barriers to entering this market were Everest-like.

The net result was that Ron and I were in the process of paying the price for needing Earth's Best to be a national company from day one. In retrospect, there was nothing organic about the way we tried to grow. The venture money was like a synthetic fertilizer. It had been necessary to move us fast and grow us fat for harvest. Ah, the irony of it all.

Aimed at the Jugular

Just to keep things interesting, in January 1991, the company entered into a serious discussion with H.J. Heinz. I don't know who contacted whom first, but the interest by Heinz got the investors' salivary juices flowing—and I have to admit mine too.

I was thinking at first that Heinz might be a preferred scenario to the ongoing venture soap opera, which was going nowhere for me and Ron. But I had no reason to believe Heinz was committed to organic or would stand behind the standards we had set for EB. For all I knew, they would put the company to sleep and rid themselves of this pesky organic-baby-food newcomer.

Big numbers were being tossed around. You could hear the chickens being counted as the money jockeyed for position. My sense was that everyone was ready for liquidity and tired of the dirty diapers. It was a collective breath-holding time. I didn't know what to want. To Heinz or not to Heinz, that was the question.

And just like that, Heinz was gone. All the mental gyrations and jockeying were for naught. Earth's Best was too early-stage for Heinz. The jury was still out on whether organic was going to be a passing fad. The losses were probably unnerving, and the supply side was still a daunting proposition for conventional wisdom to leap into.

Not to worry, there would be no lull in the action. In late February or maybe early March of 1991 came the shocking and alarming announcement that our old buddies at Beech-Nut were launching "Special Harvest," their own organic brand, to compete with Earth's Best.

The reaction to this news was another collective "holy shit" moment at the board level, followed by a call to circle the wagons and prepare to fight to the death. Beech-Nut was not serious about being in the organic-baby-food niche, but they were serious about finishing us off. Their plan was simple and it was aimed at the jugular. They would attack Earth's Best by entering the key grocery markets where EB had established beachheads. They would sell for cheap and spend like crazy to drive our market share down to zilch. They would employ the lessons we had learned by going direct to the consumer, and they would walk on us and over us to capture the market we had pioneered.

The loss of Heinz and the news that Beech-Nut was a head-on competitor forced the investor group to plan yet another round of financing, because the company was still gushing cash as it pushed its way into more markets.

Ken in particular took the news that Beech-Nut was preparing to evict us from the Denver market as a challenge to his manhood. Ken was a sales warrior, and his sense of self-worth was neatly tied up in the market scan-data results. Like that greyhound that is wired to run down that rabbit, Ken was wired to find a way to squeeze more cases into a market and slug it out, no matter how big the foe. Thankfully, Ken could take a punch, and he did so more often than he probably would care to remember.

Clearly, if we were on Beech-Nut's and Heinz's radar screens, we must have been on Gerber's also. This was great news from the vantage point of what we thought success would look like back when we used to spend our afternoons staring at the Tru-Vision office ceiling. But now, far removed from those fantastical musings, the reality was filled with fear and defensiveness.

Beech-Nut was out there talking to "our" growers. It was, as far as we know, the first time a large company ever crashed onto the stage of the organic-foods industry. I think it was intoxicating for some on the supply side, knowing the muscle they stood with. For others, there was suspicion. Beech-Nut was an outsider, and its presence was polarizing.

Competition was inevitable. In fact, way back in 1988 a Maine company called "Simply Pure" had taken a shot at organic baby food. Determined people, but they didn't make it. Baby's Garden wasn't organic, but they were competition in the natural-foods marketplace. They also eventually didn't make it. But one of the Big Three, that was another story. Our business plans and dog and pony shows had always argued that the big companies would wait and see how we did and then snap us up (and make everyone rich), rather than reinvent the wheel. Ron and I almost called that one right, but not quite, at least not yet.

And although we foresaw and were prepared for the above exit-strategy scenario, it was truly an abstraction to us, created by necessity as an adaptation to the investor reality we had landed in. Selling to the Big Three was never our dream, but it was the "home run" we believed we had to dangle out there to investors in order to get into business.

Special Harvest didn't last long; it was the proverbial flash in the pan.

By August 1991 the entire stock picture had taken several more turns. There was now a series-C class of stock and before too long, a series AA. All the series A, B, and C preferred stocks encountered a 1:10 reverse stock split. Someone with 30,000 shares of either A, B, or C now had 3,000 shares of common stock. The people in that group, which included all the original investors and the early VC investors, all got slammed by the new money coming in. Most of those guys were probably wishing they had put their money into a CD, rather than an EB.

But then again, breaking away from the model of money as the ultimate arbiter of what defines success, there are a relative few who can proudly claim that their sacrifices put organic baby food on the map in North America. Maybe this knowledge provided some consolation for those earliest waves of pioneer investment. That was my hope.

The adversarial tenor of my working relationship with the board intensified. It was an inevitable breakdown. I did my job and I fought with all my might to smartly advance the business. But you can't build a relationship upon a foundation of distrust. And how could I trust? That possibility was gone. There was nowhere to go but down, and that's what happened.

In September 1991, I took the next fateful step in separating myself from Earth's Best. I resigned my position as a director, but agreed to carry on in a consulting capacity, three days a month.

I would describe myself as a "hanger-on" at this stage. I didn't know what else to do. I had no will to fight a new fight and could not imagine the thought of looking for a job. Ironically, at this particular moment, my employability was probably never better. Although the EB board saw me too often as an obstacle to avoid, others (particularly in the natural-foods sector) perceived a talented, ambitious player. If I had been so inclined, I probably could have found a lucrative assignment as the new hired gun of an established or up-and-coming natural-foods company. Even Heinz and Gerber might have been interested in bringing me into their fold, so I could help them compete against EB. Can you imagine?

Looking ahead, life would have many twists and turns, but not that one.

By the end of 1991, EB's investors had completed yet another round of financing. The new stock flavor was a series BB preferred stock offered at $4.30 a share. It brought $4.7 million of fresh capital into the company. If you're thinking that's the round of financing that pushed the company into the black and to a positive cash flow, you haven't been paying enough attention to our story.

And We're It . . . the Lemmings

RON:

Arnie sounds so weary to me. What was most demoralizing was the experience of seeing our company, which was animated by so many wonderful people, being handled like it was a slab of meat waiting for market; and knowing that this same kind of diminished intelligence had not only cast its spell on the Earth's Best's board and venture investors, but was complicit in ravishing the natural resources and cultural heritages across the planet. Why wasn't there a deeper, more heartfelt connection to the "big picture"? It wasn't that there was a lack of heart on the board. There was plenty of heart and plenty of intelligence. It was just disconnected from those values reserved for church, synagogue, and deep knowing.

Money does have a place in this world. Our message is not at all about rejecting money. It's about using it with that higher-self connection intact. Otherwise, we have that lemming stampede . . . and we do . . . and we're it . . . the lemmings.

The other thing contributing to Arnie's deflated tone in the previous section is that all of those promises of fresh stock were amounting to virtually nothing. That express elevator was on its way down to less than 0.2 percent each of ownership in Earth's Best. When you're dropping so fast and so far, you just feel sick.

There was no light at the end of the tunnel, because at the moment, it felt more like a shaft.

How Does a Philistine Act?

ARNIE:

Roger (and his Nabisco pedigree) was shortly gone, although frankly I never experienced him as really there with the company. He seemed to just disappear, no doubt with a golden parachute.

In November 1991 the company hired Jay Anderson, past president of Grandeur Bakery, to take over the CEO helm. Jay, of course, qualified himself with the proper papers, including the requisite Harvard MBA.

I will never forget our first meeting. Ron was with me, visiting the Middlebury plant. Jay, in a bull-in-a-china-closet fashion, introduced himself to us as a "philistine." I knew that was bad, but not exactly why. Nonetheless, I kind of liked it. There wouldn't have to be any pretense between us.

Jay had either announced to us that he was an archenemy of the Hebrews, Ron and Arnie Koss, or was just a barbarous guy, antagonistic to the kind of socially responsible values that drove the founders of the company.

In any case, it was an odd beginning, but it made total sense based on what followed.

But first, all things philistinian aside, Jay was likable. He was cocky, arrogant, and had something to prove. He boasted that he was not a product guy and could have cared less about what he was selling, as long as there was a pot of gold at the end of the rainbow. I was taken by his lack of attachment to things that mattered so much to me and marveled how a person could come to see the world so differently.

In some ways I was envious and wondered why it seemed there were so many guys like Jay out there and so few like me. It brought me back to the days when I was dropping out of Wilkes, trying to figure out where I fit in or why I didn't. This was turning out to be a perpetually lonely place in life for me.

Jay did not waste time. He inherited a company that had annual revenues in the $8-million range and losses of about $7 million. And he jumped right in to fix it. I was relieved because he was a man of action, but I was also uneasy. How would his emphatic detachment from the vision and mission of Earth's Best express itself? How does a philistine act? Naturally, I was on guard. I feared something would be lost and that it would be near and dear to me. The fear came to life in dramatic fashion.

Jay's idea of moving forward included moving the company's headquarters from Middlebury to Boulder, Colorado, and soon after, shutting down the Middlebury operation. I could not have imagined a more barbarous and disheartening turn of events. Now I "got" the philistine declaration. But why did this upheaval occur? At the time, this is how I saw it.

It boiled down to this. Middlebury was not Jay's cup of tea. To him, Vermont was a backwater place with little attraction. I distinctly remember his disdain. He wanted to live in Boulder. As such, what was so near and dear to me was now being sacrificed to Jay's largely self-serving interests. A dark cloud enveloped me. The mind-set of the venture investors that would allow a new guy (albeit their guy), fresh on the scene, to dismantle all that we had established in Middlebury was incomprehensible.

But in hindsight, setting aside my pride and prejudices, it may have been very smart, the very smart that Ron and I didn't possess when we rode our own "self-serving" attachment to The Land to stay in Vermont and in turn ignore California, the mecca of organic-foods production.

It may also be that the margins at the Middlebury plant were never going to improve enough without a "do-over" because our starting point had been too far off the mark. Maybe Jay knew the bleeding had to stop and the Middlebury operation had to be a casualty, or maybe the entire company would fail, if the losses persisted.

I will always wonder if Jay would have found a way to make Middlebury work, if he had loved Vermont. Or would he have failed trying?

In order to shut down the Pond Lane operation, the company had to find a willing and able manufacturer. Remember J.R. Wood, the California fruit processor who packed up the Olsens' and Paul Buxman's stone fruit? Those guys could see the organic wave building, and when the opportunity to become EB's packer was presented to them, they found a way to grab it. By March of 1992, Earth's Best was being produced in both Middlebury and Atwater, California, the home of J.R. Wood.

Soon after, Pond Lane was closed and dismantled, the end of an era. This was like a death to me. Some fifty or sixty people lost their jobs, people whom I loved and who had given so much of themselves. It was the kind of change I had never anticipated; so much for Tru-Vision. But what was still true and intact were the standards Ron and I created for Earth's Best. We were gone. The Middlebury operation was now gone. The institutional investors were in control. But the essence of our inspiration was somehow surviving, and our dreams for the organic-foods industry were becoming true day by day.

All was not lost; far from it. Ron and I would worry obsessively about this westward migration. But we had to let go and hope that as parents, we had done a good enough job setting the foundation for the company's future.

The caveat being, when you're a parent, you never let go.

Ron Rediscovered

RON:

The end of the Pond Lane era was the beginning of a new era for me with the company. I have to say Jay was a smart philistine with good instincts. While he was in the midst of turning the company upside down, he also wanted to be sure that its essence was not being lost in the chaos. He engaged Arnie to stay connected to the supply side and me to be a guide and sounding board for the development of the first wave of Earth's Best's toddler foods. I was thrilled to do this and amazed that the company would value my participation. I had assumed I was a permanent persona non grata. Somehow, unbeknownst to me, my value was rediscovered. This was very heartening and redeeming after all of that time spent languishing in the antipathy of Paul and others.

The pivotal question I had to address for Jay was, "How does someone who is not a founder with embedded Earth's Best genes successfully navigate the myriad choices in a development process and know that the results are products worthy of the name Earth's Best?"

This process gave me hope for the future, because despite Jay's professed ambivalence to what he was selling, somewhere deep down in his bones he was really a product guy.

Chapter 11?

ARNIE:

How does fresh stock amount to nothing or thereabouts? Thought I'd never ask?

Understand this. The whole stock reality was a foreign world to Ron and me. You might say, as I know Ron would, that we were like "dumb" and "dumber."

Sometimes you don't get to flatten a steep learning curve, you fall off it. I think, in part, this happened to us. We were adapting as quickly as we could to an investment environment that was in extreme flux; meaning that the learning curve on ownership interest resisted flattening and arguably got steeper and slicker, the deeper we ventured down the venture path.

I started to pick up the lingo, as in "preferred stock this" and "ratcheting warrants that," but while understanding parts and pieces, I did not grasp the big picture sufficiently to see what might be coming down the road or how I might plan several moves ahead to protect our financial interest and control in the company. It may well have been all for naught anyway, but more knowledge and experience could have been advantageous to Ron and me. I think this is where the punch line, "Harvard MBA" is supposed to be inserted.

Along the way Ron and I did talk to a few attorneys for advice, but we didn't formally retain them, and the advice was always on the fly and under the gun. We should have had expert representation from an attorney dedicated to negotiate on our behalf, nothing less.

Here's a contrary voice. Perhaps that "should have" applies best in a "perfect world" textbook scenario and not the kind of "live" situation that was overwhelming us. I don't think we could have afforded that expert representation. The need would have been continuous. And I think there's a good chance that if we could have afforded it, our self-interest would have killed the company. In which case, instead of having almost nothing, we would have had a greater piece of absolutely nothing.

Ron and I thought we were judiciously navigating our way down the middle road. We were not. We were rocketing down a slippery slope, the middle of which was irrelevant.

In February 1992 Jay drafted a "gentleman's agreement" that outlined the consulting relationship that Ron gushes about in his last entry: 40,000 shares of options, or approximately 1 percent of the company each, were offered to Ron and me.

In September 1992 I received this cheery correspondence from

Jay: "Congratulations, Arnie. As part of your efforts to make Earth's Best a successful company, the Company's Board of Directors has decided to award you an (additional) option to purchase 16,813 shares of the Company's common stock."

Fantastic! The letter went on: "Your options can generally be exercised to purchase vested shares at any time for ten years after the date that the Board of Directors granted you your option. This is an improvement from options granted prior to June 1992, which generally permitted people to exercise their options for only three years after the shares could first be purchased."

Fantastic! "However, an option will generally terminate at an earlier time if your employment with the company ends or control of the company's ownership changes."

Does that mean what you think it means? Yes, it does.

Days after I had received this congratulations letter, a new 800-pound-gorilla investor showed up at EB's door named Sun America Life Insurance Company. Sun's interest was possibly the strongest signal yet that Earth's Best was going to survive. Their financial clout redefined the meaning of a "deep-pocketed" investor; these guys were coming in to be the last "top gorilla."

Improbably, while Sun did their due diligence, the EB board was beginning to talk about Chapter 11 bankruptcy. By this time, about $17 million had been invested by approximately two hundred investors. And still, it was not enough.

In January 1993 Jay sent me an urgent memo, asking me to help the company persuade the series-A shareholders (the original EB investors) to surrender their warrants that contained antidilution protection. I had no idea how this antidilution insulation survived the previous financings, but if Sun America was to play, the series-A guys would have to acquiesce, or else.

Given that the company was teetering on the brink of a Chapter 11 filing, time was of the essence, and apparently I was their only hope. So why was I their only hope? It's simple. Ron and I were largely responsible for attracting these investors. Our ownership interests had been beaten down. We held no power and were not the bad guys. There was at least a chance these series-A people would listen to my appeal as a dedicated founder.

A Whole Lot of Something Added Up to Almost Nothing

Greg approached me in this defining moment. He was full of angst and gravely concerned that all would be lost. It was a strange moment for both of us. He probably thought he was long past the point of coming to me on bent knee. Conversely, it was strange to suddenly be cast again in the light of savior. It was a moment of high drama.

"Arnie, this is crunch time," Greg implored.

"I understand, Greg," feeling annoyed by the groveling and syrupy, sincere tone in his voice. I added, "This is going to very tough to convince all these people to surrender their warrants. They are pissed."

Greg stammered and went on, "Arnie, you need to make them see that I am feeling the pain too. All of the venture groups are being substantially diluted. Together we have $17 million in and will only retain 7.5 percent of the company. The series-A investors have far less at risk and will still have the rights to about 2 percent."

"Greg," I said matter-of-factly, "a lot of the series-A guys have already written their investment off. The news that they still have these warrants with antidilution protection is going to embolden them to demand a better deal."

"Forget it, Arnie," Greg said in disgust. "This is it, this is the deal, and it's not getting any sweeter for them or us."

Greg paused to collect his thoughts. "Look, Arnie, I know you can do this, and the company is prepared to make it worth your while, very worth your while. Pull this off and we will not disappoint you."

"Greg," I said, with little inflection in my voice, "I would like you to put something in writing to me that reflects your intentions to reward me in the event I can work a miracle."

Greg did his usual hemming and hawing. "There is no way I can get the board to deal with this now, Arnie. We don't have time to negotiate; we need you to jump on this now, start making calls, and get people to start signing waivers."

Entrepreneurs-in-waiting, take note. There is always time. In a crunch moment like this, there may be no better opportunity to cut a deal that represents your interests. Once the crisis is over, those who were feeling vulnerable are prone to become forgetful and inflexible, especially if they are inclined to being two-hatted.

Over the weeks that followed I tracked down every series-A investor. Each signed off and surrendered his or her warrants. It was an intense and excruciatingly difficult exercise. And the result was a testimony to the goodwill of these people and their commitment to Earth's Best. Some probably would have liked nothing more than to see the institutional investors go up in flames.

During this crisis moment for the company, Ron and I also reached the zenith of our naïveté. Sometime in February 1993 we signed a document to terminate all of our outstanding options. It might seem like unfathomable stupidity, but we did it as an act of good faith to get the deal done, only after assurances that we would be reissued options in a new plan that would equal or exceed our existing shares. From that moment on, we waited in expectation for the new plan. It never happened, at least for us.

The Sun America deal closed. Jay awarded me some stock in April. I can't remember the number of shares, but it was a paltry amount reflecting the shallowness of Greg's promise not to disappoint me. I had nothing in writing, and he and the other venture directors had no qualms returning to their earlier dismissive founder prejudice.

And that's the way it went down. Whenever and wherever I promised to work with the institutional money and a return promise was reciprocally made to improve my net financial position, they, in effect, reneged or disappointed.

My ownership position in Earth's Best became an abstraction. There wasn't a founder hotline to call for updates. I was an outsider, and what would be, would be. That said, I did have an expectation that all the shares I had earned still amounted to something meaningful. However, I never translated "meaningful" into a number. I just knew I would know when the day of liquidity finally dawned.

Cruel and Unusual Punishment

I continued on as a consultant as we moved through 1993. By now I was a curiosity to the many new management hires, headquartered in Boulder, who had only heard rumors and gossip about the Koss brothers.

Unlike Ron, who was called back from his wilderness outpost on The Land and feeling redeemed, I was estranged and dissatisfied. I'm an all-or-nothing type of guy, and consulting turned out to be too close to nothing. I wasn't part of the hub of the company. I wasn't even a spoke in the wheel. I was a vestigial something or other and never found my place. This time Ron would outlast me, but not by much. I was disappearing. For a founder, this was cruel and unusual punishment, but fortunately, the company itself was doing fine without me.

I had moved on completely by 1995. I was immersed in a sustainable wood-certification project and trying to figure out how to venture into that. I was forty-four, and now in addition to Cora, who was eighteen, there was the newly arrived Ryan Kekoa Koss. I was a new dad.

When H.J. Heinz came around again to purchase Earth's Best in 1996, my ownership was as follows: I held 42 shares of common stock and had a warrant to purchase 60 shares of common stock. That's it, at least according to a February 14, 1996, correspondence I still have from the attorney representing Heinz. Ron had about the same. The fact that our share amounts were so similar proves the point that everything I received after Ron fell away was virtually worthless. It was all plenty of nothing, cleverly disguised as something.

I do not have the March closing documents that reflect the final numbers, but I think the picture is poignantly clear enough. Ron and I received around $51,000 each on a deal that was done for at least $30 million. This did not qualify as "meaningful." It seemed impossible. The outcome was disorienting.

The 10,000 option shares I received when I first started to consult in June 1990 expired well before they were worth $35,000 to purchase.

The 40,000 option shares each that Jay had touted to us in our February 1992 consulting agreement disappeared after we signed that option-termination agreement (which, to the best of our knowledge, was never reconstituted as promised).

The 16,813 option shares I received in Jay's cheery September 1992 correspondence died when the company's ownership changed to Heinz.

The paltry stock amount Jay awarded me in April 1993, for my efforts to convince the series-A investors to surrender their antidilution protection, was apparently the victim of a 1:37 stock split at some point. It was all news to Ron and me.

What happened to the 14,000 shares of warrants that were, according to the company's CFO at the time, fully vested in June 1993? I don't know what happened to them. The company did not recognize them at the time of the sale to Heinz.

One thing that's obvious, and not to our credit, is that Ron and I did not keep the paper trail of correspondence and stock-related EB documents well organized. The menagerie of stock options and warrants we held over so many years became an unintelligible tangle, an unapproachable confounding mess. "Just tell me when the ride is over."

When the Heinz deal showed up in a FedEx package on February 12, 1996, I went into shock. The ride was over. It wasn't the Heinz part. I knew some version of that was coming sooner or later. It was what the document recognized as our outstanding ownership in the company.

This outraged and confused me. What happened to the new plan and our reissued options? What happened to everything that I had earned and to all those promises of goodwill along the way for so many years by the venture capitalists? I never saw this kind of obliteration coming. It was unimaginable.

I had a one-track mind from the moment I opened that FedEx package—lawsuit. It was a reflex.

Justice Yielded to a Risk Calculation

RON:

No one wants to be the bad guy. Rationalizing has advanced to an art form in Western business culture. I believe Greg, Jay, Tony, and David did a lot of rationalizing regarding their final treatment of Arnie and me (or perhaps even worse, and more disheartening, virtually none at all). Maybe it was just a cold, hard, philistinian calculation to disregard the spirit of every offer and promise made to the founders, because there was the legal wherewithal to do so.

We retained a lawyer. Arnie and I threatened to sue. Unbelievably, we were, in turn, accused of trying to extort stock from the company. The advice we received was there was an arguable case for the outstanding 14,000 shares of warrants, but we could also be countersued by both Heinz and Earth's Best for obstructing the deal. The related legal expenses might be formidable with no guarantee of a favorable outcome to us. We were advised not to litigate, given the deep pockets we would be facing.

The prospect of depleting the small amount of money we were entitled to receive was too daunting and stressful for Carley and me. We could not risk this money for justice. Arnie reluctantly went along, but there was no consolation or resolution to be found in his decision. So, in the end, justice yielded to a risk calculation.

Setting my interests in and value to the company completely aside, Arnie's contribution literally saved the company on a number of occasions. He single-handedly rescued Jay and Greg when he succeeded in getting each series-A stockholder to surrender his or her antidilution protection to bring Sun America's investment into the company. Arnie was the difference maker to get the last money in. The company had the opportunity to finally make it to profitability and to a sale. Try to appreciate the significance of this.

And then in the end, as far as I'm concerned, they knifed him in the back, simply because they could. Again, this was a group of individuals who I believe knew better and wanted differently, but did not. The venture capitalists offered Arnie no tribute for his countless expressions of good faith. They failed on every representation to him. The results speak for themselves. Inconceivable!

The illusion is that money appears to be the epicenter of the trauma. It is not. The hurt came, not from the millions that were expected and then denied, but from the absence of any attempt at relatedness from people who appeared to genuinely respond to Arnie's commitment and loyalty to them and the company.

Who knows what the extenuating circumstances were for Greg, Tony, David, and Jay? Arnie should have known. They should have honored the relationship they had relied upon countless times and engaged him with the respect that he had earned and deserved. They abandoned him. They used him. That's the real hurt.

What do you do with a wound like that? You seethe. You go numb. You look for silver linings. You explore ideas like personal karma and embedded intergenerational family dynamics. You heal and grow stronger.

And finally you write a book and try to tell a fascinating story and feel grateful that you have one to tell.

Starry-Eyed Idealists

RON:

All of the wrong does not negate what was right. It stands opposed to it. Jay drove the company to profitability. This was no small accomplishment. He arguably saved the company. Greg went the distance. Maybe it was out of self-interest, but I believe in his own right, Greg was a champion for Earth's Best as well. His intention also saved the company and was integral to its success. There were many saviors along the way. It's just that not everyone was "our" savior. Some were saints and some were not.

This was the way the Earth's Best story went. It wasn't a fairy tale, it was an entrepreneurial tale.

Even today, I don't really understand failed relationships such as the one I had with Paul. At the time, it felt entirely personal, but now in retrospect, I think it was more situational, the result of a unique and difficult start-up situation. What mandates were imposed on him by the board? What was it like crashing into a company that was so defined by the twin-ness of Arnie and me?

I remember a West Coast trip that I took with Paul; perhaps it was to visit the Barlow Company. He had a first-class seat. I had a coach ticket. Paul very generously offered to switch, and it was the first time I flew in first class. I always wondered why people paid so much extra to sit up front. I knew the answer after that five-hour flight. Paul's softness and generosity took me by surprise. Who was that guy? I really don't know.

Convention painted Arnie and me as starry-eyed idealists. But really, in the light of today, how starry-eyed was the idea of organic baby food? We lost control of our company, and our financial interest was reduced to almost nothing. Okay, so we held values and we stood by them and we made sacrifices and mistakes. Whatever Arnie and I lost along the way, it was a small price to pay for establishing organic baby food in the United States and giving the organic-foods industry a timely boost at a critical juncture in its life.

Misguided and not starry-eyed enough are those aligned with convention who continue to spray this planet with toxic chemicals; who genetically modify organisms; who oppose mass-transportation initiatives; who exploit the poor; and who use our oceans as a dumping ground. These people are the naïve ones, who believe money and power define success and represent adulthood.

Despite all appearances to the contrary, it is and will be only the many expressions of love and relatedness that define success and represent true adulthood. We all know this or sense it; at least hopefully we did as children when the Golden Rule was more likely to be prominent. But now for some, perhaps many, this notion of love and relatedness may be received as just another preachy-sounding, inconvenient truth.

This apparently can't be helped. Interconnectedness lies at the heart of what we yearn for and value. Yet paradoxically, when in the act of relating, it also can be perceived as weak and soft.

This paradox is particularly acute in business where the R in ROI stands for "return" and not "relatedness." The two are not mutually exclusive, but the pressures of convention are great to ultimately sacrifice one of those Rs for the other.

It's amazing to think that each day, in some way, we have a fresh chance to choose which R to sacrifice and which one to take a stand for. Anyone can become a champion, express his or her conscience, and offer a voice of support or a prayer of intention for the future he or she longs for. This freedom is our power and our hope.

You Guys Are the Reason

ARNIE:

Ron and I were at the Anaheim Natural Foods Expo trade show in April of 1998 on a reconnaissance mission for another project. We walked by a booth with the company name "Gerber" emblazoned on it and baby-food jars labeled as "Tender Harvest." Gerber was in the organic baby-food business. It was a wow from head to toe. I get goose bumps writing about it.

We found an inconspicuous spot across the aisle and stopped to let the moment sink in. It was surreal. Seven years earlier, a Gerber spokesman had sniped in a Forbes article about Earth's Best that organic was "just a marketing ploy."

We had dragged Goliath into the arena, and now we were happy to see him.

Ron and I meandered over to the booth and introduced ourselves to some of the senior-looking people. I will never forget the response. "So you guys are the reason we're here doing this." In the moment, it felt like a hero's welcome.

This was the success Ron and I had dreamed about. Our odyssey that had started in September 1984 was now complete. We had accomplished what we set out to accomplish. It seemed so improbable, and yet somehow it happened.

Ron and I were wrong about so many things. The company needed almost forty times more equity than we projected. Vermont was not the best location to launch an organic baby-food company. We lost control so quickly. As a case study, the Earth's Best story offers the critical palate much to chew on and to satiate itself with. But we also got some very big pieces right, the most important pieces.

We were right about organic baby food, right about the marketplace, and right about insisting on setting standards worthy of the brand name. The organic-foods industry has evolved from a dirt path on the fringe of our national food paradigm to an avenue running through it, to a movement that has transformed it. Ron and I may have had no business stepping into the baby-food fray, but I'm so glad we did. In doing so, I learned that it is the people who are swiveling in their chairs, the people who do see the alluring specks of light on the horizon, that are the ones who must smartly crash the shores of the status quo, wave after wave, and give it a go. If Ron and I could manifest Earth's Best, what possibilities are within your reach?

The line below the bottom line has been discovered, and it remains a frontier of opportunity and personal growth for every entrepreneur. The gold there may not always be bankable, but the rewards are the kind that money can't buy.

Ron and I are the founders of the first organic baby-food company in the United States. Every time I see a jar of Earth's Best in a shopping cart or on a store shelf, I feel grateful for having dreamed and taken a chance.

Be a difference maker. And if you need a partner, pick a great one, someone you grok and who groks you.

— PART EIGHT —
Afterword

The Hain Celestial Group

RON:

Earth's Best is presently one brand in a stable of natural-foods brands controlled and managed by The Hain Celestial Group, a natural- and organic-food and personal care products company. Arnie and I are grateful that our baby has reached young adulthood and now thrives under the Hain umbrella.

For almost twenty-five years now, babies and moms and dads have depended on Earth's Best and its integrity. Naturally, as founders, Arnie and I had our own "grand vision" for the future. In it, Earth's Best was more than a 100%-organic baby and toddler food brand, but a presence and a voice for global issues affecting the lives of children. Sadly, that is a future we did not get to meet.

Publicly traded companies such as Hain Celestial are driven by maximizing the financial return to their shareholders. Grand visions are limited by the confines of this narrowly focused paradigm. As a result, Earth's Best today is also confined to being just an "ordinary extraordinary" company.

On one hand, this is fantastic because an "ordinary extraordinary" Earth's Best makes a significant contribution to the lives of many babies, parents, and growers, as well as the environment. On the other, from our inspirational starting point as founders, it's also disappointing because our aim was solely "extraordinary," and there is so much potential that remains unrealized.

Earth's Best, nonetheless, stands as a very proud achievement.

Arnie and I had no problem getting our bearings after our consulting gigs with the company wound down in 1994 and 1995. This is because the need for change and transformation on this planet of ours happens to be screaming at an alarming decibel, if you have an ear for it. Where to start when the smorgasbord of need is so grand?

First, Arnie and I jumped into a certified sustainable-wood project that failed before it got off the ground. We chose the wrong partner, and our post–Earth's Best aversion to outside money caused us to start woefully undercapitalized.

Failure is an option that you don't plan for or expect, but it happens. It hurts and you don't get used to it. But Arnie and I had another big idea waiting in the wings.

When our mom, Judith, had ovarian cancer in pre–Earth's Best 1982, Arnie and I witnessed her exasperation with the liquid-meal supplements she relied upon. For her, it was the monotony of the artificial taste and the syrupy sweetness. For Arnie and me, it was recognizing the mediocrity of these products targeted at people in a life-threatening crisis. We promised each other that someday we would revisit this product category.

Our mom had deserved so much better, even if her prognosis was unfavorable. We didn't forget. Fifteen years later, Arnie and I were ready.

And so began (1997) the "Recovery Power Foods" (RPF) chapter of our entrepreneurial lives, financed by an angel investor who attached himself to our twin star. Arnie and I set out to bring our "best" ethos to the dietary meal-supplement category.

Interestingly, this time, instead of going up against giants Gerber, Beech-Nut, and Heinz, Arnie and I made a beeline for a head-on collision with three multinational pharmaceutical companies— Mead Johnson, Ross-Abbott Laboratories, and Novartis.

Sometimes the little mutts need to lead the way because the giants are slow and clumsy, and despite their enormous size and power, are followers and not leaders. In 1997 these pharmaceutical companies were still offering products arguably entrenched in 1970s nutritional science. Where was "the best" for vulnerable people who needed "the best"?

The RPF products were cutting-edge amazing, and the public and professional response to them was gratifying and encouraging. But the marketplace was brutal, and we were again not capitalized to overcome the consequences of another stubbornly steep learning curve that demanded that we adapt and evolve our products as well as our market position.

We flirted with venture capital, but we couldn't and wouldn't pull the trigger and submit to it, and we let Recovery Power Foods sink below the waves.

But it did not entirely. Arnie and I next latched on to the idea of developing a complete-meal-supplement ice cream. Why not use ice cream as a nutrient-delivery system for people who were fatigued by those liquid products and who loved ice cream as a familiar comfort food? We weren't crazy. It just hadn't been done. Nutricopia, Incorporated, was born in 2001, and its story and our journey is another entrepreneurial tale we may someday tell.

Life is a spiritual odyssey, and business provides opportunities galore for individuals to journey to the center of their hearts and myriad rationales to travel elsewhere. I think we all know that a future driven by narcissistic greed and conceit looks pretty grim, and yet obviously and mystifyingly there's something hellishly irresistible about it. We also know that environmental stewardship, social justice, and an "all for one, one for all" ethos represent the future that looks most hopeful. Yet curiously there's something hellishly resistible about that.

We're stuck between knowing what is right and doing what is right. And unless we as individuals grok somewhere deep in our bones the reasons to choose that hopeful future, it may well elude us.

Being twins accelerated our own grokking. As youth, Arnie and I occasionally experienced acute pain when we weren't "one for all and all for one." And it was a pain far greater than that felt by our bruised egos. We had our own little mini-laboratory at home in Ellenville that taught us both how to stand alone and stand together. Unknowingly, we brought this deep understanding and value to our Earth's Best lives. The result was both our unlikely success in starting a pioneering company and the building of community at Pond Lane with a group of wonderful people. Every agony along the way was worth the ecstasy of that experience. It is an encounter every entrepreneur should aim for—the ecstasy, that is.

ACKNOWLEDGMENTS

A book that has been nineteen years in the making has many people to thank. It is the devotion of the men and women of Earth's Best Baby Foods at Pond Lane in Middlebury, Vermont, and our gratitude to them that has propelled the telling of this story. One invaluable person who did not make it into our narrative is Susan Smiley. Susan was our administrative glue in the early days and evolved to become one of the ingredient-supply pioneers for Earth's Best and, in effect, the organic foods industry.

Carley Claghorn and Anne Rillero, our dear wives, endured The Earth's Best story and a wild roller-coaster ride that wouldn't quit. They were endlessly supportive throughout, and we are eternally grateful, because without that support Earth's Best Baby Foods would have never happened. We really don't know how they did it.

Gabe and Aaron Koss (Ron and Carley's boys) involuntarily and unwittingly were trailblazers for the introduction of organic and whole baby foods. Millions of babies now have benefited from what they loved as babies and toddlers, and have been spared as well from the concoctions they spit out convincingly in our earliest days of trial and error.

A core group of family and friends contributed immensely as early readers of our manuscript. We are very grateful and want to thank Peter Claghorn, Jon Corcoran, Susan Ritz, Gus and Linda Chiarello, Tony French, Lanie Fondiller, Carolyn and Charles Clark, Gabe Koss, and Joseph Weiss.

Special thanks and gratitude go to Josie Masterson Glen, our initial copyeditor, who waded through the manuscript when we first thought we were ready for publishing and then taught us in the kindest way (with her red felt marker) that we were not. And to Cannon Labrie, our editor at Chelsea Green, who urged us to manage the tone of our storytelling and patiently and persistently showed us how to improve and sharpen it.

Joni Praded, the editor-in-chief at Chelsea Green, opened the door for us and changed our lives. She said yes to our query letter. Margo Baldwin, president and publisher, has been a fan from the beginning, and it has been heartening to feel her support along the way. Jonathan Teller-Elsberg, associate editor, has cheerfully guided us through the many steps of the publishing process. We could not have been more fortunate than to find our way to Chelsea Green.

ABOUT THE AUTHORS

RON KOSS   ARNIE KOSS

Ron and Arnie Koss founded Earth's Best Baby Food in 1985. In addition to baby food, **Ron Koss** is a natural foods product innovator. During his long-term employ with the aio Food Group, Ron has secured patents for his work on complete meal supplement ice cream and has also introduced specialized complete meal supplements for people in health recovery situations. Presently, he is working on nutritional products for a global relief aid project. Ron enjoys working as a consultant for socially responsible enterprises and has a special interest in group dynamics, organizational development, and conflict resolution. He lives in Montpelier, Vermont, with his family.

Arnie Koss honed his business skills by founding and operating a number of small entrepreneurial companies in Vermont. He was actively involved in the development of organic certification standards, which eventually led to the Organic Foods Act of 1990. Arnie has served as a consultant to several prominent natural products companies and is presently the Managing Partner at aio Food Group, a Hawaii-based product development company that has created patented nutritional supplement products and also owns the Punalu'u Bakeshop and Visitor Center on the Big Island of Hawaii. He lives in Kula, Hawaii, with his family.

green
press
INITIATIVE

Chelsea Green Publishing is committed to preserving ancient forests and natural resources. We elected to print this title on 30-percent postconsumer recycled paper, processed chlorine-free. As a result, for this printing, we have saved:

21 Trees (40' tall and 6-8" diameter)
7 Million BTUs of Total Energy
1,991 Pounds of Greenhouse Gases
9,589 Gallons of Wastewater
582 Pounds of Solid Waste

Chelsea Green Publishing made this paper choice because we and our printer, Thomson-Shore, Inc., are members of the Green Press Initiative, a nonprofit program dedicated to supporting authors, publishers, and suppliers in their efforts to reduce their use of fiber obtained from endangered forests. For more information, visit: www.greenpressinitiative.org.

Environmental impact estimates were made using the Environmental Defense Paper Calculator. For more information visit: www.papercalculator.org.

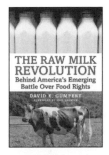

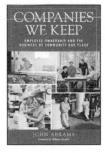

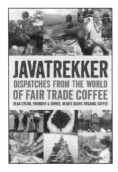